KU-821-781

London's Hidden Walks

Volume 1

London's Hidden Walks

by Stephen Millar

Volume 1

London's Hidden Walks
(Volume 1)

Written by Stephen Millar
Photography by Stephen Millar
Edited by Abigail Willis
Additional research by Tony Whyte
Book design by Lesley Gilmour and Susi Koch
Illustrations by Lesley Gilmour

All rights reserved. No part of this publication may be reproduced, stored in a retrieval system or transmitted in any form or by any means electronic, mechanical, photocopying, recording or otherwise without the prior consent of the publishers and copyright owners. Every effort has been made to ensure the accuracy of this book; however, due to the nature of the subject the publishers cannot accept responsibility for any errors which occur, or their consequences.

Published in 2013 by
Metro Publications Ltd, PO Box 6336, London, N1 6PY

Metro® is a registered trade mark of Associated Newspapers Limited. The METRO mark is under licence from Associated Newspapers Limited.

Printed and bound in India. This book is produced using paper from registered sustainable and managed sources. Suppliers have provided both LEI and MUTU certification.

© 2013 Stephen Millar
British Library Cataloguing in Publication Data. A catalogue record for this book is available from the British Library.

ISBN 978-1-902910-45-1

For Helen and the kids

Acknowledgements

My thanks go to Helen, without whose support I would never have been able to finish this book. My children – Patrick, Annapurna, Blythe and Arran – also deserve a big thank you for being dragged around London on many of the walks, suffering snow, rain, summer heat and general bewilderment as to why daddy had to visit yet another church before they could go home and play.

The book would not have been possible without Tony Whyte, fact checker extraordinaire and the first real friend I made after moving to London so many years ago. The staff at Metro Publications (Susi, Andrew, Abigail and in particular Lesley) have been enormously supportive and helpful as always.

I would also like to thank all the many people along the way who helped with queries and showed such great patience. In particular, John 'Hoppy' Hopkins who gave me tea, sound advice, and made me think about London in a different way.

Contents

"Sir, if you wish to have a just notion of the magnitude of this city, you must not be satisfied with seeing its great streets and squares, but must survey the innumerable little lanes and courts. It is not in the showy evolutions of buildings, but in the multiplicity of human habitations which are crowded together, that the wonderful immensity of London consists."
from Boswell's *Life of Johnson* (1791)

Introduction

In writing this book I researched about 25 walks around London. Thirteen of those walks are in this volume. Having been resident in the capital for many years I had – admittedly – become rather jaded by it. Despite having lived in a number of places during this time, my experience of London was becoming increasingly narrow; the commute to work, the area around my workplace, and the occasional excursion with the kids at weekends.

This book gave me the excuse to rip up my increasingly mundane London rule book, swim against the tide of humanity and wander the capital's streets in search of the interesting and often unnoticed. In the course of hundreds of miles of wandering I have discovered the churches of Hawksmoor, the narrow alleyways where Jack the Ripper stalked his prey, where John met Yoko, and the location of the church hall where Pink Floyd played their early gigs. I now know the site of Christopher Marlowe's murder and where Peter the Great trashed John Evelyn's house, the pub famous for a cocktail invented by the Satanist Aleister Crowley and the block of flats where the Kray twins were arrested.

I hope this book will encourage you to follow in my footsteps. So go on, try something different. Wake up one weekend and explore Shadwell instead of making the regular trip to IKEA, or take a detour around the back streets of Southwark when you next visit Borough Market. Don't forget to stop, look up at buildings and search for clues – they are all there if you choose to find them and your instincts will probably be right.

This book contains a great deal of history, but it is not a history book. It is a mix of myth, gossip, fact and geography. Everyone has their own experience of London and I would appreciate any comments or suggestions on the less obvious or hidden aspects of the capital that would help me improve the walks in future editions. You can email me directly or contact me via the publisher. I hope you enjoy the walks. **Stephen Millar**

stephenwmillar@hotmail.com

HAMPSTEAD WALK

7

CAMDEN ROAD

MAIDA VALE

REGENT'S PARK

HARROW ROAD

MARYLEBONE ROAD

FITZROVIA & BLOOMSBURY WALK

2

WESTWAY

NOTTING HILL WALK

8

OXFORD STREET

3

SOHO WALK

BAYSWATER ROAD

1

MAYFAIR WALK

KENSINGTON GARDENS

HYDE PARK

VICTORIA

4

WESTMINSTER & WHITEHALL WALK

KING'S RD

VAUXHALL BR.

CHELSEA EMBANKMENT

River Thames

BATTERSEA PARK RD

WANDSWORTH RD

River Thames

1 Mayfair Walk

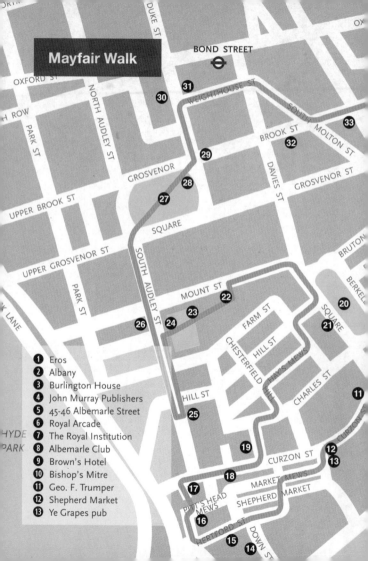

Mayfair Walk

BOND STREET

1. Eros
2. Albany
3. Burlington House
4. John Murray Publishers
5. 45-46 Albemarle Street
6. Royal Arcade
7. The Royal Institution
8. Albemarle Club
9. Brown's Hotel
10. Bishop's Mitre
11. Geo. F. Trumper
12. Shepherd Market
13. Ye Grapes pub

OXFORD STREET

GREAT MARLBOROUGH ST

HANOVER ST

MADDOX ST

NEW BOND ST

CONDUIT ST

REGENT ST

SAVILE ROW

VIGO ST

PICCADILLY

ROYAL ACADEMY

HAY HILL

DOVER ST

ALBEMARLE ST

OLD BOND ST

BERKELEY ST

PICCADILLY

JERMYN ST

REGENT ST

GREEN PARK

ST JAMES ST

GREEN PARK

Mayfair Walk

Start/Finish: Piccadilly Circus underground station
Distance: 3 miles

Mayfair has been arguably the most prestigious district of London for over 300 years, although today the offices of hedge fund managers and expensive boutiques are more prevalent than the grand mansions that once dominated the area. This walk begins in Piccadilly Circus, laid out in 1819 to connect Regent Street to Piccadilly.

Piccadilly Circus's most famous feature is the statue of ❶ **Eros**, which stands on top of the memorial to the 7th Earl of Shaftesbury, one of the great Victorian philanthropists. The monument was erected in 1893 and it has become common currency that the statue represents the Angel of Christian Charity. In fact Sir Alfred Gilbert (1854-1934), the sculptor, intended the statue to portray Eros's twin Anteros, the Greek god of unrequited love, but this choice was not acceptable to the more prudish members of the organising committee behind the monument.

The monument was not constructed entirely to Gilbert's design, with the result that the embittered sculptor went into a self-imposed exile abroad for many years. This was the first aluminium statue in the world, and Gilbert used his 16-year-old studio assistant Angelo Colarossi as the model. The statue's bow and arrow were originally meant to have pointed towards Wimborne St Giles in Dorset, Shaftesbury's country estate, but this instruction was ignored and they now face Regent Street. A second copy was made by Gilbert in the late 1920s and stood in Sefton Park in Liverpool, although it has recently been moved to the National Conservation Centre in the same city.

Head down Piccadilly – named after a type of starched collar known as the 'piccadil' once sold here in the 17th century – where on the right hand side next to number 46 is the entrance to ❷ **Albany**, an apartment block set back from the road. It was originally built in the 1770s for Viscount Melbourne, and later occupied by George III's son Prince Frederick, Duke of York – the famous 'Grand old

Duke of York' of the children's nursery rhyme. In 1802 the house was converted into 69 bachelor apartments known as 'sets' – tenancies were restricted to male bachelors who were not involved in 'trade' and had impeccable social credentials.

Albany become the most fashionable address in London and the list of notable bachelors who have lived here includes Lord Byron, William Gladstone, Aldous Huxley, J. B. Priestley, Isaiah Berlin, Terence Stamp, and Edward Heath. It was also the home of Raffles, the fictional gentleman burglar created by E. W. Hornung. In recent years women have also been allowed to rent a 'set', although it remains the case that having social connections is the only way to help secure a tenancy.

Continue on past The Royal Academy of Arts based in ❸ **Burlington House**. The Royal Academy is the oldest art school in England, founded in 1768. However, Burlington House is also notable for being a rare survivor of the grand Mayfair mansions that were once common in the area. The 1st Earl of Burlington bought the house, still unfinished, in 1667 – hence the name.

3 The Royal Academy of Arts, Burlington House

Burlington House remained in private hands until it was purchased by the British Government in the mid 19th century to be used by a number of learned societies, the Royal Academy of Arts among them.

In July 1858 the Linnean Society met at Burlington House to hear a natural history paper authored by Charles Darwin and Alfred Russel Wallace. The paper outlined for the first time the revolutionary theory of natural selection more fully explored in Darwin's later book *On the Origin of Species* (1859). Neither Darwin nor Wallace attended the meeting, and the paper was only included at short notice and read out at the end of a very long session. Almost certainly few – if any – of the 30 members who attended the meeting understood the significance of what they were hearing.

Pass the Academy to take a right up **Albemarle Street**. On the left-hand side is ❹ **John Murray Publishers** at number 50, the building dating from 1719. Although it has recently been taken over by a bigger publishing company, John Murray has been based here since 1812 and counts Sir Arthur Conan Doyle, Jane Austen, Goethe, and Charles Darwin among its past authors. The company was founded by the first John Murray in 1768, and a descendant of the same name became Lord Byron's publisher and made the office into London's great literary salon of the early 19th century.

It was the same John Murray who carried out one of the most infamous acts in literary history. On 17th May 1824, after Byron's death, Murray persuaded Byron's executors and friends to burn the poet's unpublished – and apparently scandalous – autobiography in the fireplace at number 50. Byron enthusiasts to this day make a pilgrimage to the original fire grate and mourn what might have been. Benjamin Disraeli, the 19th-century author and politician, once grew so frustrated at Murray's delay in giving feedback on a draft novel that he wrote to the publisher asking 'as you have had some small experience in burning manuscripts perhaps you will be so kind as to consign [mine] to the flames'.

The archive of John Murray Publishers from 1768 to 1920 (including the original manuscript of *On the Origin of Species*) was recently sold to the National Library of Scotland for over £30 million.

The modern building at **5** **number 45-46** on this street was completed in 1957 to a design by the Hungarian-born Ernö Goldfinger (1902-1987). Goldfinger was one of the most influential architects in England during the middle decades of the 20th century, and his London buildings include The Trellick Tower in North Kensington and 2 Willow Road in Hampstead. He is also thought to have been the inspiration for the Bond villain Auric Goldfinger.

Continue up Albemarle Street looking out on the right hand side for the **6** **Royal Arcade** at number 12. This elegant shopping arcade was built in 1879. Continue north to visit **7** **The Royal Institution of Great Britain** at number 21. The Institution was founded in 1799, and some of the country's most eminent scientists have worked here including Sir Humphrey Davy (who invented the miner's lamp and discovered sodium and potassium), Sir Lawrence Bragg (who won the Nobel prize for his work on x-ray diffraction), and Michael Faraday.

During the 19th century Faraday (1791-1867) contributed greatly to the study of electricity, and the RI's Faraday Museum is worth a visit. Ten chemical elements were discovered at the Institution, and since its foundation fourteen of its resident scientists have won a Nobel Prize. Its public lectures (including the famous Christmas lectures for children) were once so popular that the street outside became London's first one way traffic system in order to reduce congestion.

The infamous **❽ Albemarle Club** was once located at number 13, and it was here in the late 19th century that London's bohemians would gather, and where in 1895 the writer Oscar Wilde's downfall began. The Marquess of Queensbury, father of Wilde's lover Lord Alfred Douglas – or 'Bosie' – left his card for Wilde at the Club with the note 'For Oscar Wilde, posing somdomite' (sic). The incident led to Wilde's failed libel action against the Marquess, then his own subsequent criminal prosecution for gross indecency. Wilde never recovered and died a broken man in 1900.

Opposite the Royal Institution is **❾ Brown's Hotel**, the oldest hotel in London, which first opened in 1837. Alexander Graham Bell (1847-1922), inventor of the telephone, made the first telephone call in Britain from here in 1876, and American President Theodore Roosevelt stayed at Browns in 1886 before walking to his wedding at St George's, Hanover Square – a church seen later on in the walk. Another American president – Franklin D. Roosevelt also stayed at the hotel in 1905 during his honeymoon with wife Eleanor.

Follow the map to Dover Street, noting at number 37 on the right-hand side a **❿ Bishop's Mitre** visible above the first floor window. This recalls that the house was originally built in the 1770s for the Bishop of Ely.

Head into Hay Hill and then Lansdowne Row, the latter lying directly over the path of the now hidden River Tyburn which flows underground from Hampstead through London to meet the Thames near Vauxhall Bridge. Continue down Curzon Street, passing number 1-4 which was home to the Registry of MI5 (and their most secret files) from 1976-1995. Continue down Curzon St looking out on the right hand side for the fantastic Victorian barbershop of **⓫ Geo. F. Trumper**, 'Court hairdresser and perfumer'.

'Trumpers' has served generations of Mayfair's well-heeled residents and seated within its mahogany interior you can get the best shave in London.

On the left-hand side at number 47 head through a low arch into **12 Shepherd Market**, the heart of old Mayfair, and named after Edward Shepherd who laid out the original street plan in 1735. A fair was held here for 15 days every May (hence 'Mayfair') from 1686 until 1708, when local residents could no longer stand the scenes of debauchery and forced it to close. Whilst the area has since moved upmarket, it remains a red-light district. In 1986 the politician and writer Jeffrey Archer came to the market and picked up a prostitute named Monica Coghlan, an event he would deny in court and which led ultimately to his imprisonment for perjury in 2001. Just inside the entrance is **13 Ye Grapes** public house, an excellent place for a break if you are flagging.

Take the opportunity to explore the narrow streets of the market, today mostly lined by the fine restaurants and expensive art galleries that are so typical of wealthy Mayfair. When finished continue into Hertford Street and keep left. Walk ahead along Down Street for a short detour. On the right-hand side just before Piccadilly is the former entrance to **14 Down Street underground station**.

This station was part of the Piccadilly Line and was in use from 1907 to 1932. During WWII it was used as a deep-level shelter by the Emergency Railway

Committee, and Winston Churchill and members of his Cabinet also stayed here occasionally when the Cabinet War Rooms in Whitehall were not available. Churchill liked sleeping here because it offered good noise insulation against the sounds of bombing above and he nicknamed the place the 'Burrow'. More recently, the station has been the setting for several films including *Creep* and *Die Another Day*.

Head back onto Hertford Street where outside number 20 is a plaque to former resident **15** **Sir George Cayley** (1773-1857), a mostly forgotten figure now but who is regarded as the 'Father of Aerodynamics'. His ground breaking research was highly influential in the decades leading up to the first powered flight by the Wright Brothers in 1903. Between 1849 and 1853 Cayley successfully tested his own gliders using first a ten-year-old boy, and then later his coachman. Their names are now lost to us, but they were arguably the first true aviators.

Follow the map to pass by the **16** **Hilton Hotel** which opened in the 1960s. It was here in 1964 that Ronnie Kray met his counterparts in the American Mafia to try to establish a trans-Atlantic crime partnership, and also where in August 1967 the Beatles first met the Maharishi Mahesh Yogi. The band later went to the Maharishi's ashram in India where they wrote some of the songs that would appear on the *White Album* and *Abbey Road*.

Follow the map into Pitt Head Mews and immediately on the left head up Curzon Place. It was at Flat 12, on the top floor of **17** **number nine Curzon Place** that two of the most famous rock stars in the world met their deaths at different times. Mama Cass Elliott, singer with the Mamas and the Papas, died here in 1974 when the flat was owned by singer-songwriter Harry Nilsson. Legend has it she died choking on a sandwich in bed, but it was officially from a heart attack. Four years later Keith Moon, drummer with The Who, died from an overdose in the very same bed.

Head north to Curzon Street where on the right at number 30 is **⑱ Crockfords**, one of London's oldest and most exclusive gambling establishments. It has been accepting the wagers of London's aristocracy since 1828 when it was founded in St James's and now has an international clientele of the super rich. It was founded by a fishmonger named **William Crockford** whose amazing natural gambling talent allowed him to raise enough money to demolish four homes in St James's in order to build his original gambling hall. He retired in 1840, already a millionaire.

Opposite Crockfords is Chesterfield Gardens where during WWII the infamous British spies Philby, Burgess and Blunt were regulars at parties organised by Tomás Harris – owner of number 6. Head up Chesterfield Street with its gorgeous Georgian town houses that today sell for more than £2 million. Writer **Somerset Maugham** lived at **⑲ number six** and past residents of number four include the Regency dandy Beau Brummell and Prime Minister Anthony Eden.

Follow the map along Charles Street, then Chesterfield Hill and Hays Mews, passing chic houses and squadrons of four-by-four vehicles with personalised number plates. You come out into **⑳ Berkeley Square**, the first of Mayfair's three great squares visited on the walk, and made famous by the song *A Nightingale Sang in Berkeley Square* (1940) (Maschwitz/Sherwin).

Number 44 on the west side of the square is home to the **㉑ Clermont Club** where Lord Lucan (b. 1934) used to gamble with his aristocratic chums. He was due to meet them on the evening of 8th November, 1974; however, he disappeared following the murder of his family's nanny. The basement is home to **Annabel's** – London's most upmarket nightclub since the 1960s. Number 40 housed the American Office of Strategic Services (OSS) – forerunner of the Central Intelligence Agency (CIA) – in 1942.

If you have an interest in the Royal Family you may be interested in visiting Bruton Street on the north-east side as the Queen was born at number 17 in 1926, and later lived at nearby 145 Piccadilly until 1936. Otherwise head along Mount Street on the north-west side, bearing left until you see the entrance to the rarely visited but fantastic **㉒ Mount Street Gardens**. This was once the burial ground of St George's church in Hanover Square, and by the entrance is the British headquarters of the Jesuits.

Enter the gardens and the first thing you see is the **㉓ Church of the Immaculate Conception** on Farm Street, an elegant neo-Gothic building that

was commissioned by the Jesuits and completed in 1849. It is one of London's most atmospheric churches; Pugin designed the altar, and it was here that the writer Evelyn Waugh converted to Catholicism in 1939.

In the 18th century the parish workhouse stood just to the north (where 103 Mount Street is now located), evidence that even in its aristocratic heyday Mayfair was not immune to the social deprivation that blighted many other areas of London. Continue through the gardens and on the other side you will see the elegant **㉔ Grosvenor Chapel**, built in 1730 for the Grosvenor Estate and later popular with American servicemen stationed in London during WWII. The estate was first laid out in 1720 by Sir Richard Grosvenor along a grid plan, and the family (now headed by the 6th Duke of Westminster) continues to own much of the area.

The origin of the Grosvenor family's great wealth began in 1066 when William Gros Veneur (meaning 'fat hunter') first arrived in England with William the Conqueror, and acted as the King's Master of the Hunt. He was rewarded with land in the north-east of England, and in 1677 his descendant Sir Thomas Grosvenor married Mary Davies, heiress to 500 acres of rural land on the then outskirts of London. However, after the Great

Fire of 1666 many of the wealthier inhabitants of the burnt-out City moved westwards, and the family's fields were developed into what became Mayfair and Belgravia, today some of the most valuable real estate in the world.

Walk south down South Audley Street until you reach Audley Square on the left. Outside **㉕** **number two** is a lamp post used by Russian agents to leave messages during the Cold War in the 1950s. They would mark the lamp post with a chalk-marked number '8' if a covert operation was about to begin and a little trap door at the rear of the lamp post was used to leave messages. Walk back up South Audley Street retracing your steps. **㉖** **Number 33** on this street has another spying connection as it was here in the early 1960s that Sir Roger Hollis – then director general of MI5 – was interrogated by fellow intelligence officers. They suspected he was a Soviet mole, an accusation that has never been proven.

Continue north to reach **㉗** **Grosvenor Square**, the second largest square in London, although very little of its Georgian origins survive. The modern and rather ugly 1960s US embassy building dominates the west side and looks out over a statue of President Franklin D Roosevelt in the middle of the square. In the late 1960s a number of large demonstrations took place outside the embassy against US involvement in Vietnam. During one demonstration in 1968 8,000 protestors besieged the embassy and more than 200 were arrested. This inspired Mick Jagger to write the song *Street Fighting Man* (about Tariq Ali, who led the demonstration with Vanessa Redgrave) after apparently watching the incident from his Bentley.

A quiet **㉘** **memorial garden** dedicated to the memory of those affected by the

September 11th terrorist attacks is situated on the eastern side of the Square. Just beyond this at number nine, on the north-east corner, is an original Georgian house that was home in the 1780s to **㉙ John Adams** (1735-1826), the first American ambassador to England. He was also a signatory to the American Declaration of Independence, and the second President of the United States.

When the embassy originally moved to the square the US authorities followed their normal policy and sought to buy the freehold to the land, but the Grosvenor Estate refused to sell. This is therefore the only tenanted US embassy anywhere in the world. When pressed personally by President J. F. Kennedy, the then Duke of Westminster offered the freehold in exchange for the return of his family's huge former landholdings in US, which had been confiscated during the American War of Independence – an offer the Americans turned down. In 2008 it was announced the embassy would leave the square and relocate to Nine Elms (between Vauxhall and Battersea).

A previous building at **44 Grosvenor Square** was once home to the Earl of Harrowby, and the Cabinet were dining here in 1815 when news of Wellington's victory at Waterloo was received. Four years later a group of revolutionaries planned to murder the Cabinet whilst they dined at number 44. The conspirators were arrested at their base in Cato Street (near Edgware Road) – an incident that became known as the Cato Street Conspiracy.

Leave the Square on the north-east corner and head up Duke Street. Ahead on the left is an odd building that houses an **electricity substation**, and above which stands **㉚ Brown Hart Gardens**. The substation and Italian-style paved gardens were designed in 1903 by Stanley Peach. The gardens re-opened in 2007 after 20 years of closure. The site is run by the Grosvenor Estate and frequently hosts free classical music concerts, an open air theatre and children's days (visit brownhartgardens.co.uk).

Opposite the substation is the **31** **Ukrainian Catholic Cathedral** on Weighhouse Street. This intriguing place is moments away from busy Oxford Street, and yet the interior is an oasis of calm that gives no hint that you are in the middle of London. The building was formerly the home of a Free Chapel congregation that was founded by Queen Matilda in 1148, and which moved over the centuries from the Tower of London area to Weighhouse Street in the late 19th century. The church was designed by Alfred Waterhouse, architect of the Natural History Museum, and can seat 900 people.

The Ukrainian Catholics originally worshipped at a church in Saffron Hill near Clerkenwell but took over this building in the 1960s after its original congregation had dwindled away. The first sizeable group of Ukrainians settled in London after WWII; these were often soldiers displaced by the war, and unable to return home because of the Communist suppression of the Ukrainian

30 *Brown Hart Gardens*

Greek-Catholic Church. Following the collapse of the USSR, the Ukraine regained its independence in 1991 and this has led to more Ukrainians coming to London and swelling the congregation.

Follow the map across Davies Street and into South Molton Lane, then almost immediately through South Molton Passage into the cosmopolitan and pedestrianised South Molton Street. At the end cross Brook Street. This street is named after the hidden Tyburn river (or 'brook') that flows directly underneath and was once open to the air. Brook Street is now home to a number of embassies and high-class art galleries, some of which sell museum-quality ancient artefacts. Do not be afraid to go into the private art galleries – they do not charge, although you may want to buy a glossy catalogue to fully understand the exhibits.

On the right is ㉜ **Claridges Hotel**, one of the finest in London. A sad tale from the Jewish Holocaust is associated with the hotel, as it was here that Szmul Zygielbojm (1895-1943), a Jewish-Polish member of the Polish government in exile, met the American Office of Strategic Services (OSS) on 11th May, 1943. Zygielbojm had already tried to convince the Allies to bomb the train lines leading to the Nazi concentration camps in order to stop the genocide, and had made broadcasts about Nazi atrocities on BBC radio as early as June 1942. But in Claridges the OSS, forerunner of the CIA, informed Zygielbojm that Roosevelt himself had decided no war planes could be spared to help the Jews. Distraught, Zygielbojm committed suicide the next day and his final letter spoke bitterly of the Allies and how 'By looking on passively upon this murder of defenseless millions [of] tortured children, women and men they have become partners to the responsibility'.

Continue east along Brook Street where the rock star **Jimi Hendrix** lived briefly at number 23 in 1969. The 18th-century composer **George Frideric Handel** lived next door at number 25 for 36 years until his death in 1759, and this building is now occupied by the excellent **㉝ Handel Museum**. You can reach the entrance on Lancashire Court to the rear.

Handel composed some of his most important works here including *Messiah*, *Zadok the Priest* and *Music for the Royal Fireworks*. Handel was appointed court composer to George I, his original patron back in Hanover, and the museum is a great place to find out more about the man and his music (open Tuesday to Sunday). If you feel a strange presence in the building you are not alone – in 2001 two people reported seeing a ghost here and the Handel House Trust called in a Roman Catholic priest to perform an exorcism. The museum hosts regular concerts in the same room that Handel performed in although you need to book ahead for these (telephone 020 7495 1685 or visit www.handelhouse.org for more information).

The museum also allows access to part of number 23, where there is an exhibition of photographs showing Hendrix living here with his girlfriend Kathy Etchingham. Twice a year with advance booking you can also visit the upper floors where Hendrix actually lived, normally used as office space.

Courtyard behind Handel's Museum

Continue east until you reach **New Bond Street**. Many Londoners do not realise that 'Bond Street', famous for its galleries and expensive boutiques, is actually two streets – New Bond Street, which runs south from Oxford Street, and Old Bond Street, which continues on at the southern end and stops at Piccadilly. They are both named after 17th-century developer Sir Thomas Bond who also built Dover Street and Albemarle Street when Mayfair was semi-rural.

New Bond Street was once home to the Soviet spy **Guy Burgess** (1911-1963) who lived at **34** **10 Clifford Chambers** just before he fled to the USSR in 1951 with fellow traitor Donald Maclean. Burgess, an alcoholic and openly homosexual, never enjoyed living in exile in the USSR, and continued to order his clothes from his former Savile Row tailor. Anthony Blunt, another member of the same spy ring, was one of the first people sent by the British security services to search the flat after Burgess had fled, allowing Blunt to hide potentially incriminating evidence that would have brought forward his own exposure as a spy by many years.

Cross over New Bond Street and continue along Brook Street to reach **35** **Hanover Square**, originally laid out in the early 18th century. Head south down St George Street until you see **36** **St George's Church**. It was built in the 1720s by John James, apprentice to Sir Christopher Wren, and has always been a popular choice for society weddings, including those of the actor and clown Joseph Grimaldi, the poet Percy Shelley, Prime Minister Benjamin Disraeli, US President Theodore ('Teddy') Roosevelt, and writer George Eliot.

The church is where Eliza Doolittle's father Alfred is married in George Bernard Shaw's *Pygmalion*. In *My Fair Lady*, the musical version, St George's is the subject of the famous song *Get Me to the Church on Time*. In 1797 Horatio Nelson – then a resident at 147 New Bond Street and having recently lost his arm in a naval battle – left a thanksgiving note at the church stating 'an officer desires to return thanks to Almighty God for his perfect recovery from a severe wound...'. Handel was also a regular in the congregation here. If you look inside the church there are a number of wooden boards that list past church wardens – among them knights, high-ranking soldiers and various members of the nobility stretching back hundreds of years.

Walk along Maddox Street and around the back of the church to head down Mill Street. Cross over Conduit Street into **Savile Row**, home of London's finest bespoke tailors. Indeed the term 'bespoke' is thought to have originated here as the cloth for a suit was said to have been 'spoken' for by particular customers.

The oldest tailors is **37** **Gieves and Hawkes** at number one, an amalgamation of two earlier businesses founded in the late 18th century. Past customers have included Lord Nelson and the Duke of Wellington. **38** **Henry Poole & Co** at number 15 was founded in 1806 and has been in Savile Row since 1846. It has made clothes for Winston Churchill, Napoleon III, Charles Dickens and General de Gaulle. It is also where the first smoking jacket – later known as the tuxedo – was designed for the Prince of Wales in 1860.

The Beatles opened their **39** **Apple Corps headquarters** at number three Savile Row in the late 1960s, a brave attempt to combine a money-making enterprise with the high ideals of hippy culture. Things did not go well as the band was falling apart, and their last ever concert was held on 30th January, 1969 on the roof of the headquarters. As captured in the documentary film *Let it Be*, the Beatles ran through a number of songs from their last album before the police intervened to shut down the gig after 40 minutes, acting on complaints received from angry office workers opposite. Later in 1969, the Rolling Stones practised in the basement studio with new guitarist Mick Taylor in the two days between the death of the band's founder Brian Jones and their seminal Hyde Park concert.

At the end of Savile Row you can head left and follow the map towards Regent Street and Piccadilly Circus to complete the walk. ●

35 *Hanover Square*

SHOP...

Piccadilly Market
Piccadilly, W1
www.st-james-piccadilly.org/market.html

VISIT...

Royal Academy of Arts (see p.9)
Burlington House,
Piccadilly, W1J
www.royalacademy.org.uk

Handel Museum (see p.23)
25 Brook Street, Mayfair, W1K
www.handelhouse.org

EAT, DRINK...

Ye Grapes Public House
(see p.14)
Shepherd Market, W1J

Claridges (see p.22)
49 Brook Street, W1K
www.claridges.co.uk

Waterstones
5th Floor,
203-206 Piccadilly, W1J
www.5thview.co.uk
Café, bar and lounge located
on the fifth floor of this art
deco building.

27

2 Fitzrovia & Bloomsbury Walk

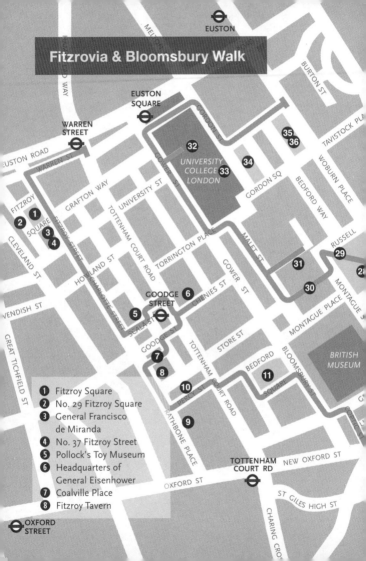

Fitzrovia & Bloomsbury Walk

① Fitzroy Square
② No. 29 Fitzroy Square
③ General Francisco
de Miranda
④ No. 37 Fitzroy Street
⑤ Pollock's Toy Museum
⑥ Headquarters of
General Eisenhower
⑦ Coalville Place
⑧ Fitzroy Tavern

1 Fitzroy Square

Fitzrovia & Bloomsbury Walk

Start: Warren Street underground station
Finish: Euston rail station/Euston Square underground station
Distance: 4.5 miles

The walk begins at Warren Street tube station, from where you head west along Warren Street then down Fitzroy Street to ❶ **Fitzroy Square** – all part of an area known as Fitzrovia. This district is bounded to the north by Euston Road, to the east by Tottenham Court Road, to the south by Oxford Street and to the west by Great Portland Street.

The square is named after the Fitzroy family who used to own the land here. The origins of the family's wealth and influence began with Henry FitzRoy, one of Charles II's many illegitimate children. Henry became the Duke of Grafton, with a subsidiary title being Earl of Euston (in Suffolk) hence the name of the nearby train station. Fitzroy square was designed by James and William Adam (brothers of the more famous Robert) and developed from the early 1790s. In the early 20th century the area became synonymous with the hard-drinking bohemians and artists who gathered at the Fitzroy Tavern on Charlotte Street, hence the soubriquet 'Fitzrovia'.

The first sign of this artistic legacy can be seen at ❷ **number 29**; it was here that Virginia Stephen (1882-1941) (better known as Virginia Woolf) lived with her brother Adrian from 1907 to 1911. The house had previously been occupied in the 1890s by the writer and playwright George Bernard Shaw. The Stephen siblings (Virginia, her older sister Vanessa, and brothers Thoby and Adrian) – formed the nucleus of the Bloomsbury Group, a loose artistic association which had its origins in the Apostles Society at Cambridge University, and whose members continued their artistic endeavours and sexual adventures after moving to London.

Membership of the Group was fluid, but centred around the Stephen family and their close friends such as the economist John Maynard Keynes, writer E. M. Forster, artist and critic Roger Fry and the biographer Lytton Strachey. They chose to live in Fitzrovia and Bloomsbury at a time when the upper-classes regarded it, according to Henry James, as an 'antiquated, ex-fashionable area'. Virginia was the queen bee of the 'Bloomsberries', and her lifestyle exemplified the description of the group as 'couples who live in squares and have triangular relationships'.

On the south side of the square is an unusual statue to former resident ❸ **General Francisco de Miranda** (1750-1816), a Venezuelan revolutionary and flamboyant adventurer who fought for the independence of Spain's South American colonies and died in a Spanish jail. Continue south along Fitzroy Street, passing ❹ **number 37**, where George Bernard Shaw lived with his mother between 1881 and 1882, and where in the 1950s L. Ron Hubbard (1911-1986) – founder of Scientology – based his first headquarters.

Continue down Fitzroy Street to Charlotte Street, once a magnet for hundreds of anarchists and radicals from France and Germany who moved to London during the late 19th and early 20th centuries. The Anglers' Club, then located on this street, was used by the Foreign Barbers of London Association – a front for radical activity whose meetings were attended by the future Soviet leader Lenin (1870-1924) during his time in London before the 1917 Russian Revolution. The Communist Club once based at 107 Charlotte Street was also visited by Stalin and Trotsky in the pre-Revolution era.

Follow the map to take a left up Scala Street. At the end on the corner is one of London's quaintest museums, the little-known ❺ **Pollock's Toy Museum**. It contains a wide range of Victorian toys and paper theatres popularised by Benjamin Pollock in the 19th century and is open Monday to Saturday 10am-5pm.

Follow the map to reach Tottenham Court Road where you cross over and walk down Chenies Street. On the left are some unusual round buildings now used as storage facilities but which during WWII were the only visible part of the deep underground ❻ **headquarters of General Eisenhower** (1890-1969). The extensive underground buildings were later used as an army transit camp until the mid-1950s and could hold up to 2,000 men. The storage company that uses the tunnels re-named the pill box entrances The Eisenhower Centre, although they remain closed to the public.

The tunnels – including those under Goodge Street underground station nearby – were originally part of a grand plan to create an express underground line to run parallel to the Northern Line and thus ease congestion. The plans were shelved when WWII started and were never resurrected. To this day certain stations on the Northern Line are only separated by a few feet of concrete from their long-hidden counterparts.

Follow the map back across Tottenham Court Road to walk down ❼ **Coalville Place**, an unusual residential road full of plants and flowers tended by the green-fingered residents.

Back on Charlotte Street head south to reach the ❽ **Fitzroy Tavern** at number 16 – named after the creator of Fitzroy Square, Charles FitzRoy. The Tavern, which was at its bohemian peak from the 1920s until the 1940s, became a meeting place for various artists, writers and voracious drinkers of the era including Dylan Thomas, Julian Maclaren-Ross, Augustus John, George Orwell and Nina Hamnett. The Satanist Aleister Crowley drank here and even invented a cocktail for the pub. However, regulars were in danger of catching 'Sohoitis', an ailment afflicting aspiring artists who ended up wasting their talents by staying in the Tavern all day and night and never getting any work done.

Those interested in the Tavern might want to also visit the ❾ **Wheatsheaf** public house in nearby Rathbone Place. In the late 1930s some of the in-crowd at the Tavern migrated to the Wheatsheaf and a core group including Dylan Thomas, George Orwell, Philip O'Connor and Edwin Muir became known as the 'Wheatsheaf writers'.

Cleveland Street runs parallel to Charlotte Street on the west side and has a strange connection with Jack the Ripper and Prince Albert Victor, known as 'Prince Eddy' (1864-1892), eldest son of Edward VII and grandson of Queen Victoria. It has been suggested by some Ripper theorists that the Prince worked incognito as an apprentice to the painter Walter Sickert (1860-1942) whose studio was located on Cleveland Street. Eddy was later implicated, probably unfairly, in a damaging public scandal after the police raided a high-society male brothel on the same street in 1889, and the prince was soon sent off on a long tour of India by his despairing family.

In the 1970s a man claiming to be Sickert's illegitimate son alleged that Prince Eddy, whilst working for Sickert, had fathered a child with the lowly-born Annie Cook who was a model for Sickert. The conspiracy theory runs that the Establishment tried to protect the monarchy from the potential scandal by locking away Annie Cook (who it was said had married the prince) in an asylum, but not before Cook had entrusted her child to a prostitute friend named Mary Jane Kelly. Kelly – one of the Ripper's victims – and her friends then tried to blackmail the monarchy over the scandal, only to be murdered in quick succession in 1888 by the Establishment in order to silence them. It is unlikely the real identity of Jack the Ripper will ever be discovered; however, in 2002 crime novelist Patricia Cornwell announced her theory that Sickert himself was the murderer, and tried (inconclusively) to match DNA taken from his paintings with extracts taken from the original taunting letters the Ripper sent to the police in 1888.

Continue past the Tavern along Percy Street where Alois Hitler, Jr is thought to have lived at ⑩ **number four**, and where his half

brother Adolph (1889-1945) may have visited him in 1912. Cross over Tottenham Court Road again to head down Bayley Street.

This leads into ⑪ **Bedford Square**, the finest of many elegant squares in Bloomsbury and often used for filming period dramas. It was built between 1775 and 1783 and takes its name from the Russell family whose most senior member is the Duke of Bedford. The Russells were the main landowners in Bloomsbury and the Russell and Bedford names crop up throughout the area. Notable past residents of this square

11 *Bedford Square*

include Prime Minister Herbert Asquith (number 44), Sir Edwin Lutyens, architect of New Delhi (number 31) and scientist Sir Henry Cavendish (number 11).

On the far side, walk down Bloomsbury Street then turn left along Great Russell Street on the south side of the British Museum. Head down Coptic Street (look out for the Cartoon Museum on Little Russell Street) until you reach New Oxford Street. Just over the road is **⑫ James Smith & Sons**, London's oldest and best umbrella and walking stick shop. Founded in 1830, it boasts an ornate Victorian shop front which remains almost unaltered after 140 years. The shop is still family-run and is worth a visit solely to see the unusual animal-headed walking sticks.

Continue east along Bloomsbury Way where shortly on your left is **⑬ St George's Bloomsbury** – perhaps the least known of Nicholas Hawksmoor's six London churches. This flamboyant building was completed in 1731. Its unusual tower is modelled on the Roman writer Pliny's description of the 4th century BC Mausoleum of Mausolos at Halicarnassus in Turkey, one of the seven wonders of the ancient world. The church also features in the background of William Hogarth's famous engraving, *Gin Lane* (1751).

Gin Lane depicts the squalor of the gin addicted poor living in a notorious slum – or 'rookery' – that bordered St George's. The slums were largely demolished during the Victorian construction of New Oxford Street and Shaftesbury Avenue.

St George's was the sixth and final London church designed by Hawksmoor (1661-1736) in his distinctive English Baroque style. The church hosted the memorial service for Emily Davison, the suffragette who died after throwing herself under George V's horse at the Epsom Derby in 1913. An interesting exhibition on the church and Hawksmoor can be visited inside.

Continue east to see **14** **Bloomsbury Square** on your left. This is the oldest official 'square' in London, and was laid out in the early 1660's. The name 'Bloomsbury' is thought to derive from 'Blemondisberi', meaning 'the manor of (William) Blemond', who acquired the land in the early 13th century. The land remained rural until the 1660s when the 4th Earl of Southampton began developing the area, attracting an influx of wealthy citizens from the over-crowded City, particularly after the Great Fire of 1666. It was originally designed so the houses on three sides were inhabited by the wealthy, with their servants based on the remaining side. Today it is a fairly soulless place although it's worth looking out for a fine bronze statue of the Whig leader Charles James Fox (1749-1806). The writer Isaac D'Israeli lived at number 6 between 1817 and 1829 and his son, the writer and future Prime Minister Benjamin Disraeli, also stayed here for a while.

Continue east and at the junction with Southampton Row look to the right to see a strange lane behind some gates that disappears into the depths of London underneath the road. This was the **15** **Kingsway entrance** of a tram system that functioned from the early 1900s until the last tram left the Kingsway tunnel in July 1952. The tunnel dates from when Kingsway was first built and the tram underpass ran from Holborn via Kingsway and Aldwych before emerging at the surface near Waterloo Bridge. It is generally impossible for the public to visit the tunnels and long-closed tram stations, but there are a number of web-sites such as Subterranea Brittannica (www.subbrit.org.uk) that have a wealth of information and photographs on these hidden parts of London.

Continuing the underground theme you may be interested to know that not far from here, and hidden 100 feet below street level, is the huge **Kingsway Telephone Exchange**. It extends for one mile and covers an area equivalent to 14 football pitches underneath Chancery Lane underground station and Red Lion Street. The complex was built during WWII as one of eight deep tunnel shelters underneath the Northern and Central Line routes. As its name suggests, it acted as a communications centre and was extensively developed after WWII, coming under the control of the General Post Office until it was closed in the 1990s. In 2008 British Telecom announced the complex was for sale for £5 million.

In 1980 the New Statesman journalist Duncan Campbell entered London's secret network of government tunnels from a traffic island in Bethnal Green and cycled for miles unobserved by the authorities. His route took him past various interchanges in the tunnel system and he passed under St Martin le Grand in the City, then Holborn and Covent Garden and as far as Whitehall and its telephone exchange just south of Nelson's Column. Allegedly

there are lifts and staircases here leading up to 10 Downing Street and various government ministry buildings. On his return trip Campbell passed the Kingsway Telephone Exchange before re-emerging in the Holborn Telephone Exchange near the offices of the New Statesman.

Continue east along Theo-bald's Road for a few minutes looking out on the right for the antiquated frontage of ⑯ **Conway Hall**. This has been the home since 1929 to one of London's most obscure groups – the South Place

TO THINE OWN SELF BE TRUE

Ethical Society. Describing themselves as the oldest 'freethought community' in the world, the society began in 1793 as a dissenting congregation. It was then mostly concerned with rebelling against the doctrine of eternal hell, but is now a non-religious foundation that runs a programme of lectures and activities concerning basic ethical principles.

From Theobald's Road turn left up Great James Street then Northington Street, which leads onto John Street. Head north onto adjoining **17** **Doughty Street** with its fine Georgian town houses, an elegant part of Bloomsbury that most tourists and Londoners rarely see.

At number 48 is the **18** **Charles Dickens Museum**, situated in the only surviving London house the great writer inhabited. Dickens lived here between 1837 and 1839 during which time he wrote *Oliver Twist*, *Nicholas Nickleby* and much of *The Pickwick Papers*. It was here too that Mary Hogarth, Dickens's sister-in-law, died in 1837 in Dickens's arms aged only 17. It has been suggested Dickens was more in love with Mary than his own wife Catherine. The author was so stricken by Mary's death that he expressed a desire to be buried beside her and, for the only time in his life,

missed a writing deadline. Mary's demise was fictionalised by Dickens in the death of Little Nell in *The Old Curiosity Shop* – an account that caused scenes of hysteria among some of the writer's fans when the book was serialised in the 1840s. Not all were impressed, however – Oscar Wilde later remarking that 'One would have to have a heart of stone to read the death of Little Nell without laughing'. The museum is open Monday to Saturday 10am-5pm, Sunday 11am-5pm (www.dickensmuseum.com).

At the top of Doughty Street head north into Mecklenburgh Square, then left at Heathcoate Street. At the end is the entrance to one of London's most hidden spots, ⑲ **St George's Gardens**. Covering three acres, the Gardens began in 1713 as a burial ground for St George the Martyr, and St George's Bloomsbury. It is thought to have been the first graveyard in London to be located separately from its associated parish churches. Among those buried here are Oliver Cromwell's daughter, Anna Gibson, and eight officers who were executed in 1746 for fighting on the side of Bonnie Prince Charlie. The first recorded case in London of body-snatching took place here, although this stopped in the 1850s when the burial ground was closed after becoming full. It re-opened in the 1880s as a park, although it still contains grave-stones and tombs.

Re-trace your steps back to ⑳ **Mecklenburgh Square**. Those interested in Virginia Woolf should note that William Goodenough House stands on the site of number 37 where Virginia and Leonard Woolf lived from 1939 until her suicide in March 1941.

On the north side is a small alleyway that skirts Coram Fields to the south, and leads you to the ㉑ **Foundling Museum** at 40 Brunswick Square. The museum tells the fascinating story of the Foundling Hospital that once stood on Coram's Fields and was founded by Sir Thomas Coram (1668-1751).

Coram, a retired sea captain, was shocked by the way abandoned children in London were treated. His first hospital was founded in Hatton Garden, and in 1739 he obtained a royal charter from George II to establish a 'hospital for the maintenance and education of exposed and deserted young children'. The Foundling Hospital was built in the 1740s and was the first incorporated charity in the world. Coram encouraged the rich and famous to support the hospital, among them the painter William Hogarth who was one of the first governors. His portrait of Coram, along with other important paintings given to the hospital, can be seen inside the museum. Hogarth also designed the children's uniforms and the hospital's coat of arms.

22

Another great 18th-century figure associated with the hospital was George Frideric Handel. He gave a charity concert performance of *Messiah* at the hospital and donated to it an original copy of the musical score. This, as well as Handel's will, can be seen in the room dedicated to the composer at the museum. On arrival at the hospital children were sent to wet nurses in the countryside and returned as toddlers; on reaching their teens the girls were apprenticed as domestic servants whilst boys entered the Navy. The museum displays the personal tokens left by the mothers as keepsakes for their babies. In the 1920s the hospital moved out of London and its buildings were mostly demolished. However, its legacy continues to this day in the form of the Coram charity for children. The museum is open Tuesday to Saturday 10am-6pm and Sundays 12noon-6pm.

Head out of the museum and cross over the park outside to reach Lansdowne Terrace, then head left along Guildford Street. On the left is the entrance to ㉒ **Coram's Fields**, and the small enclave by the gates is where, on the day the hospital opened, over 100 babies were left by their desperate mothers. A park now occupies the site of the hospital, which cannot be visited without being accompanied by a child.

Opposite Coram's Fields is Lambs Conduit Street and if you are in need of refreshment try ㉓ **The Lamb** public house at number 94 – said to have been a favourite with Charles Dickens. This is a great old-

23 The Lamb

fashioned Victorian boozer, with original glass slats – or 'snob screens' – that were designed to protect the respectable drunks in the lounge bar from the stares of the poor drunks in the public bar.

Head west along Guildford Street where shortly on your left you will see the entrance to ㉔ **Queen Square**, another secluded Bloomsbury gem that is surrounded by several medical institutions. The square was completed by 1725 and a statue of a queen stands on the north side. For many years it was thought to represent Queen Anne and the square was once called Queen Anne's Square. However, more recent thinking suggests the statue was in fact meant to represent Queen Charlotte (1744-1818), wife of King George III (1738-1820). The name of the square is now an elegant compromise.

Head through the square to reach the church of ㉕ **St George the Martyr**. Originally a chapel of ease in the early 18th century, it became a parish church in 1723. Hawksmoor added the four columns and circular dome, and you can still see the reredos on the eastern wall where the altar used to be situated before the Victorians moved it to the south side. Until 1875 the church held an annual Christmas dinner for 100 chimney sweep apprentices and is still known today as the Chimney Sweeps' church. The poets Ted Hughes and Sylvia Plath were married here in 1956, and some of Hughes's lines (and also those of Philip Larkin) are etched into the paving stones beside a memorial to the Queen's Jubilee on the south side of the square.

Beside the church is the ㉖ **Queen's Larder** public house. The name is thought to have originated from when Queen Charlotte rented a cellar beneath the pub in order to store her husband George III's favourite foods whilst he stayed in the square undergoing medical treatment for his many bouts of apparent insanity (now thought to have been porphyria).

On the eastern side of the square is Great Ormond Street, best known for its ㉗ **children's hospital**. J. M. Barrie (1860-1937) donated the copyright of Peter Pan to the hospital in 1929 and when the copyright expired the UK government granted the hospital a perpetual right to collect royalties on the work, although this was later revised under recent changes in European Union law. The hospital has often fought to protect its rights to Peter Pan against unauthorised derivative works, particularly against the Hollywood film studios.

Head down Cosmo Place and cross over Southampton Row to bear right until you reach ㉘ **Russell Square**, the second largest square in London. It was founded by the Duke of Bedford in 1799, and built by the prolific developer James Burton – one of the first to have a permanent labour force of builders. It is closely associated with the poet T. S. Eliot (1888-1965) who lived at number 28 Bedford Place nearby, and worked at the venerable publishing house Faber & Faber, then based at number 24 Russell Square (see the plaque on the western corner). Whilst working here he had to endure his estranged wife marching up and down outside the office building wearing a sandwich board that proclaimed 'I am the wife that T. S. Eliot abandoned'. He often slept at the office on Tuesday

28 Russell Square

nights during WWII whilst on fire-watching duty. It was at these premises in 1944 that Eliot received – and rejected – George Orwell's manuscript for *Animal Farm*.

The western corner of the square contains one of London's 13 remaining **㉙ cab shelters**, arguably among the most exclusive establishments in the capital given you need to pass the 'knowledge' to drive a black cab and hence use the shelters. The shelters were the product of the Cabmen's Shelter Fund established in London in 1875 to provide an alcohol-free alternative for cabbies between fares. All are now Grade II listed buildings.

The suffragette Emmeline Pankhurst (1858-1928) lived as a child with her family in the square and their home became a prominent meeting place for many of London's socialists, anarchists and Fabians. This experience had a huge influence on the young Emmeline and laid the foundations of her later struggles to obtain the vote for women.

This part of Bloomsbury is now dominated by University College London (UCL) and on the west side you can see the imposing sight of ❸⓿ **Senate House**, the administrative centre of the college and home to the second largest library in London. Walk through the gates and under Senate House to reach Malet Street.

Senate House was built in the 1930s to an Art Deco design by architect Charles Holden, and was at the time the tallest building in London. Legend has it that during the 1930s Oswald Mosley, leader of the British Union of Fascists, intended to house Parliament in the building in the event of his taking power. The Ministry of Information was based here during WWII and its staff included writers Graham Greene and George Orwell (1903-1950). Orwell's frustrations at the degree of censorship imposed by the Ministry partly inspired him to write his great novel *Nineteen Eighty-Four* (1949), with its Ministry of Truth housed in an ominous building similar to the Senate House and controlled by Big Brother (the Ministry of Information was run by Brendan Bracken – nicknamed 'BB').

Walk north along Malet Street and head right into the UCL complex following the sign for SOAS (School of Oriental and African Studies). Opposite, and also signposted, is the ❸⓵ **Brunei Gallery**. The gallery hosts a programme of changing exhibitions reflecting Asian themes, and also gives you access to one of London's most hidden places – a tranquil **Japanese roof garden**. It is normally open to the public for free when the Brunei Gallery has an exhibition, Tuesday to Saturday 10.30am-5pm (see www.soas. ac.uk/gallery for details).

Continue up Malet Street and left at Torrington Place to reach Gower Street. Head north, passing on the right a University building that stands on the site where Charles Darwin used to live. Shortly after this you will see the grand entrance to **University College**, nicknamed the 'Godless college on Gower Street' by its detractors when founded in 1826 because it controversially admitted non Anglican students. King's College London was set up three years later as an Anglican alternative. Head over to the right-hand corner and into the building itself, following the sign for ❸⓶ **Auto-icon.** This is one of the strangest sights in London – the preserved body of the great philosopher Jeremy Bentham (1748-1832).

In his will, and consistent with his Utilitarian principles, Bentham requested his body be preserved and stored in a wooden cabinet described as his 'Auto-icon'. The college acquired the Auto-icon in 1850 and put it on public display. For the 100th and 150th anniversaries of the college the Auto-icon attended the meeting of the College Council, where Bentham was listed as 'present but not voting'. However, contrary to popular myth, he does not put in regular appearances at council meetings. The Auto-icon has a wax head because of damage done to the original (now in storage) during the preservation process, and also through endless student pranks carried out over the years.

If you have time follow the signs to visit the excellent ❸❸ **Petrie Museum of Egyptian Archaeology** (open Tuesday to Friday 1pm-5pm, Saturday 11am-2pm – www.petrie.ucl.ac.uk). It is a welcome alternative to the crowds at the British Museum. The Petrie houses one of the greatest collections of Egyptian and Sudanese archaeology in the world.

When finished continue up Gower Street then turn right at Gower Place and then head south down Gordon Street. This brings you into ❸❹ **Gordon Square**, which was developed by Thomas

Cubitt in the 1820s as one of a pair with neighbouring Tavistock Square. Virginia Woolf lived at number 46 from 1905 to 1907, and later the house was taken over by the economist John Maynard Keynes (1883–1946). The biographer Lytton Strachey lived at number 51 from 1919, and Clive Bell, the art critic and husband of Virginia's sister Vanessa, lived at number 50 from 1922-1939. All this talent caused Virginia to remark smugly in 1922 that 'everyone in Gordon Square has become famous'.

Continue to ㉟ **Tavistock Square**. Virginia Woolf lived at number 52 (now demolished) from 1924-1939 after marrying Leonard Woolf, and it was here that she wrote some of her best-known works such as *Orlando, The Waves* and *To the Lighthouse*.

The square contains a statue to ㊱ **Mahatma Gandhi** (1869-1948), the great Indian figure who studied law nearby at University College between 1888 and 1891. You will also find here a cherry tree planted as a memorial to the victims of Hiroshima.

On July 7 2005 a bomb exploded on a bus near the British Medical Association building, part of a wider terrorist attack on London that same day. A memorial to the victims of the bombings can be visited in Hyde Park. The BMA building on the east side of the square, and dating from 1911, was designed by Sir Edwin Lutyens and stands on the site of a house where Charles Dickens lived between 1851 and 1860. During this period he wrote classics such as *Bleak House, Little Dorrit, Hard Times* and *A Tale of Two Cities*. The Fitzrovia/Bloomsbury walk ends on this final literary connection.

If you head north you can cross over Euston Road to reach Euston railway station or head right towards St Pancras and King's Cross. ●

VISIT...

British Museum
Great Russell St, WC1B
www.britishmuseum.org

Brunei Gallery (p.53)
10 Thornhaugh St, WC1H
www.soas.ac.uk/gallery

**Charles Dickens
Museum** (p.44)
48 Doughty St, WC1N
www.dickensmuseum.com

Foundling Museum (p.46)
40 Brunswick Square, WC1N
www.foundlingmuseum.org.uk

Cartoon Museum
35 Little Russell St, WC1A
www.cartoonmuseum.org

Petrie Museum (p.54)
6 Gower St, WC1E
www.petrie.ucl.ac.uk

Pollock's Toy Museum(p.35)
1 Scala St, W1T
www.pollockstoymuseum.com

EAT, DRINK...

Fitzroy Tavern (see p.37)
Wheatsheaf (see p.37)
The Lamb (see p.47)
Queen's Larder (see p.50)

3 Soho Walk

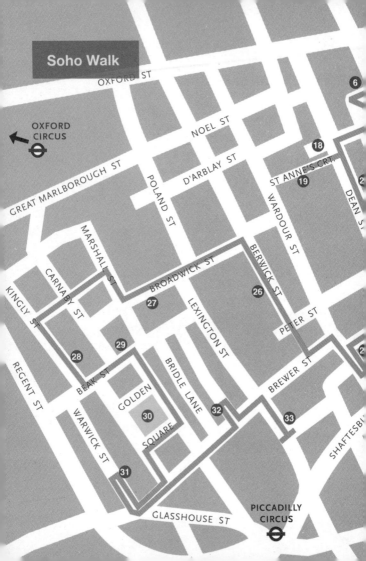

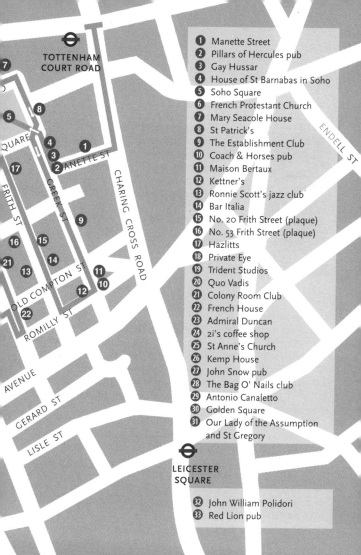

ENDELL ST

CHARING CROSS ROAD

FRITH ST

GREEK ST

SQUARE

ANETTE ST

OLD COMPTON ST

ROMILLY ST

AVENUE

GERARD ST

LISLE ST

Soho Walk

Start: Tottenham Court Road station
Finish: various options
Distance: 2 miles

Follow the map from Tottenham Court Road underground station down Charing Cross Road to enter Soho on its eastern perimeter along ❶ **Manette Street**. This street, formerly Rose Street, was renamed in honour of Dickens's character Dr Manette from *A Tale of Two Cities* (1859) who lived 'in a quiet street corner not far from Soho Square... In a building at the back, attainable by a courtyard where a plane tree rustled its green leaves, church organs claimed to be made, and likewise gold to be beaten by some mysterious giant who had a golden arm starting out of the wall... as if he had beaten himself precious...'. A modern replica of the golden arm can be seen protruding from the wall on the left.

Soho is contained geographically within the boundaries of Oxford Street, Shaftesbury Avenue, Charing Cross Road and Regent Street. Chinatown, based along Gerrard Street south of Shaftesbury Avenue, is also considered by many to be part of Soho. During the Middle Ages the Church owned the area, leasing it out as farmland, but after the Dissolution it came under the control of Henry VIII. Hunting still took place here, and the ancient hunting cry 'so-ho!' may explain the area's name.

On the right hand side of the street is the chapel of the House of St Barnabas – an institution we will find out more about shortly. Straight ahead is the back of the ❷ **Pillars of Hercules** public house, which first opened on this site in 1733, and is mentioned in *A Tale of Two Cities*. The current building dates from 1935 and in recent years became a favourite meeting place for writers such as Ian McEwan, Martin Amis and Julian Barnes.

Walk through the narrow alleyway that passes under the pub – an entrance in Soho described by the author Christopher Petit as 'a border post, the crossing-point where obligations could be left behind'. You come straight out into the bustle of Greek Street, which together with three parallel streets running to the west (Frith, Dean and Wardour Street), forms the heart of Soho.

Most of Soho's street-plan has its origins in the 1670s when the first building development began. The early squares and streets were favoured by the aristocracy and the wealthy, but these classes began to move westwards to newer developments such as Mayfair and were often replaced over time by newly arrived immigrant groups. These included French Huguenots who had fled Catholic France after the Edict of Nantes was revoked in 1685. By the early 18th century nearly half of the parish of Soho was French, giving rise to the area's nickname of 'Petty France'. It was natural that Dickens imagined Dr Manette living here during the era of the French Revolution.

The Huguenots' success in London encouraged further immigration, including Greeks escaping persecution by the Turks (hence Greek Street, where many of them settled from 1670), Germans and Italians fleeing revolutions at home, and Jews building new lives away from the pogroms of Eastern Europe. The last surge came in the mid-20th century when the Chinese began to move from their traditional strongholds in the East End to create Chinatown.

Turn right up **Greek Street** looking out on the right for the ❸ **Gay Hussar** at number two. Opened in 1953, this restaurant became known as the haunt of left wing politicians such as Tony Benn, Roy Hattersley, Michael Foot and Tom Driberg as well as Soviet agents based in London. It was also frequented by General Eisenhower and the Queen of Siam. Its golden age was the late 60s when Driberg, a Labour MP and suspected Soviet spy, tried to persuade Mick Jagger and his girlfriend Marianne Faithful to help target young people for Labour. The rock star evidently decided that playing to thousands in Hyde Park was more attractive and the encounter came to nothing.

Next door is the ❹ **House of St Barnabas in Soho** (number one), which was built in the 1740s and is one of the finest examples of a Georgian mansion in London. In the early 19th century the building served as the offices of the Westminster Commissioner for Works for Sewers (which became the Metropolitan Board of Works), and from here Sir Joseph Bazalgette planned the creation of 86 miles of sewers and 120 miles of drainage that still serve Londoners – in various states of repair – to this day. It has also been speculated that the house was the inspiration for Dickens's description of Dr Manette's Soho home with its courtyard and plane tree (see the quote at the beginning of this chapter).

In 1863 the house was taken over by a charity to help homeless women, a function it serves to this day. Three of its historic rooms can be hired for events and the house is occasionally open to the public on selected days (see website for details www.atthehouse.org.uk). Particularly notable is the cantilevered 'crinoline' staircase extending through five floors, so named as the railings were shaped to accommodate the wide ladies' skirts of the day. There is also a small, hidden garden and a fine chapel (the entrance to which you passed on Manette Street) that is an early example of ecclesiastical architecture inspired by the Oxford Movement.

Carry on to ❺ **Soho Square**, looking out for the unique penny chute attached to railings alongside the House of St Barnabas that has been used to receive charitable donations for over one hundred years. The square was laid out in the 1680s and originally named King's Square after Charles II. The statue of the monarch in the middle of the square dates from 1681 and was returned here in 1938 after being in private ownership for many years. In the 18th century the square was a highly fashionable residential address.

Today the houses have been mainly replaced by modern office blocks. Sir Paul McCartney's company, MPL Communications Ltd, occupies number one. The basement contains an exact replica of EMI studio number two – the legendary venue at EMI's Abbey Road studios where the Beatles recorded. McCartney first came to the square in the 1970s when he was in *Wings* and ran the band's business affairs from the second floor of number one. Underneath the square itself are a number of secret underground tunnels and shelters last used to protect Londoners during the Blitz.

❺ *Soho Square*

Soho Square is usually full of people moving too fast to appreciate its two churches, but they are both worth visiting. On the north-east side beside MPL is Soho's only remaining Huguenot church, the ❻ **French Protestant Church** (or Eglise Protestante Française de Londres) completed in 1893 and architecturally notable for its tiled façade. The architect was Sir Aston Webb, best known for the Victoria and Albert Museum. In the very early 19th Century, London had around 30 French Huguenot churches, with the primary 'mother church' located in Threadneedle Street in the City. However the French congregation was already dwindling, and by 1841, when the church in Threedneedle Street was demolished to make way for the Royal Exchange, only three Huguenot churches remained.

Despite the survival of a few French derived street names (Beaumont Place, Dufour Place, Foubert's Place, Romilly Street) the Huguenot influence on Soho after decades of assimilation has largely disappeared. However this church is a rare legacy and services are still conducted in French. It also houses important historical archives which are invaluable for those seeking information on the Huguenots (see www.huguenotsociety.org.uk for more information).

Number 14 on the north east side of the Square is where the pioneering nurse ❼ **Mary Seacole** (1805-1881) lived during 1857 whilst writing her autobiography *Wonderful Adventures of Mrs Mary Seacole in Many Lands*. Seacole was born in Jamaica, her mother

a Jamaican and her father a Scottish army officer. In the Victorian era Seacole's mixed race meant she encountered great obstacles and prejudice as she tried to help wounded soldiers during the Crimean War. Florence Nightingale is far better known for her efforts to improve medical care during the war, but Seacole's work had considerable practical impact. Unlike her English rival, Seacole ventured onto the battlefields to alleviate the suffering of the injured. It is a pity her work has not been more widely recognised.

6 French Protestant Church

On the east side is **8** **St Patrick's**, a substantial Catholic church dating from 1891 and designed in an Italianate style by John Kelly. The church stands on the site of an 18th-century Catholic church that served the Irish community then living in Soho. St Patrick's is the oldest place of worship in London dedicated to Ireland's patron saint. Today the church is sparsely attended, although it provides assistance to many homeless people to be found on Soho's streets.

The church stands on the site of Carlisle House, where in the 1760s the flamboyant Venetian opera singer and courtesan Theresa Cornelys hosted extravagent masked balls and other entertainments that became the highlight of London's social calendar. Her occasional lover **Casanova** also visited her here during his brief stay in London (see Greek Street below).

From the square return to Greek Street and head south. Number 18 Greek Street (on the left) once hosted **9** **The Establishment**, a club at the centre of the satirical comedy movement that became influential in the early

60s. Ironically titled, the club was always controversial given its founder Peter Cook's desire to create somewhere 'where we could be more outrageous than we could be on stage'.

In 1963 the Home Secretary banned American comedian Lenny Bruce from performing at the club, although others such as Barry Humphries (aka Dame Edna Everage) and Dudley Moore were able to progress their careers here. Also in 1963, and on the first floor of the same building, Lewis Morley took his iconic photograph of Christine Keeler sitting naked astride an Arne Jacobson chair. The photo shoot was intended to publicise a film about Keeler's role in the Profumo Affair, but the film was never made. The shoot was a tense affair as Keeler was reluctant to pose naked, but she was put under considerable pressure by the producers of the film who insisted it was required under her contract. The iconic photograph has, however, kept Keeler in the public consciousness for more than 40 years. Today the suitably named Zebrano at the Establishment bar and restaurant occupies the building.

Number 47 Greek Street is where the world-famous 18th-century romancer **Giacomo Casanova** (1725-1798) lived for several months in 1764. Usually associated with Venice rather than Soho, Casanova nevertheless immersed himself in London society. Casanova had previously fathered an illegitimate child by Theresa Cornelys (see above – Carlisle House) and arrived in Soho after escorting another of Cornelys's children to London. Casanova left England following several brushes with the law having run up debts and contracted venereal disease.

Greek Street was also home to the literary critic **Thomas de Quincey** (1785-1859) whose book *Confessions of an English Opium Eater* (1821) was the first to properly deal with the subject of drug addiction. In it he describes arriving in Soho as a poor teenager and squatting at number 38 where he was shocked to discover a destitute ten-year-old girl living alone. He later befriended a young prostitute named Ann who saved his life when he fell seriously ill. One day in Soho's Golden Square he said goodbye to Ann before leaving on a short trip out of London, returning to find she had disappeared. Despite his desperate searches he never found her again – Golden Square is visited later on in the walk.

Continue south and cross over Old Compton Street until you reach the **⑩ Coach and Horses public house** (number 29). Whilst it does not look like much today, this is one of London's most famous pubs and was founded in 1847. It later became popular with the bibulous artists of Soho's golden age after WWII.

The Soho of that era was notorious for the eccentrics, artists and gangsters who rubbed shoulders in the district's numerous drinking dens, creating a bohemian atmosphere that resulted in the area's 'Boho' nickname. The gangsters – who over the years included the Krays, Billy Hill and Jack Spot, and various Jewish, Maltese and Albanian mafiosi – controlled the clip joints, pornography shops and brothels that made this the centre of London's sex industry.

Corrupt local policemen largely turned a blind eye to what went on, encouraging a relatively high degree of tolerance that inadvertently benefited London's homosexual community and turned Soho into an enclave of unorthodoxy within austere post-war Britain. The more extreme elements of Soho have been cleaned up since the 1970s, although enough remains to attract – in the words of legendary Soho resident Quentin Crisp – 'the safaris that still love(d) to penetrate this exotic land'.

For several decades Norman Balon, the notoriously rude former landlord of the Coach and Horses, served hard drinks to his regular clientele of writers, journalists and actors – including Tom Baker and John Hurt. Vodka was the favourite tipple of the alcoholic columnist Jeffrey Bernard (1932-1997) and Bernard's resulting stupor often resulted in the Spectator magazine having to cancel his Low Life column with the excuse that 'Jeffrey Bernard is unwell'.

Playwright John Osborne wrote that Bernard's column was 'the longest suicide note in history'. The Spectator's printed excuse became the title of the smash hit play written by Keith Waterhouse with Peter O'Toole playing Bernard in the first production. Today the pub remains the venue for satirical magazine Private Eye's fortnightly lunches. Balon retired in 2006, marking the end of a Soho era; however, you can read about his time in Soho in his charmingly-titled autobiography *You're Barred, You Bastards: Memoirs of a Soho Publican*.

Beside the Coach and Horses is ⓫ **Maison Bertaux** – London's oldest French patisserie and café with a bohemian feel that has served some of the best cakes and pastries in Soho since it was founded in 1871. It is popular with students from St Martins College of Art nearby and former student Alexander McQueen – the world famous fashion designer – used to pop in.

Head west along Romilly Street, passing ⓬ **Kettner's** restaurant on the corner at number 29. In its glamorous heyday in the late 19th century the restaurant and the private rooms above were a favourite haunt of Oscar Wilde and his lover Lord Alfred Douglas. Other pleasure-seeking customers included Edward VII and his mistress Lily Langtry.

Join Frith Street and head north to stop at Old Compton Street. This street – originally built in the 1670s – was named after the Bishop of London, Henry Compton. Today it is home to London's most vibrant gay scene.

For many years **Wheelers** restaurant occupied numbers 19-21 Old Compton Street. This was a favourite haunt of the artist Francis Bacon (1909-1992) who regularly lunched here and held court among an assorted group of artists, intellectuals and Soho bruisers. It was also where, in a private room during the 1950s, the Duke of Edinburgh hosted a regular gathering of male friends that became known as the Thursday Club. Attendees included Peter Ustinov, David Niven, James Robertson Justice, Larry Adler, Patrick Campbell and the Soviet spy Kim Philby. The secretive nature of what actually went on at these gatherings led to much gossip about how the Queen's husband liked to relax when not on duty at Buckingham Palace, although from most accounts the participants did no more than sing rowdy songs and tell jokes.

A young and financially-challenged Richard Wagner (1813-1883) stayed at an unknown address on Old Compton Street with his wife in 1839, recovering after a bad sea journey that he later claimed had inspired him to compose the opera *The Flying Dutchman*. The creator of *The Ring* operatic cycle recorded how 'I found my knowledge of English quite inadequate when it came to conversing

with the landlady of the King's Arms'. The couple's dog, Robber, ran away causing the composer some distress, but later returned after having 'wandered as far as Oxford Street in search of adventures'.

Continue up **Frith Street**, well known for its restaurants and ⓭ **Ronnie Scott's jazz club**. Famous for its world-class jazz performances, the club was also the venue for the first public performance of The Who's rock opera *Tommy* in 1969, and for Jimi Hendrix's final public performance in 1970. On your right is ⓮ **Bar Italia**, opened in 1949 by an Italian family, and many a Londoner's final stopping-off point after a late night in the West End. It oozes atmosphere despite the tourists, most of whom will be unaware that an upstairs room hosted the world's first live television broadcast in 1925.

The inhabitant then was the Scottish engineer and inventor **John Logie Baird** (1888-1946) who had arrived in Soho after being evicted from his previous premises, having caused an explosion. Baird constructed the first television equipment and his experiments culminated in October 1925 when (as the inventor later recalled) 'I ran down the little flight of stairs to Mr Cross' office and seized by the arm his office boy, William Taynton, hauled him upstairs, and put him in front of the transmitter'.

Baird had to bribe a terrified Taynton 2s 6d to take part in the experiment, and the office boy thus became the first televised person in history. The experiment was interrupted by angry local prostitutes who banged on Baird's door to complain that his strange looking equipment was being used (they thought) to spy on them. Baird's experiments began to attract wide public and scientific attention and he soon moved out to larger premises.

Continue north up Frith Street. Almost immediately on your right at ⓯ **number 20** is a blue plaque indicating the site of the house where the composer **Wolfgang Amadeus Mozart** (1756-1791) stayed in the mid 1760s. As a musical child prodigy already renowned throughout Europe, he had come to London with his father Leopold and talented four-year-old sister Nannerl, entertaining visitors in return for a fee. In a newspaper advertisement of the time Leopold promised potential clients that they 'may not only hear this young Music Master and his Sister perform in private; but likewise try his surprising Musical Capacity, by giving him anything to play at sight'. Mozart was presented to the Royal Society, and played three times for the court of George III during his 15 months in London. He even found time to begin work on his first symphony.

A blue plaque at ⓰ **number 53** Frith Street commemorates the former residence of **Dr John Snow** (1813-1858) who helped defeat the scourge of cholera (see below).

Frith Street was also home to the painter John Constable in 1810-1811, and the diarist **William Hazlitt** (1778-1830) in the year of his death. Hazlitt, who lived at number six, is widely regarded as England's greatest literary critic after Samuel Johnson and was the author of an influential biography of Napoleon. This is now the site of ⓱ **Hazlitts**, one of London's finest and most discreet hotels. The hotel building incorporates three Georgian houses, and the largely original interior is very atmospheric. Bill Bryson enjoyed a stay here before setting off on his travels around the UK, which were subsequently immortalised in his popular travelogue *Notes from a Small Island* (1995). Those interested in Hazlitt can visit his grave in St. Anne's Churchyard (see below). On his deathbed his last words were 'Well, I've had a happy life'. His landlady then hid his body behind the furniture in order to show his lodgings to new prospective tenants.

Walk up to Soho Square where on the west side you cut through Carlisle Street (where the satirical magazine ⓲ **Private Eye** is based at number 6) to reach Dean Street and head south. On the right hand side take a small detour along St Anne's Court until you reach number 17 on the right hand side. It was here in 1967 that Barry and John Sheffield opened ⓳ **Trident Studios** – most famously used by The Beatles to record *Hey Jude* on 31 July 1968. The Beatles also recorded a number of songs from *The White Album* here, attracted by the studio's 8-track recording equipment which was then far superior to the four-track recorder on offer at the more famous Abbey Road studio. Other artists who have recorded some of their best work here include David Bowie (*Ziggy Stardust*, *Hunky Dory*), The Boomtown Rats (*I Don't Like Mondays*), Elton John (*Your Song*), Lou Reed (*Transformer*), Genesis (*A Trick of the Tail*) and Queen (*Bohemian Rhapsody*). Each of the former members of The Beatles also recorded here during their solo careers.

The Sheffield brothers later sold the studio, but the current owners clearly respect the building's rock and pop legacy and a tour of the studio is available. You can reserve tickets from the studio's reception which is open Monday to Fridays 9.30am-5.30pm. The studio recommends phoning beforehand to confirm when the next tour is on (020 7734 6198).

Retrace your steps to Dean Street. Whilst Frith Street can boast of having once been home to Mozart, Dean Street has closer ties with an even more influential world figure. **Karl Marx** (1818-83), philosopher, political economist and revolutionary, lived in poverty with his wife and children in two locations on this street, writing many of his great works, including *Das Kapital*, in the former British Museum Library just ten minutes walk away.

Marx first lived for a few months in 1850 at the now demolished number 64 with his wife Jenny, their children and their maid Lenchen. Jenny wrote of how they 'found two rooms in the house of a Jewish lace dealer and spent a miserable summer there with our four children'. Marx largely survived on handouts from his collaborator Friedrich Engels, all the while being spied upon by Prussian secret agents. During this era Soho and the area around Charlotte Street to the north were home to hundreds of European radicals and anarchists who had settled in London, so Marx had plenty of fellow agitators with whom to debate.

Three of Marx's children died during his stay in Dean Street (including one during a cholera epidemic – see more on the epidemic below). At one point the family finances were so stretched they could not even afford a coffin in which to bury one of their children. At the same time Marx's relationship with Jenny was further strained over his affair with Lenchen. Even the great communist could not, it seems, escape the temptations of Soho.

The Marx family moved to **28 Dean Street** where they stayed for six years, paying an annual rent of £22 pounds. Their apartment was described by a Prussian spy as being 'in one of the worst, and hence the cheapest quarters of London... Everything is broken, tattered and torn, finger-thick dust everywhere'. The well-known restaurant **㉛ Quo Vadis** now occupies the site; sadly, Marx's former rooms are not open to the public.

Despite the fact that Communist doctrine disapproved of people benefiting from an inheritance, when Jenny received one in 1856 the Marx family were off like a shot to better quarters in the affluent suburb of Kentish Town, leaving the slums of Soho far behind. For more on Marx and Soho see **The Red Lion** below.

Continue south down Dean Street, home to a number of Soho's historic drinking dens. The members-only **㉑ Colony Room Club** at number 41 (the green doorway) – a grungy bar opened in 1948 by the famously difficult Muriel Belcher – was perhaps the most exclusive. It attracted the cream of London's bohemian society including painters Lucian Freud, Frank Auerbach and Francis Bacon; musician George Melly; actors Peter O'Toole, Tom Baker and Trevor Howard; and *Absolute Beginners* author Colin MacInnes. Perhaps more surprisingly, Princess Margaret once visited and ordered a pink gin. Bacon, not yet a successful painter, received £10 pounds a week from Belcher to attract suitable customers. In recent years artists such as Damien Hirst and Tracey Emin were also regulars, and the model Kate Moss once served behind the bar. Unfortunately, the Club has now closed to make way for luxury flats.

22 French House, Old Compton Street

Just past the Colony Room Club site is the Groucho Club at number 45 – the favoured Soho drinking-hole of London's media figures. Cross over Old Compton Street and reach the ㉒ **French House** at number 49.

A pub has been on this site for centuries; however, it entered Soho legend in the 20th century under the eccentric proprietorship of Belgian born Victor Berlemont and (from 1951) his son Gaston. During WWII the pub (then known as the York Minster) became the unofficial headquarters of the Free French under Charles De Gaulle, with strategy meetings being held in the room upstairs. When De Gaulle used to visit the normally vibrant pub everyone within it would become very quiet, the French drinkers standing to attention. Many years later in 1960 De Gaulle, then the President of France, visited London and spotted Gaston in the crowd. He pointed to the landlord's flamboyant moustache, calling out 'Not as fine as your father's'.

The atmospheric French flavour continues to this day with beer lovers having to make do with half-pints under the stares of famous customers of the past, whose photographs are pinned to the walls. This establishment is particularly associated with artists and writers such as Lucian Freud, Françis Bacon, Brendan Behan, Dylan Thomas and even Salvador Dali during his visits to London.

Dylan Thomas left his only manuscript copy of *Under Milk Wood* here in 1953 during a drunken pub crawl. When he sobered up the distraught poet asked his BBC producer Douglas Cleverdon to try to find it, offering the manuscript as a prize. Cleverdon duly trawled the pubs of Soho and managed to locate it the following morning, later selling the manuscript for a substantial sum after the poet's death. In 1966 Cleverdon gave evidence about how he came to own the manuscript during a court case brought by Dylan's widow Caitlin against a later owner.

The French House has always attracted a diverse clientele ranging from local prostitutes to one down-and-out who left after last orders every night to return to a tree he lived in on Hampstead Heath. Today the atmosphere is still interesting (the hard-core regulars occupy the right-hand side of the bar as you enter) although,

25

as with many of Soho's iconic venues, the pub is perhaps trading a little on past glories.

Re-trace your steps slightly back onto Old Compton Street and turn left. On the other side of the street look out for the ㉓ **Admiral Duncan** public house at number 54 – a popular gay venue. This was one of the places bombed in 1999 by the right-wing extremist David Copeland, killing three people. The pub is named after the Scottish naval hero who won a naval victory against the Dutch in 1797.

Continue west looking out on the left-hand side for a plaque outside number 59 commemorating the ㉔ **2i's coffee shop** (pronounced 'two eyes'). The bar is regarded as the birth-place of rock 'n' roll in the UK, as it was here that in the late 50s many rock stars cut their teeth performing, including Tommy Steele, Adam Faith, Marty Wilde, Hank Marvin and Cliff Richard. The **2i's** was the basis for the bar depicted in *Expresso Bongo*, the 1959 film that captured the British style of rock 'n' roll that the Beatles would consign to the dustbin of history in 1963. Peter Grant – later the notorious manager of Led Zeppelin – learnt some of his strong-arm tactics whilst working as a doorman at the coffee bar.

You soon meet Wardour Street where you turn left (south) to visit ㉕ **St Anne's Church**. This is notable not only because decadent Soho seems an unlikely area for a place of worship, but also because if you try to enter the apparently substantial building it takes a few seconds to realise the frontage is all that remains. Built between 1677 and 1686, possibly to a design by Wren, only the tower and parts of the exterior survived the Blitz; a post-war campaign led by the poet Sir John Betjeman helped save the remains from demolition. The former churchyard – now a garden – has recently been revitalized through the efforts of the Architecture Ensemble and is a pleasant place to stop before continuing further into the bustling streets of Soho. At the rear (reached from Dean Street) a friendly modern chapel doubles up as a community centre and also boasts a secret little garden open to the public.

The churchyard contains the headstone of essayist William Hazlitt (see above) and **Baron Theodore von Neuhoff** (1694-1756). The baron was a German adventurer who led Corsican rebels in their fight against Genoese control. The rebels elected him King

Theodore I of Corsica but he eventually had to flee that island and ended up in Soho. He later spent time in a debtor's prison, only satisfying his creditors by making over the kingdom of Corsica to them. Horace Walpole, Theodore's friend and supporter, wrote the epitaph seen on the outside wall. Legend has it that the king's secret treasure remains buried in Epping Forest and his influence is still remembered to this day in the Moor's Head motif he added to the Corsican flag.

The crime writer **Dorothy L Sayers**, creator of the literary character Lord Peter Wimsey, was once churchwarden here, and her ashes were buried beneath the tower following her death in 1957. St Anne's has another literary connection, as it was here that Lucie Manette was married in Dickens's *A Tale of Two Cities*.

A final interesting feature of St Anne's is the long-abandoned southern entrance about halfway along Shaftesbury Avenue between Dean Street and Wardour Street. Keep an eye out and you will see a sign for the church underneath a modern shop.

Although not worth a detour on this walk, number 33 Wardour Street (on the south side of Shaftesbury Avenue) is notable for having once been home to the Flamingo Jazz Club. It was here in 1963 that the *Rolling Stones* first performed with the line-up of Mick Jagger, Keith Richards, Charlie Watts, Brian Jones and Bill Wyman. The same building was later home to the Whiskey-A-Go-Go, one of the coolest clubs of 60s London and where stars such as Hendrix, McCartney and

Pete Townsend were regulars. The club's name was later abbreviated to the Wag Club which transformed itself into an iconic establishment of the 1980s. Today, sadly, this venue is home to an Irish theme pub.

Re-trace your steps and walk north up Wardour Street before turning left into Brewer Street and immediately into Walkers Court on the right. Ahead you enter Berwick Street, an almost entirely Jewish area in the late 19th century. This rather dingy street is named after the Duke of Berwick, an illegitimate

Berwick St Market

son of James II, and is best known for its street market and record shops. A photograph of the street was used for the front cover of the 1995 Oasis album (*What's the Story*) *Morning Glory*? In Robert Louis Stevenson's famous story of *Dr Jekyll and Mr Hyde* (1886), the unsavoury character of Hyde lives in down-at-heel Soho – in a place not dissimilar to Berwick Street – described by a character in the book as being 'like a district of some city in a nightmare'.

This street is dominated by ㉖ **Kemp House**, the only tower block built as part of an ambitious plan in the 1950s to construct a number of towers and a glass ceiling over Soho. Each tower was supposed to have its own helipad, with canals dug at ground level. In 1997 Soho legend Jeffrey Bernard died of kidney failure at his home at number 45 Kemp House.

At this point, if you carry on north up Berwick Street you will reach Noel Street. In the 1920s the Italian Fascist headquarters in Soho were based at number 25, and were visited by Benito Mussolini during his visit to London in 1922. However, on this walk we turn left from Berwick Street into Broadwick Street (formerly Broad Street). You pass some public conveniences in the middle of the road that featured – along with John Lennon in a cameo role – in a sketch filmed in November 1967 for Peter Cook and Dudley Moore's television comedy show *Not Only But Also*. Lennon played a toadying commissionaire looking after the entrance to a private gentlemen's club supposedly located in the lavatory.

Ahead is the **㉗** **John Snow** pub on the corner, which is named after the teetotaller **Dr John Snow** who made medical history when he proved the connection between infected water supplies and cholera. London suffered a number of devastating cholera outbreaks between 1831 and 1860 and in 1849 alone 53,000 Londoners died of the disease. During one such outbreak in 1854 Snow realised the victims had one thing in common: their use of a water pump on Broad Street. He persuaded a sceptical medical establishment – many of who believed cholera was an airborne disease – of his concerns and the handle of the pump was removed. Almost immediately the epidemic abated, thus proving his case. In 2003 a poll of doctors in Hospital Doctor magazine voted Snow greatest doctor of all time, placing him just ahead of ancient Greek Hippocrates. Today the original site of the pump is indicated by a dull red granite kerbstone in Broadwick Street, just outside the pub (there is a small sign on the wall as well). There is also a replica water pump a few yards away near the corner of Poland Street.

Follow the map to reach Marshall Street and bear right. On the right-hand side is a dismal tower block, which stands on the site of the birthplace of the poet and visionary artist **William Blake** (1757-1827). His parents ran a hosiery shop here (originally 27 Broad Street, now 73 Marshall Street), and as a four-year-old William believed he saw a vision of God's face pressed against his bedroom window.

Blake later opened a printing shop beside his parents' business and hosted largely unsuccessful exhibitions of his work there. The Blakean connection continues in nearby Poland Street where Blake lived at number 28 from 1785 to 1791 and wrote his famous *Songs of Innocence*, among other works.

Walk past Blake's birthplace and turn left down Ganton Street. Cross over into Carnaby Street, the fashion heartland of 60s London. Before the 1960s the street had little association with the fashion industry but that changed when entrepreneur John Stephen opened a boutique here in 1958, going on to own around 15 shops in the area and becoming the 'King of Carnaby Street'. In 1966 *Time Magazine* published its famous report on *London: the Swinging City* and helped turn Carnaby Street into a world-famous fashion centre. However this fame proved its downfall, and by 1968 the real trend-setters had gone elsewhere, leaving Carnaby Street largely to the tourists. John Stephen is commemorated by a plaque on the south side of Carnaby Street (facing Beak Street).

On the other side of Ganton Street turn left into Kingly Street. Continue south along Kingly Street, looking out on the left hand side for number eight. This site was once home in the 1960s to ㉘ **The Bag O' Nails club** where members of The Rolling Stones, The Beatles, The Who and Jimi Hendrix amongst others would socialise together. It was also where Paul McCartney met his future wife Linda Eastman in May 1967 as they both attended a Georgie Fame concert.

28

At the end of Kingly Street you reach Beak Street and turn left. Today it is a busy, prosperous looking street lined with shops,

30

however Charles Dickens once described it as 'tumbledown... with two irregular rows of tall meagre houses'.

Shortly on the left hand side you pass number 41 where the Venetian artist  **29** **Antonio Canaletto** (1697-1768) lived between 1749 and 1751. He came to London to capitalise on the popularity of his pictures amongst the aristocrats who had seen his work while passing through Venice on the 'Grand Tour'.

Opposite the Canaletto house is Upper James Street which you walk up to reach the relative calm of **30** **Golden Square**, possibly named after the castrated male horses – or geldings – that were kept on land here before the area was developed in the 1670s. Some have suggested Sir Christopher Wren designed the Square, however if he did it was not one of his most memorable creations and today the rather bland atmosphere of the place has probably not changed that much since Dickens described the area in *Nicholas Nickleby* (1838) as 'not exactly in anybody's way to or from anywhere'. Dickens placed Ralph Nickleby's house here and referred to the 'mournful statue' of George II that can still be seen

– notable for being the last British monarch to be depicted in historical costume

The square was completed in the early 1700s, and was originally very popular with the aristocracy. However, the proximity of less desirable features such as breweries (on nearby Brewer Street) drove fashionable society away and their place was taken by hotels and foreign embassies. The Portuguese embassy, which occupied numbers 23-24 on the west side of the square in the mid 18th century, is commemorated

by a plaque and the chapel at the rear is now one of Soho's most secret churches.

You can reach the church by walking out of the square on the south-west corner and then turning right onto Brewer Street. Head right again onto Warwick Street where about half-way up you will see ③ **Our Lady of the Assumption and St Gregory**, now home to the Eritrean Catholics. In the past it served as a chapel for the Portuguese and Bavarian legations in London, and is the only surviving Catholic former embassy chapel to have been built before the Catholic Emancipation of 1829. The original church was pillaged during the anti-Catholic Gordon Riots of 1780, and the current building was finished in 1788. It is one of the quietest churches in this part of London, and a real Soho gem.

Retrace your steps and continue along Brewer Street to **Great Pulteney Street** named after Sir William Pulteney who laid out Brewer Street in the 1660s. A plaque on the left-hand side at number 38 remembers former resident ② **John William Polidori** (1795-1821) who served as physician to the poet Lord Byron. The latter, during his stay in Geneva in 1816, came up with the idea of having a ghost story writing competition

amongst his house guests. The most famous result was Mary Shelley's *Frankenstein*, but Polidori contributed the influential early Gothic work *The Vampyre*.

Polidori's vampire was a more human, erotic creature than Bram Stoker's much later creation *Dracula*; however, Polidori's story was ridiculed by Byron and Polidori returned dejected to London. An unknown person later sent Polidori's story to a London magazine who published it, incorrectly attributing it to Byron. Polidori tried to rectify this error but was accused of plagiarism. He became depressed, and subsequently committed suicide at this address (where he was also born) by drinking prussic acid.

Back on Brewer Street continue east until you reach Great Windmill Street on the south side, named after a 16th-century windmill that once stood here. Head down Great Windmill Street as far as the corner with Archer Street. Now a trendy bar, this site was until recently the ❸❸ **Red Lion** pub. Soho resident **Karl Marx** (see above) once gave lectures in an upstairs room of the Red Lion, and the Communist League held its Second Congress here in November 1847.

It was here that Marx and Engels submitted proposals to the League to secure a commission to write what became *The Communist Manifesto*. A bitter ten-day debate ensued, but Marx and Engels were successful and the resulting manifesto has been described as the most influential written work in history after the Bible. Prussian spies infiltrated the Congress and made false reports to Lord Palmerston that its members were plotting to assassinate Queen Victoria. However, the great English statesman wisely decided not to be drawn into the political intrigue and refused to act.

The walk ends here. For those who may find it hard to imagine 'normal' life taking place in Soho, look out for the primary school in Great Windmill Street, which serves the local population of about 5,000 people. From here you can continue south to reach Shaftesbury Avenue. A number of tube stations are nearby including Piccadilly Circus, Leicester Square and Tottenham Court Road. ●

SHOP...

Carnaby St, W1 (see p.83)
www.carnaby.co.uk

Berwick St Market
Berwick St, W1F
Daily 9am-5pm

EAT, DRINK...

Gay Hussar (see p.62)
2 Greek Street, W1D
www.gayhussar.co.uk

Coach & Horses (see p.68)
29 Greek Street, W1D

Maison Bertaux (see p.69)
28 Greek Street, W1

Kettner's (see p.69)
29 Romilly Street, W1D
www.kettners.com

Bar Italia (see p.71)
22 Frith Street, W1D
www.baritaliasoho.co.uk

Quo Vadis (see p.75)
26 Dean Street, W1D
www.quovadissoho.co.uk

French House (see p.77)
49 Dean Street, W1D
www.frenchhousesoho.com

4 **Westminster & Whitehall Walk**

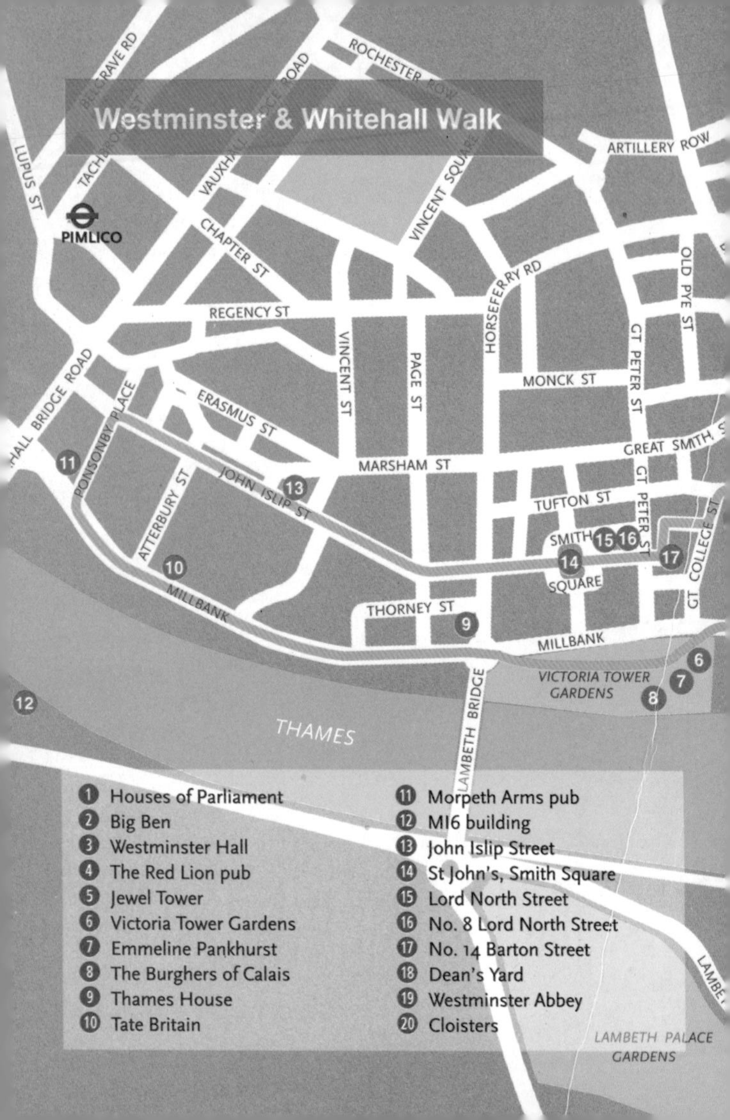

PIMLICO

VAUXHALL BRIDGE ROAD
BELGRAVE RD
TACHBROOK ST
ROCHESTER ROW
ARTILLERY ROW
LUPUS ST
CHAPTER ST
VINCENT SQUARE
OLD PYE ST
REGENCY ST
HORSEFERRY RD
GT PETER ST
GREAT SMITH S
VINCENT ST
PAGE ST
MONCK ST
ERASMUS ST
HALL BRIDGE ROAD
PONSONBY PLACE
ATTERBURY ST
JOHN ISLIP ST
MARSHAM ST
GREAT SMITH S
GT PETER ST
TUFTON ST
SMITH
SQUARE
GT COLLEGE ST
MILLBANK
THORNEY ST
MILLBANK
VICTORIA TOWER
GARDENS

THAMES

LAMBETH BRIDGE

LAMBE

LAMBETH PALACE
GARDENS

①	Houses of Parliament	⑪	Morpeth Arms pub
②	Big Ben	⑫	MI6 building
③	Westminster Hall	⑬	John Islip Street
④	The Red Lion pub	⑭	St John's, Smith Square
⑤	Jewel Tower	⑮	Lord North Street
⑥	Victoria Tower Gardens	⑯	No. 8 Lord North Street
⑦	Emmeline Pankhurst	⑰	No. 14 Barton Street
⑧	The Burghers of Calais	⑱	Dean's Yard
⑨	Thames House	⑲	Westminster Abbey
⑩	Tate Britain	⑳	Cloisters

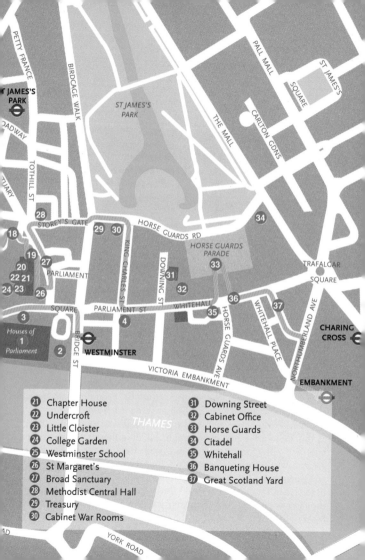

Westminster & Whitehall Walk

Start: Westminster underground station
Finish: Embankment/Charing Cross station
Distance: 3 miles

From Westminster underground station head down St Margaret's Street with the ❶ **Houses of Parliament** on your left. Surprisingly few visitors know its official name is the Palace of Westminster and that it is the oldest royal palace in the country. Before the palace was built – during Saxon times – this part of London was a barren, desolate place, full of briar bushes and known as Thorney Island.

It was an island at this time: cut off from the rest of London by tributaries of the now hidden Tyburn river (which runs south from Hamp-stead before emptying into the Thames near Pimlico). An isolated church dedicated to St Peter was established here perhaps as early as the 7th century AD, according to legend after the Saint appeared in a vision to some fishermen.

The Anglo-Saxon King Edward the Confessor moved his court to this area in the mid 11th century, building the first royal palace here and enlarging St Peter's into what became the Benedictine Westminster Abbey. The name 'Westminster' itself derives from the fact the minster (or church of a monastery) was located to the west of the more established St Paul's Cathedral in the City. The English monarchy occupied the palace until the early 1500s when after a fire Henry VIII moved his court to the nearby Palace of Whitehall.

Walk westwards with Big Ben to your left and Parliament Square and Westminster Abbey to your right. The current Parliament building dates largely from the mid 19th century after a fire in 1834 destroyed almost all of the old palace complex. The fire is thought to have started when the burning of redundant wooden sticks or 'tallies' (used by the Exchequer for tax accounting purposes) in a furnace situated in the palace cellars got out of control.

The architect of the famous neo-Gothic design was Sir Charles Barry (1795-1860), assisted by Augustus Pugin (1812-1852). Inside is a warren of 1,200 rooms and over two miles of passages. The members of the House of Commons and House of Lords can also relax in one of the 19 bars, a gymnasium, a hair salon, and even a miniature rifle range.

❷ **Big Ben** is the best-known feature of the palace, although the name refers to the great bell inside Elizabeth Tower rather than the tower itself. Inside are five bells of which Big Ben – officially the Great Bell of Westminster – is the biggest at over 13 tonnes, ringing the note of 'E' every hour.

The original great bell cracked during testing, and Big Ben was cast as a replacement at the Whitechapel Bell Foundry on Whitechapel Road in 1858 (see page 366). When it was transported from Whitechapel to Westminster huge crowds turned out to see Big Ben being pulled along by 16 brightly beribboned horses. It was either named after Benjamin Hall, the then Commissioner of Works, or the 18-stone heavyweight boxer Ben Caunt. The tower contains a secret prison cell used for trouble-makers within the palace, and the suffragette Emmeline Pankhurst was held here following a protest in the early 20th century.

Tight security measures ensure that visiting the palace is not easy. Tickets for a guided tour of the two main chambers and Westminster Hall are normally sold from a kiosk opposite, but only when Parliament is not sitting. If you want to see the proceedings

of the House of Commons or the House of Lords you can obtain tickets in advance through your local MP, or alternatively join the queue outside St Stephen's Entrance. Visit the website at www.parliament.uk for more information.

Continue west with the palace to your left. Even if you don't visit the inside, remnants of the palace's Saxon and medieval past are visible to the casual visitor from the roadside. The most obvious is ❸ **Westminster Hall** which overlooks Parliament Square (whose own claim to fame lies in becoming the country's first official roundabout in 1926).

The hall was built around 1097 by William (Rufus) II (c.1056-1100). It is arguably the birthplace of English democracy as it was the original meeting place for the King's Council, the forerunner of the present House of Lords. The hall was also the location of the first true English parliament to include elected representatives, summoned by Simon de Montfort in 1265.

The magnificent oak hammer-beam ceiling was added in the 1390s during the reign of Richard II. During restoration work in 1913 the authorities were struggling to find wood of sufficient quality to replace some of the rotting timbers. Sir George Courthope MP suggested using trees from his family estate near Wadhurst in Sussex, the source of the original timber, his ancestors having had the foresight to plant new trees in anticipation of future repairs.

For many centuries the hall was used as a law court. Some of the most dramatic trials in British history took place here, including those of Scotland's 'Braveheart' William Wallace (1305), Sir Thomas More (1535), Queen Anne Boleyn (1536), Guy Fawkes (1606) and Charles I (1649). Oliver Cromwell was declared Lord Protector in the hall in 1653, although after his death his decomposing head was stuck on the roof of the hall where it stayed for 25 years until being finally blown down. Over the following centuries Cromwell's head passed through many hands until 1960 when it was buried at a secret location within the chapel of his old Cambridge college.

Westminster Hall remained an important law court right up until the 1880s when the Royal Courts of Justice on the Strand were opened. Peter the Great of Russia (1672-1725) visited it during his stay in London and was struck by the numbers of lawyers visible in their wigs and gowns, causing him to remark 'Lawyers! Why I have but two in my whole dominions and I believe I shall hang one of them the moment I get home'.

The palace contains a few other relics of the pre-1834 complex, most notably the late 13th-century crypt under St Stephen's Hall, the Tudor cloisters, and the Jewel House (see below).

Today the House of Commons within the palace is the heart of British democracy. However, for hundreds of years the members of the Commons were shunted around between the palace and Westminster Abbey like poor relations. They often met in the hall, or the Chapter House of the Abbey, before eventually securing a permanent berth in the Royal Chapel of St Stephen which had been emptied of its priests after Henry VIII's Dissolution.

The Commons continued to meet in the chapel until it was destroyed in 1834; the current St Stephen's Hall is built on the same site. Brass studs on the floor mark the location of the old Speaker's

Chair and Table of the House. It was in the old chapel that King Charles I confronted the Commons in 1642, demanding the arrest of five MPs for treason. The Speaker famously replied, 'May it please your Majesty, I have neither eyes to see nor tongue to speak in this place but as the House is pleased to direct me, whose servant I am here'. The bitter Civil War followed, which ended with Charles I's execution (see below). To this day by tradition the monarch is not allowed to enter the Commons.

Sir Charles Barry was commissioned to construct the post-1834 Parliament complex in a Gothic design, despite his classical preferences. At this time classical designs were associated with republicanism – as exemplified in the government buildings then being built in Washington – and so Barry commissioned Pugin, the champion of Gothic design to provide the medieval details. It was not always a happy partnership, Pugin remarking acidly about Barry's restoration of the Great Hall 'All Grecian, sir; Tudor details on a classic body'. Pugin was a workaholic, a habit that helped drive him into a mental asylum whilst still relatively young.

Votes in the Commons are called by the ringing of the Division Bell. Before modern technology such as mobile phones, many local public houses and restaurants were connected to the Commons so their own bell could let MPs know when to head back to the House to vote. An example of such a bell can still be seen in ❹ **The Red Lion** public house situated at 48 Parliament

Street, about halfway between the Palace of Westminster and Downing Street.

If you die in a royal palace you are in theory entitled to a state funeral. The implications of this mean that deaths within the Palace of Westminster have traditionally been registered as taking place elsewhere, often at St. Thomas' Hospital nearby. When Prime Minister Spencer Perceval was shot and killed in the lobby of the House of Commons in 1812, the only British Prime Minister to have been assassinated, he 'officially' died (rather conveniently) as his body crossed the threshold of 10 Downing Street.

Follow the map west passing the statues of Cromwell and Richard II on the left. On the right – on the other side of St Margaret Street – is the medieval **⑤ Jewel Tower**, a rare survivor of the old palace, built in around 1365 as a stronghold for Edward III's treasure. It later housed the records of the House of Lords before becoming the office for weights and measures. Today the tower houses a small museum (which is open daily 10am-4pm November to March, 10am-5pm April to October).

6

Continue into ❻ **Victoria Tower Gardens** past the statue of ❼ **Emmeline Pankhurst** (1858-1928), leader of the Suffragette movement. You soon reach Auguste Rodin's ❽ *The Burghers of Calais* – one of the finest pieces of public art in London. Rodin's inspiration was the siege of Calais by the English under Edward III in 1347 during the Hundred Years War. The city was forced to surrender, and the King offered to spare its inhabitants on the condition he received six of their most prominent citizens wearing

8

nooses and carrying the keys to the city. The burghers walked out to meet their fate, however Edward's queen, Philippa of Hainault, persuaded her husband to spare them believing their death would be a bad omen for her pregnancy. This statue was purchased in 1911, and is one of twelve casts made of the original after Rodin's death – the maximum permitted under French law.

Walk through the gardens, taking in one of the finest views of the Thames in London, and continue along **Millbank** – named after the medieval mill that once stood by the river bank. Since 1995 ❾ **Thames House** at number 11 Millbank (opposite Lambeth Bridge) has been home to **MI5** (Military Intelligence, section 5), the counter-intelligence and security agency concerned with Britain's domestic security. After about five minutes you reach ❿ **Tate Britain** on the right-hand side.

The Tate stands on the site of one of London's most peculiar experiments – the Millbank Penitentiary. Built on seven acres of marshland, it was for a time the largest prison in London when completed in 1821, and could hold 1,120 prisoners. The design was based on the 'panopticon principle' developed by philosopher Jeremy Bentham, with the corridors of prison cells being connected along a six-pointed star to a central point which allowed the warders to sit in the middle and keep an eye on the prisoners, who had to live in almost total silence. Bentham had the contract to build the prison until his funding fell through, although he influenced the design.

Many ancestors of today's Australians began their journey from here as nearly all male and female prisoners sentenced to deportation in England passed through Millbank. The prisoners would cross over from the prison onto barges moored in the Thames. Around 4,000 people a year until 1867 began their transportation in this way. The prison was finally shut in 1890 and demolished two years later. Also, opposite the Morpeth Arms public house (see below), you can see a stone bollard in a small garden, which stood by the river steps. Prisoners being transported to Australia passed by here along a passageway from the prison.

The Tate is a great place to spend a few hours as it has one of the best art collections in the country. The collection contains many works by J. M. W. Turner, and you might want to look out for his painting *Moonlight, a Study at Millbank* (1797). It also contains a pleasant café if you just need a rest.

Continue past the Tate looking out for the Victorian ⑪ **Morpeth Arms** public house. Built originally for the prison's warders, it contains the remnants of a **tunnel and cellar** said to have been part of the prison and used to take prisoners to the Thames. The cellar is not generally open to the public, however if you are interested it is worth asking someone in the pub to let you have a look. Be careful if you do – it is said that a prisoner died in the tunnel and that his ghost still haunts the pub. In any event this is another good place to stop for a break, particularly the upstairs room with great views of the Thames. The room's small collection of photographs of famous spies is appropriate given the modern ⓬ **MI6 building** clearly visible on the other side of the river. MI6 – the Secret Intelligence Service – looks after Britain's foreign security interests, and the construction of this building aroused huge controversy in the late 1990s because of the cost (estimated at around £200 million) and its less-than-subtle design.

Follow the map down Ponsonby Place and then up ⓭ **John Islip Street**, with its magnificent avenue of plane trees, passing alongside the rear of the Tate. Continue for a few minutes, crossing Horseferry Road, until you reach Smith Square ahead. The eastern side of Horseferry Road is where an ancient horse-ferry once operated, taking passengers between Thorney Island and Lambeth and earning revenue for the Archbishop of Canterbury who occupied Lambeth Palace.

Smith Square was laid out in the 1720s and is dominated by ⓮ **St John's, Smith Square** – one of London's finest small concert venues. The building, designed by

Thomas Archer (1668-1743), started life as the church of St John the Evangelist and is regarded as one of the finest examples of English Baroque architecture in London. It became known as 'Queen Anne's Footstool' on account of the legend that when asked about her preference for the church's design, the Queen kicked over her footstool with the legs facing upwards like the four towers of the church, crying 'like that!'. The church opened in 1728 but surprisingly its design was never very popular – Dickens describing it in *Our Mutual Friend* as 'a very hideous church... resembling some petrified monster'. However, most regard it as an elegant piece of Rome in the heart of Westminster. You may notice its slightly slanted appearance, the result of having its foundations on marshy ground.

The north side of the square contains some of the finest Georgian houses in London, dating from the early 18th century. Number 32 on the square was until very recently the headquarters of the Conservative Party. Continue along ⑮ **Lord North Street**, dating from the 1720s, and look out on the left-hand side near ⑯ **number 8** for an extremely rare reminder of the Blitz in London. A faded sign reads 'Public Shelters in Vaults under Pavements in this Street', and the shelters are still hidden underneath having been blocked up after WWII. The disgraced Tory minister Jonathan Aitken used to live here before being jailed for perjury in 1999, and Prime Minister Harold Wilson used to live at number 5 in the mid 1970s.

Continue up Cowley Street (the Liberal Democrat headquarters are at number 4) and into Barton Street. Along with Lord North Street, these quiet streets with their elegant Georgian town houses are where the wealthier politicians choose to live and are a far cry from the tourist-dominated streets around Westminster Palace. The locale was evidently hidden enough to attract the famously reclusive **T. E. Lawrence (of Arabia)** (1888-1935). He lived in the attic at ⑰ **number 14** and wrote much of *The Seven Pillars of Wisdom* (1922) whilst living here.

Follow the map into Great College Street and then right through the gates into the wide expanse of ⑱ **Dean's Yard**, part of Westminster Abbey. The yard is also home to two other historic British institutions – **Westminster School**, and the headquarters of the Church of England (inside Church House).

As with Parliament, the Abbey is covered extensively in the main tourist guides. However there are some features which are often overlooked by many tourists and you can reach these by following the signs for the cloisters on the other corner of the yard.

20 Cloisters, Westminster Abbey

19   **Westminster Abbey** is properly known as the Collegiate Church of St Peter, Westminster; the term 'Abbey' persists despite the Benedictine monks who once occupied it having been forced out during Henry VIII's Dissolution in the 1530s. The coronation of almost every monarch has taken place here since 1066 and seventeen monarchs are buried in the grounds, including St Edward the Confessor. However, St Peter's is neither a cathedral nor a parish church but a 'Royal Peculiar', meaning it falls under the jurisdiction of the monarchy and is run by an independent Dean and Chapter.

Most of the current Gothic building dates from the 13th century and following the Dissolution St Peter's was re-founded by Elizabeth I. It was actually a cathedral for a few years, Henry VIII granting it this status because of its Royal connections and his desire to protect it from the full impact of the Dissolution (which resulted in nearly all other abbeys in the country being shut down). The Abbey ceased to be a cathedral in 1550 and it is thought the expression 'robbing Peter to pay Paul' dates from this period when revenues meant for St Peter's were diverted by the Bishop of London to St Paul's Cathedral.

To see the most hidden parts of the Abbey head through the medieval **20** **cloisters**, following signs for the Chapter House. Just to the right of the entrance to the Chapter House is a small wooden door dating from the 1050s – making it the oldest door in Britain. Experts think it was originally part of the Saxon Abbey constructed by Edward the Confessor.

The octagonal **㉑ Chapter House** dates from the 1250s, and was regularly used by the House of Commons in the mid 14th century before it found a permanent home inside the palace. It was also here that the monks met every day for prayers and to read a chapter (hence the name) from the rule of St Benedict and discuss their day's work. The room contains elaborate sculptures and wall paintings of the Apocalypse, with the Last Judgement depicted on the east wall. It also contains one of the finest medieval tile pavements in England.

Beside the Chapter House further traces of the medieval monastery can be found in the round arches and massive supporting columns of the **㉒ Undercroft**. This was originally part of the domestic quarters of the Benedictine monks and today is home to a fascinating museum. The unusual exhibits include the funeral effigies of several English monarchs and other notables, and rank as some of the strangest items of any collection in London. An effigy would be paraded during a funeral procession, and many were made using the clothes of the deceased, with the facial features moulded from a death mask to ensure a true likeness.

The effigies on display include those of Edward III, Henry VII (taken from a death mask), Elizabeth I, Charles II, William III, Mary II, Horatio Nelson (wearing some of the naval hero's own clothes) and Prime Minister William Pitt. Elizabeth I's effigy was recently found to contain a corset dating from 1603, the same year she died, and is displayed separately. The museum also contains the late 13th-century Westminster Retable – one of the oldest altars in England, and in terms of workmanship as good as any found in Europe from this period.

21 - Chapter House

Just past the museum head through the ㉓ **Little Cloister** into the ㉔ **College Garden**, England's oldest garden. This verdant one-acre site is over 900 years old and originally served as the Abbey's infirmary garden, where the monks grew medicinal herbs. Herbs are still grown in the garden today, which is open Tuesday to Thursday 10am-4pm (in winter) and until 6pm (April-September). The Abbey is usually open to visitors from Monday to Saturday, but it is best to check if services are due to take place (telephone 020 7222 5152). There is an entrance charge to the Abbey, unless you are visiting to worship, and tickets include admission to the museum. Admission is free to the cloisters and College Garden (although donations are invited).

Near the garden is ㉕ **Westminster School**, officially known as the Royal College of St Peter in Westminster. Almost hidden from public view, this historic institution has thrived in the heart of London for over 900 years, although understandably it cannot be visited by the public except for certain tours available during the Easter holidays.

It is the only great public school in London founded by a religious institution to have remained in its original location

(Charterhouse and St Paul's schools having moved from their original sites). The school, incorporating parts of the original Benedictine monastery, dates from 1179. Following the Dissolution of the Monasteries the school was re-founded by Elizabeth I. Past pupils including Ben Jonson, Sir Christopher Wren, Henry Purcell, Edward Gibbon, Jeremy Bentham, A. A. Milne, Sir John Gielgud, Tony Benn, Andrew Lloyd Webber, Martin Amis and, last but not least, Shane MacGowan of the Pogues.

24 *College Garden*

The pupils have not always been easy to handle. In 1679 a group of scholars killed a bailiff who was threatening the Abbey's traditional right of sanctuary. The enterprising headmaster of the time bought a royal pardon from Charles II, and then added the cost to the school bills sent to parents.

The original monastery can still be glimpsed in Ashburnham House, which dates from the 1660s but incorporates a medieval lodging house. The 'school' building was also once part of the monastic dormitory, its single hall serving as the place where all classes within the school were held for three hundred years until 1884. 'College Hall' was built in the 14th century and was once the Abbot's state dining hall. It was here that Elizabeth Woodville took sanctuary in 1483 with her family, although that did not spare her son Richard from his fate as one of the tragic Princes in the Tower. In the following century Elizabeth I used to visit in order to see scholars act out their traditional Latin Plays.

The monarch's scholars are the first commoners to acclaim each new sovereign during the coronation ceremony in Westminster Abbey and their shouts of 'Vivat Regina' ('Long Live the Queen') are incorporated into the Coronation Anthem. On a more populist level, the school helped develop the modern game of football when the original rules of the game were being drawn up in the 1860s. The school persuaded the rule-makers to respect an open passing game with a generous off-side rule, in stark contrast to other institutions such as Eton who wanted a more restrictive approach. For information about tours of the School during the Easter holidays call 020 7963 1003 or e-mail: registrar@westminster.org.uk

Leave the Abbey and walk around to see the 900-year-old church of **26** **St Margaret's**, which is sited discretely between the Abbey and the palace. It was founded when the Benedictine monks of the Abbey decided they no longer wished to share their services with the local inhabitants of Westminster, and so built a separate church for the parish.

The current structure dates largely from the late 15th century and past parishioners include poet John Milton (married here) and pioneering printer William Caxton (buried here). Sir Walter Raleigh

28 Methodist Central Hall

(1552-1618) was buried under the altar here after being executed in Old Palace Yard (opposite the Jewel House). Others executed in the yard include Guy Fawkes and three others involved in the famous Gunpowder Plot to blow up the Commons, all of whom were hanged, drawn and quartered in the Yard in 1606. Being the parish church of the House of Commons, St Margaret's hosts many politicians' weddings, and Samuel Pepys and Winston Churchill were both married here. The church also features a stained-glass window commemorating the marriage of Prince Arthur – Henry VIII's brother – to Catherine of Aragon (later wife to Henry as well). The churchyard contains a Roman boundary stone embedded in the ground.

Beside the church is ㉗ **Broad Sanctuary** – named after the sanctuary that operated here in medieval times, and where criminals could live in relative safety under the protection of the church provided their crimes were not treasonable or heretical.

Follow the map up Storey's Gate pausing beside ㉘ **Methodist Central Hall**, which opened in 1912 and can accommodate over 2,000 people. In 1946 it was the venue for the inaugural General Assembly of the United Nations. The UN soon moved to New York and its origins in London are largely forgotten. The first meeting for the Campaign for Nuclear Disarmament (CND) also took place here in 1958, with speakers including Bertrand Russell and J. B. Priestley. The construction of the hall was bankrolled by the '20th Century

Fund' which was set up to commemorate the 100th anniversary of John Wesley's death; in the main lobby you can ask to see the 50 vast volumes containing the signatures of the one million donors, who each contributed one guinea. Sir Andrew Lloyd Webber's father was the director of music and an organist at the hall for many years, and the younger composer chose the hall for the premiere of *Joseph and the Amazing Technicolor Dreamcoat* in 1968. If you need a break there is a nice café on the lower ground floor. The basement was England's largest WWII air raid shelter with a capacity of 2,000 people.

Continue up Storey's Gate, leading you into the heart of HM Government where the key ministries are based. Cross over Great St George Street into Horse Guards Road, which runs along side St James's Park. The ㉙ **Treasury** is housed in the building on the right-hand side, and on the corner with King Charles Street is the entrance to the ㉚ **Cabinet War Rooms**.

The War Rooms served as the underground headquarters of Winston Churchill and his cabinet during WWII, protecting them from the heavy air raids suffered by London. They contain the secure telephone used by Churchill to discuss secret wartime matters with President Roosevelt, and also the Churchill Museum. Soon after the War, the rooms were shut and hidden from public view for 40 years until being taken over by the Imperial War Museum in 1984. Some believe the underground complex extends far beyond what can be seen by the public, with secret tunnels connecting the rooms to 10 Downing Street and possibly far beyond. Opening times are daily 9.30am-6pm (http://cwr.iwm.org.uk).

Continue along King Charles Street with the Foreign Office on your left. Ahead is Parliament Street where you head north past Sir Edwin Lutyens' Cenotaph monument to the dead of both World Wars. Shortly on the left is ㉛ **Downing Street**, famous as the official home of the Prime Minister and the Chancellor of the Exchequer. What is less well known is that it is named after the unscrupulous 17th-century statesman, Sir George Downing (1623-1684), who first developed the street. Downing spent much of his childhood in Salem, Massachusetts and was the second graduate of the now-famous Harvard University. Regarded as a skilled yet untrustworthy diplomat, his behaviour resulted in his name becoming American slang for a man who betrays another's trust.

Downing Street retains four of the original houses that its founder built here after buying the land in 1680. Number 10 began its association with the office of Prime Minister when George II offered the house to Sir Robert Walpole in 1732, and it became, and technically remains, the office of the First Lord of the Treasury. It was joined to a much bigger house at the rear and the small frontage belies the 160 rooms that lie within. Number 14 was the scene of the only meeting between Lord Nelson and the Duke of Wellington, a purely coincidental encounter that took place in the waiting room of the Exchequer.

Just north of Downing Street at number 70 is found the ㉜ **Cabinet Office**, which dates from the mid 19th century and is situated on part of the former Palace of Whitehall. It was on this site that the young Henry VIII carried out his numerous sporting activities such as tennis, bowling, cockfighting and jousting. The remains of his tennis courts are visible inside, and the building also contains a Cockpit Gallery named after the site of Henry's cock-fighting pit. The medieval building was later converted into a private residence by Charles II and was first used as a Cabinet office in around 1720. Given its role as a government building it is not currently open to the public.

The Palace of Whitehall was the main Royal residence in central London after Henry VIII moved out of Westminster Palace in the early 16th century. Whitehall was the largest palace of its kind in Europe until its destruction by fire in 1698. At its peak it covered 23 acres and contained over 1,500 rooms. It was originally founded as York Place by the Archbishop of York in the 13th century, and was later home to Cardinal Wolsey. Henry VIII took over the palace and it was here that he married Anne Boleyn and Jane Seymour, where both he and Charles II died, and the setting for the first performance of Shakespeare's *The Tempest* in 1611. After its destruction there were plans for the palace to be rebuilt by Sir Christopher Wren, but William III decided to live elsewhere and the plan was never realised.

Continue north past the elegant 18th-century Dover House on the left where the Scotland Office is based and turn into 33 **Horse Guards**, the official entrance into Whitehall. Head past the guards and into the vast open space of Horse Guards Parade, best known

today as the location of the annual Trooping of the Colour ceremony. In the 16th century Henry VIII used to practise his jousting in the tilt yards that once stood here, surrounded by the Palace of Whitehall complex. The Horse Guards were originally based here to guard the entrance to the Palace of Whitehall, and the buildings later became the headquarters of the British Army. However, today the site only serves a ceremonial function. If you have time, visit the Household Cavalry Museum – a living museum in the heart of Horse Guards where visitors can see troopers working with their horses in the original 18th-century stables. The museum is open daily 10am-6pm March to September and 10am-5pm October to February (www. householdcavalrymuseum.co.uk).

On the far right (looking north) you can see an odd-shaped brick building covered in ivy known as the ➌➍ **Citadel**, a bomb-proof building erected during WWII and said to still be used as a communications centre by Navy intelligence.

33 Horse Guards Parade

Head back onto ㉟ **Whitehall** and cross over to the ㊱ **Banqueting House**. Completed in 1622 and designed by Inigo Jones for James I, it is the only surviving part of the Palace of Whitehall. It was from a window on the first floor of this building that Charles I walked out onto a scaffold to be beheaded on 30th January, 1649. Inside, the ceiling paintings by Sir Peter Paul Rubens are the finest feature. The Banqueting House's Italianate Renaissance style was regarded as highly innovative in Jacobean England, and even today its beautifully proportioned exterior does not seem out of place beside the modern buildings nearby. It is normally open to visitors Monday-Saturday 10am-5pm.

The Ministry of Defence building to the south of the Banqueting House contains **Henry VIII's Wine Cellar**. This hidden undercroft originally belonged to Cardinal Wolsey, and was built around 1515. It contains a Tudor brick-vaulted roof 70 feet long and 30 feet wide. In 1949 the cellars were skillfully relocated when the MOD building was being constructed. It is now closed to the public.

The fire that destroyed Whitehall Palace also destroyed Michelangelo's sculpture of *Cupid* – bought by the monarchy along with the rest of the Gonzaga collection in the 17th century. Michelangelo made it in 1496, and sold it to an Italian Cardinal as an ancient Greek statue. His deception was uncovered and he was lucky to survive the scandal.

Head north and turn up **37** **Great Scotland Yard**, originally part of the precincts of the Palace of Whitehall. Its name may be derived from the tradition that the Kings of Scotland and their courtiers stayed in this area. Sir Robert Peel founded the Metropolitan Police here in 1829, and the force became known as 'Scotland Yard'. The Met moved out in the late 19th century but the current headquarters of the force is still called New Scotland Yard.

Continue along until you reach Northumberland Avenue, where the walk ends. You can either turn left to reach Trafalgar Square with Charing Cross train station and underground on the eastern side, or turn right to reach Embankment tube. ●

VISIT...

Houses of Parliament &
Westminster Hall (see p.94)
Parliament Square, SW1P
www.parliament.uk

Jewel Tower (see p.97)
Abingdon Street, SW1P
www.english-heritage.org.uk

Tate Britain (see p.99)
Millbank, SW1P
www.tate.org.uk

Westminster Abbey (see p.105)
20 Dean's Yard, SW1P
www.westminster-abbey.org

Cabinet War Rooms (see p.114)
King Charles Street, SW1A
www.iwm.org.uk

Household Cavalry Museum
Whitehall, SW1A (see p.117)
www.householdcavalrymuseum.co.uk

Banqueting House (see p.119)
Whitehall Palace, SW1A
www.hrp.org.uk

EAT, DRINK...

The Red Lion (see p.96)
Morpeth Arms (see p.100)

5 Inns of Court Walk

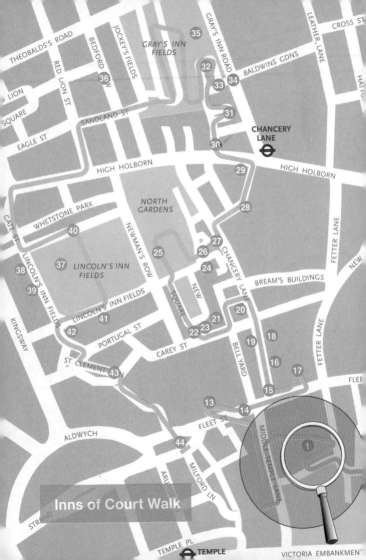

Inns of Court Walk

THEOBALD'S ROAD

BEDFORD

JOCKEY'S FIELDS

GRAY'S INN FIELDS

GRAY'S INN ROAD

LEATHER LANE

CROSS ST

35

36

RED LION ST

LION

SQUARE

EAGLE ST

SANDLAND ST

32

33 34

BALDWINS GDNS

31

CHANCERY
LANE

HIGH HOLBORN

30

29

HIGH HOLBORN

FETTER LANE

WHETSTONE PARK

NORTH
GARDENS

28

GATE ST

40

NEWMAN'S ROW

27

26

25

CHANCERY LANE

NEW

37

LINCOLN'S
INN FIELDS

24

BREAM'S BUILDINGS

38

LINCOLN'S INN FIELDS

39

LINCOLN'S INN FIELDS

41

SQUARE

20

FETTER LANE

NEW

42

PORTUGAL ST

21

22 23

BELL YARD

19

18

KINGSWAY

CAREY ST

16

17

ST CLEMENT

43

15

13

14

ALDWYCH

44

FLEET ST

FLEE

MIDDLE TEMPLE LANE

1

STRAND

ARUNDEL

MILFORD LN

TEMPLE PL

TEMPLE

VICTORIA EMBANKMENT

FARRINGDON

FLEET STREET

BARBICAN

GREVILLE ST

FARRINGDON RD

TEMPLE CHURCH

CHURCH COURT

BRICK COURT

ALDERSGATE ST

KING'S BENCH WALK

FOUNTAIN COURT

MIDDLE TEMPLE HALL

MIDDLE TEMPLE LANE

HOLBORN VIADUCT

GARDENS

CITY THAMESLINK NEWGATE

OLD BAILEY

ST PAUL'S

LUDGATE HILL

CHEAP

CITY THAMESLINK

IRELAND YARD

QUEEN VICTORIA ST

BLACKFRIARS

UPPER THAMES ST

1. Inner Temple (nos 1-12)
2. Tudor Street gate
3. Inner Temple Gardens
4. King's Bench Walk
5. Paper Buildings
6. Inner Temple Hall
7. Temple Church
8. Elm Court
9. The Inn of Middle Temple
10. Middle Temple Hall
11. Middle Temple Gardens
12. Middle Temple Lane
13. Royal Courts of Justice
14. Temple Bar
15. Chancery Lane
16. Serjeant's Inn
17. Clifford's Inn
18. Public Record Office
19. The Law Society
20. Ede & Ravenscroft
21. Victorian public toilet

22. Seven Stars pub
23. Lincoln's Inn Gateway
24. Lincoln's Inn Old Hall
25. Great Hall & Library
26. Lincoln's Inn chapel
27. Lincoln's Inn Gate House
28. Southampton Buildings
29. Staple Inn
30. Cittie of Yorke pub
31. South Square of Gray's Inn
32. Gray's Inn Square
33. Gray's Inn Chapel
34. Gray's Inn Hall
35. Gray's Inn Gardens
36. Bedford Row
37. Lincoln's Inn Fields
38. Farrer & Co
39. No. 59/60 Lincoln's Inn Fields
40. Sir John Soane's Museum
41. Hunterian Museum
42. The Old Curiosity Shop
43. Clement's Inn
44. St Clement Danes

Inns of Court Walk

Start: Blackfriars underground/rail station
Finish: Temple underground station/various
Distance: 3 miles
(This walk is best done during the week – at the weekend Inner and Middle Temple are accessible, but Gray's Inn and Lincoln's Inn are largely closed).

The first Inn on the walk – ❶ **Inner Temple** – is reached by following the map from Blackfriars station along Tudor Street and entering through the ❷ **Tudor Street gate.** Before the 18th century the area to the east of Inner Temple was known as Alsatia – a lawless area full of thieves and desperados who frequently clashed with the lawyers who worked and lived nearby. In 1691 Inner Temple tried to brick up the Tudor Street gate to stop 'Alsatians' from entering; however, the latter attacked the workers, killing one and knocking down the sheriff who arrived to try to restore order.

There are four Inns of Court – collectively serving as the headquarters of the branch of the legal profession known as barristers. These wigged and black-gowned advocates have had a virtual monopoly on the rights of audience in the English courts since medieval times, and a student wishing to become a barrister-at-law must be affiliated to one of the Inns – Inner and Middle Temple, Lincoln's Inn and Gray's Inn. Upon qualification the student is called to the 'bar' (originally the railing that enclosed a judge in the courtroom).

Inner Temple's origins – like those of the other three Inns – are obscure. Some have suggested the Inns began after an ordinance

1 Inner Temple

of Edward I in 1292 placed barristers under the control of the judges rather than the church, thus creating a secularised profession. During the early 14th century it is likely that lawyers began to leave the schools of law based within the City to congregate around new 'inns' – lodging houses originally – just west of the City wall, although most of the official records of the Inns do not begin until the 15th century.

Each Inn is an unincorporated association of students and barristers governed by a central body comprising the Masters of the Bench, normally drawn from senior members of the judiciary or Queen's Counsel – the highest rank of practising barrister. The Inn provides certain key services: assistance with training for students, the provision of office space for barristers' chambers, a library for research, a chapel for spiritual needs and a central hall that serves as the focal point for the Inn's social and ceremonial calendar.

The Temple area – covering Inner, Middle and Outer Temple – was once owned by the Knights Templar, the religious-military order that was founded in Jerusalem in 1119 during the Crusades. Originally founded to protect pilgrims visiting the Holy Land, the Templars built up a vast network of estates and mercantile interests throughout Europe and the Crusader kingdom of Outremer. The English branch of the order moved to this area in the 12th century from their original headquarters in Holborn, and their lands stretched from what is now Fleet Street right down to the Thames. However, from 1307 a number of European monarchs, supported by Pope Clement V, decided the Templars were becoming too powerful for their own good and began to persecute them.

In 1312 the Order's London properties were taken over by the Crown and given over to another similar religious-military order also founded in Jerusalem – the Knights Hospitallers. The Hospitallers leased their new lands to the lawyers who were already congregating there, and the Inns of Inner Temple and Middle Temple are first mentioned by name in a manuscript yearbook of 1388. After the Hospitallers were themselves suppressed during Henry VIII's Dissolution, the land reverted to the Crown. In 1609 James I granted the land to the two Inns in perpetuity on the condition they maintain the church and Master's House. Whilst it is not entirely clear why two Inns developed on the Templar lands instead of just one, today they remain separate, albeit neighbouring, institutions.

To the south as you enter Inner Temple are ❸ **Inner Temple Gardens**. Covering three acres, this is one of the City's most attractive open spaces and, as noted by Dickens in *Barnaby Rudge*, 'who enters here leaves noise behind'. The gates date from 1730 and are adorned with the figures of a griffin and Pegasus, taken respectively from the coats of arms of Gray's Inn and Inner Temple which have historically had close ties. All along the walk you will frequently see the arms of each Inn – look out also for the sheep of Middle Temple and the rampant red lion of Lincoln's Inn. The Gardens are normally open to the public on weekdays 12.30pm-3pm.

On the eastern side is ❹ **King's Bench Walk**, the buildings dating largely from the 1670s and designed by Sir Christopher Wren. If you look at the entrances to each building you will see the list of barristers who form a set of chambers. 11 King's Bench Walk Chambers was founded by Alexander Irvine (now Lord Irvine) in 1981, and counted Tony and Cherie Blair among its early barristers. In 1997 Blair – as Prime Minister – appointed his former boss Irvine as Lord Chancellor. Another Inner Templar chose a political career over a legal one – Mohandas Gandhi (1869-1948). The great Indian nationalist was called to the bar in 1891 although disbarred in 1922 following a conviction for sedition. He was posthumously reinstated in 1988.

Ahead is ❺ **Paper Buildings**, originally constructed in 1610, although the current buildings date from 1838. In Dickens's *Barnaby Rudge* the character Sir John Chester lived here. In addition to featuring in many novels, Inner Temple has also had many members who have become more famous as writers, including John Mortimer (creator of Horace Rumpole – himself an Inner Templar), Bram Stoker, and possibly the poet Geoffrey Chaucer.

To the right are ❻ **Inner Temple Hall**, the Treasury and the library. Each Inn has its own hall, normally closed to the public, where examinations are held, as well as the ceremonies in which students are called to the bar, and formal dinners (students have to attend a certain number of dinners each year as part of their qualification). Like much of Inner Temple the hall is a neo-Georgian reconstruction from the 1950s following terrible damage inflicted during the Blitz.

Ahead is the distinctive round nave of ❼ **Temple Church**. This church is the only substantial remnant of the Knights Templars' occupation of the area, and was built by them to resemble the Church of the Holy Sepulchre in Jerusalem. The Church – recently featured in Dan Brown's best selling book *The Da Vinci Code* – is shared by both Inner and Middle Temple. It was consecrated in 1185 by Heraclius, Patriarch of Jerusalem during the reign of Henry II, and despite much rebuilding over the centuries including after the Blitz, it remains a fascinating place. The 13th-century effigies of Templar knights are the most striking feature. There is also a stairwell which contains a former cell where disobedient knights were held and, it is said, sometimes starved to death.

Outside the church is a column marking where the Great Fire of 1666 finally stopped on the western side of the City, and the statue of the two knights riding a single horse commemorates the Templar's frugality. The Order's original title was The Poor Fellow Soldiers of Christ, and the later 'Templar' name was derived from the fact the knights' first headquarters were situated on the ruins of Solomon's Temple in Jerusalem. The church is usually open Wednesday to Friday 11am-4pm and hosts excellent lunchtime concerts (see website for details at www.templechurch.com).

Continue on the southwest side to ⑧ **Elm Court**, where a plaque on the wall to the left indicates this was once part of the original Templar 'buttery' – or food store. Continue west onto Middle Temple Lane, where most of ⑨ **The Inn of Middle Temple** can be found on the other side.

PLEASE DO NOT LEAN AGAINST OR SIT ON THESE RAILINGS

10 Middle Temple Hall

Just across the Lane in Fountain Court you reach ⑩ **Middle Temple Hall**. It dates from 1573, and is one of the best examples of an Elizabethan hall in the country. Boasting a fine double hammerbeam ceiling, it has served as the heart of activities in Middle Temple for more than four hundred years.

One of its most notable features is the 29 feet long **Bench Table**, thought to have been a gift from Elizabeth I and cut from a single oak tree from her estate at Windsor. The Benchers who run the Middle Temple still dine here just as they did when Sir Francis Drake arrived to a huge welcome in August 1586 upon his return from a successful expedition against the Spanish Indies, also bringing back with him the survivors of Sir Walter Raleigh's colony in Virginia.

Drake (1540-1595) was a regular visitor, and the **Cupboard** – a small table in front of the Bench Table where newly-called barristers stand to sign the register – is thought to have been carved from the hatchcover of Drake's *Golden Hinde*. The *Hinde's* lantern hung in the entrance to the hall until it was destroyed during the Blitz in 1941.

Shakespeare's play *Twelfth Night* was premiered in the hall in 1602. During this period it was fashionable for the offspring of the wealthier classes to spend some time studying at one of the Inns even if they never intended to pursue a career in the law. As a result, the students were a cosmopolitan bunch who often excelled in artistic pursuits. It was therefore entirely natural that London's greatest playwright would premiere a new play to an appreciative audience of lawyers.

Another literary connection relates to the stained glass window in the hall that contains the shields of Josephus Jekyll and Roburtus Hyde. The writer Robert Louis Stevenson, a Middle Templar, may have taken these names for the main character(s) of his novel *The Strange Case of Dr Jekyll and Mr Hyde* (1886). The hall contains original paintings of Queen Elizabeth I, said to have dined here many times, Charles I & II, James II, William III, Queen Anne and George I.

In the days of the British Empire lawyers often came from the colonies to train here before returning home. Five Middle Templars were among the original signatories of the **American Declaration of Independence**, whilst seven more helped draft the **Constitution of the United States**. Americans often received their legal training at the Inns even after their country became independent, and this tradition only stopped when England went to war with America in 1812. The hall is normally open to the public Monday to Friday (10am-noon, 3pm-4pm).

Leave the hall and head south down the lane to reach ⑪ **Middle Temple Gardens**. The gardens, with their red and white rose border, were portrayed by Shakespeare in *Henry VI Part I* as the place where the red rose of Lancaster and white rose of York were first plucked, marking the beginning of the English War of the Roses (1455-1485):

PLANTAGENET
Since you are tongue-tied and so loath to speak,
In dumb significants proclaim your thoughts:
Let him that is a true-born gentleman
And stands upon the honour of his birth,
If he suppose that I have pleaded truth,
From off this brier pluck a white rose with me.

SOMERSET
Let him that is no coward nor no flatterer,
But dare maintain the party of the truth,
Pluck a red rose from off this thorn with me.

The gardens were also once home to the Royal Horticultural Society Great Spring Show during the 19th century before moving west and becoming today's Chelsea Flower Show.

Head north along ⑫ **Middle Temple Lane** until you reach the Strand. On the other side are ⑬ **The Royal Courts of Justice**, which were opened in 1882 by Queen Victoria and house the Supreme Court. This consists of the High Court of Justice, principally dealing with civil cases, and the Court of Appeal. Before 1882 London's main courts were dotted around

the capital, including at Westminster Hall and the Old Hall of Lincoln's Inn. Over 35 million bricks were used in the construction of the Royal Courts, each faced with Portland stone.

You can visit the Courts during working hours (9am-4.30pm) although it is easy to get lost amongst the 1,000 rooms that are arranged along three and a half miles of corridors. The building is so large that a man was once found living in the basement. Lists show what cases are taking place each day within the 50 court rooms, and most can be visited by the public. Tours of the Courts are run on the first and third Tuesday of each month and cost £6 (call the tour organiser on 020 7947 7684).

Just outside the Courts on the eastern side is the statue of a dragon, symbol of the City, which marks the former site of ⑭ **Temple Bar**. This was a gateway on the western side of the City, its name derived from a chain or bar between posts that marked the entrance in medieval times. By tradition the monarch could not pass through Temple Bar on official business without first receiving an escort from the Mayor of London.

The gateway was rebuilt in 1672 by Sir Christopher Wren. Whilst the other gateways into the City had been removed by 1761, Temple Bar survived until 1878 when it was dismantled in order to reduce traffic congestion on Fleet Street. It was moved to a country estate outside London but has recently returned to the capital and now stands beside St Paul's Cathedral. The gateway still retains the spikes upon which the heads of executed traitors were placed, heavily salted beforehand to prevent the birds picking at them.

Cross over to the start of ⑮ **Chancery Lane**. On the right at number five is a plaque marking the former location of the now defunct ⑯ **Serjeant's Inn**. The Serjeants-at-law were a superior rank of barrister that originated in the Middle Ages. A barrister, upon being appointed as a Serjeant, had to leave their own Inn of Court and join Serjeant's Inn. Judges were appointed from the small band of Serjeants, and this monopoly lasted until the late 19th century when legal reforms made this rank of lawyer obsolete. The last remaining Serjeants sold their Inn at number five in 1877 for a vast sum and they each then returned to the Inn of Court to which they had originally belonged.

If you take a small detour just west down Fleet Street on the left you can see the old entrance to ⑰ **Clifford's Inn**, one of the defunct Inns of Chancery. These Inns were founded in the late medieval period and were always the poorer relations of the main Inns of Court. In those days it was very difficult to join one of the Inns of Court, so students would often join one of the Inns of Chancery to begin their studies. However, it was not possible to be called to the bar at an Inn of Chancery, so students would later try to move on to one of the more prestigious Inns of Court. Over the centuries it became easier to join an Inn of Court directly, and so the role of the Inns of Chancery – essentially preparatory colleges – became increasingly redundant.

By the 18th century the Inns of Chancery had effectively become social clubs, often used by solicitors (the branch of the legal profession that does not traditionally have rights of audience in the English courts), and by the late 19th century most of the Inns of Chancery had been disbanded and the buildings sold on. **Clifford's Inn** was founded in around 1345 and the main building survived until the early 20th century. The entrance off Fleet Street is the only remaining part that can be seen today. The other Inns of Chancery were Clements's Inn, Lyon's Inn, Strand Inn, New Inn, Furnival's Inn, Thavie's Inn, Staple Inn and Barnard's Inn.

Continue up Chancery Lane where on the right is the vast building that served as the ⑱ **Public Record Office** from the 1860s until 1996. Today it is a library for King's College. On the left is ⑲ **The Law Society**, headquarters of the institution

that governs the solicitors' profession. In recent years it has been possible for solicitors to become advocates in the English courts, and so the traditional demarcation line between barristers and solicitors has become slightly blurred. The building dates from 1832.

The oldest tailor in London, ⑳ **Ede & Ravenscroft**, is situated at number 97 Chancery Lane. Operating since 1689, it is the traditional outfitter to barristers working at the Inns. The famous wigs worn by barristers can be bought here with prices starting at around £500. They were originally made out of human hair, but in the 1830s Humphrey Ravenscroft patented the current design, which uses horse hair.

Head towards Chichester Rents and then through Star Yard where the premises of the lawyers Krook were located in Dickens's *Bleak House* (1852).

Look out for the historic and very rare green-metal ㉑ **Victorian public toilet** in Star Yard. It features in the fascinating documentary film *The London Nobody Knows* (1967), with the actor James Mason recreating the original toilet attendant's habit of keeping goldfish in the water tank.

Continue along Carey Street with the formidable gated entrance to Lincoln's Inn on the right. Just past the entrance is the atmospheric ㉒ **Seven Stars pub** – popular with lawyers since it was founded 400 years ago and a good place to stop if you want to see them letting their horse-hair wigs down.

Enter Lincoln's Inn through the ㉓ **gateway** which leads into the south side of

New Square. This is perhaps the best preserved of all the Inns of Court, and covers around 11 acres. Past members have included Sir Thomas More, Oliver Cromwell, John Donne, William Pitt, Margaret Thatcher and Tony Blair.

Lincoln's Inn's official records begin in 1422, 80 years before the other three Inns. However, like the other Inns, it was probably in existence far earlier. The name is derived from Henry de Lacy, third Earl of Lincoln (d. 1311). He was probably the Inn's first great patron and lived in nearby Shoe Lane.

It is worth taking a few minutes just to walk up and down the centre of the Inn, which is open to the public during weekday lunchtimes. On the eastern side is Old Buildings. This contains **24** **Old Hall**, built in the 1490s during which time Sir Thomas More would have dined here. One of the paintings displayed inside is Hogarth's vast Biblical canvas of *Paul Before Felix*, commissioned courtesy of a bequest to the Inn of £200 by Lord Wyndham in 1745.

The Old Hall used to be one of London's main courts and features in the opening scene of Dickens's *Bleak House* in connection with the fictional case of 'Jarndyce vs Jarndyce':

London. Michaelmas Term lately over, and the Lord Chancellor sitting in Lincoln's Inn Hall. Implacable November weather... Fog everywhere. Fog up the river, where it flows among green aits and meadows; fog down the river, where it rolls defiled among the tiers of shipping, and the waterside pollutions of a great (and dirty) city... And hard by Temple Bar, in Lincoln's Inn Hall, at the very heart of the fog, sits the Lord High Chancellor in his High Court of Chancery.

'Jarndyce vs Jarndyce' became a by-word for the greed of lawyers and futility – and cost — of endless litigation. Dickens is thought to have been inspired by two cases – *The Thellusson Will Case* and the *Great Jennings Case*. The *Thellusson Case* concerned a wealthy merchant named Peter Thellusson who died in 1797 leaving an estate that was still being fought over by his heirs as late as 1859, by which time the estate had been largely exhausted by legal fees.

25 *Great Hall & Library, Lincoln's Inn*

The Great Jennings Case was partly heard within the Old Hall and concerned a rich miser named William Jennings who died in 1798 aged 97 and leaving no heir. A number of lawsuits were launched by distant relatives seeking part of Jennings's estate. The main settlement took place in 1821 but litigation nevertheless continued, particularly because in America speculative lawyers encouraged anyone called Jennings to stake a claim. The last such claim was filed as late as 1934.

By the mid 19th century the Old Hall was too small to cope with the demands being placed upon it, and on the west side the Inn built the **㉕ Great Hall and Library**. It was opened in 1845 by Queen Victoria and designed by Philip Hardwick. The Great Hall serves all the normal purposes of a hall in an Inn such as dining, although Old Hall is still used for examinations and lectures. Sadly neither hall is generally open to the public.

The **㉖ chapel** beside the Old Hall was built 1619-23, with the original dedication ceremony conducted by poet and Inn member John Donne (1572-1631), then also the Dean of St Paul's Cathedral. It stands over a fascinating undercroft with gravestones set flat in the ground. Women were not allowed to be buried here until Lord Brougham successfully argued for a rule change that allowed his daughter to be interred here in 1839, her father wishing to be buried beside her when he died. Poor mothers left their babies in the undercroft knowing the Inn would look after their upbringing, and many of these foundlings were given the adoptive surname 'Lincoln'.

The chapel bell is said to have been brought back from Spain as part of the booty taken during the raid on Cadiz in 1596. It has long been the custom to toll the bell between 12.30pm and 1pm when news of the

death of a Bencher of the Inn is received, and barristers send their clerks to enquire as to the identity of the deceased. The tradition inspired Donne's famous lines 'No man is an island, entire of itself; every man is a piece of the continent, a part of the main... and therefore never send to know for whom the bell tolls; it tolls for thee'. The chapel is open to the public between 12noon and 2.30pm during the week.

Head east from Old Buildings through the 27 **Gate House**. This was built around 1520 and the oak doors date from 1564. Legend has it that dramatist Ben Jonson (1572-1637) worked as a bricklayer during the construction of the Gate House. Above the Gate House are a number of original heraldic arms including those of Henry de Lacy, Earl of Lincoln and Henry VIII.

Leave Lincoln's Inn to walk north up Chancery Lane and then through 28 **Southampton Buildings**. This takes you out onto busy High Holborn where you can see the timbered frontage of 29 **Staple Inn**. This building is the only one to survive from the now defunct Inn of Chancery described above. The front of the building dates from around 1580 and is one of the oldest structures in London.

The word 'Staple' originates from a tax imposed on wool introduced in 1275 and the building was originally used by wool dealers (or 'wool-staplers'). From the early 15th century the building was used by the lawyers of the Inn of Chancery and became known by its current name. However by the

19th century, along with the other Inns of Chancery, Staple Inn had gone into terminal decline and its members sold the building in 1884. The site now houses the Institute of Actuaries.

Head over High Holborn and take the tiny passageway beside the ㉚ **Cittie of Yorke** pub, which may have been founded here as early as 1430. You enter the ㉛ **South Square** of **Gray's Inn**, the final Inn of Court visited on this walk. In South Square there is a statue of Sir Francis Bacon (1561-1626), philosopher, statesman, scientist, and a prominent member of Gray's Inn in the 16th century. Number 1 on South Square was once the offices of Ellis & Blackmore, where the teenage Charles Dickens worked as a law clerk in 1827 (a high desk he used during his time at Gray's Inn can be seen in the Dickens Museum in Doughty Street, Bloomsbury).

Head north into the larger ㉜ **Gray's Inn Square**. Gray's Inn is named after Reginald de Grey, a Chief Justice whose London mansion housed the original Gray's Inn after he died in 1308. Much of the Inn was damaged during WWII, although the rebuilding work was tastefully done.

The ㉝ **chapel** on the south side of the square dates from 1689 and was built on the site of the Inn's original chapel (built in around 1315). Beside the chapel is the ㉞ **hall** dating largely from 1556-8, although extensively renovated after Blitz damage. Luckily the glass, pictures and Treasurer's shields had been removed to a place of safety and so were returned after the war. The screen on the west side is said to have been a gift from Queen Elizabeth I and made from the wood of a captured Spanish galleon. Some of the stained glass in the windows dates back to the 16th century.

The third Earl of Southampton, patron of William Shakespeare, was a member of Gray's Inn. This probably explains why Shakespeare's company premiered *A Comedy of Errors* in the Hall. The Inn's records state that a performance was given by 'a company of base and common fellows' on 28th December, 1594 during Christmas celebrations, probably with Shakespeare himself taking one of the roles.

This was during the 'Golden Age' of Gray's when Elizabeth I was the Patron Lady and many of her inner circle were members of the Inn including Admiral Lord Howard of Effingham (who masterminded the defeat of the Spanish Armada in 1588), and Sir Francis Walsingham (a key player in the development of the secret service). Currently Gray's Inn Hall is open by appointment only. You can write for more information about access to the Treasury, South Square, Gray's Inn, London WC1 (or call 0207 458 7800).

On the west side head through a narrow passage to see ㉟ **Gray's Inn Gardens** – better known as 'The Walks' – on the right. The Walks are one of the loveliest parts of this area of London and often overlooked by people who think access is restricted to members of Gray's. However, the public can visit during every weekday lunchtime. The Walks were first laid out by Sir Francis Bacon in 1606 when he was Treasurer of Gray's, and were popular for promenading by fashionable society during the 17th century.

In 1660 the diarist Samuel Pepys went 'to Gray's Inn where I saw many beauties' and proceeded to Walks where he saw a 'great store of gallants, but above all Mrs Frances Butler is the greatest beauty'. On the east side is a twisted trunk of an ancient catalpa which is all that remains of a larger tree crushed during the hurricane of 1987, and which is said to have been planted by Sir Francis Bacon.

Leave Gray's Inn on the western side through a gate and walk along Sandland Street. On the right you can see ㊱ **Bedford Row** – a fine street of Georgian houses, historically popular with firms of

35 Gray's Inn Gardens

solicitors. Take a left down Red Lion Street and follow the map along High Holborn for a short while before crossing over and walking down the winding and atmospheric Little Turnstile that takes you out into the vast expanse of **37** **Lincoln's Inn Fields**.

This is London's largest square and covers 12 acres. It is said to have the same dimensions as the base of the Great Pyramid at Giza, and to have been the inspiration for Central Park in New York. The land here consisted of rural fields before the square was laid out by Inigo Jones (1573-1652) in the early 17th century. Before then it had been a popular site for duellists and was also used for public executions. In 1586 Sir Anthony Babington was half-hanged before being drawn and quartered here because of his part in a plot against Elizabeth I. He suffered so horrendously that the Queen allowed his fellow plotters to be hanged until death before also being drawn and quartered.

38 **Farrer & Co** solicitors have been based at number 66 since 1790, and count the monarchy and much of England's landed aristocracy amongst their clients. **39** **Number 59/60** dates from around 1640 and has been attributed to Inigo Jones. It was home to Spencer Perceval, the only British Prime Minister to have been assassinated. At number 13, on the north side, is **40** **Sir John Soane's Museum**. Soane (1753-1837) was the son of a bricklayer who became an architect. His work includes the Bank of England and the Dulwich Picture Gallery. He married into money and began his collection of art and oddities, including Hogarth's *Rakes Progress*, three Canalettos, and many fine Egyptian, Roman and other classical pieces. The house became a public museum after Soane's death and has hardly been altered since. One of the best museums in London, it is open from Tuesday to Saturday, 10am-5pm and admission is free. Special candlelit openings take place on the first Tuesday evening of each month, 6pm-9pm.

Walk through the middle of Lincoln's Inn Fields. Underneath is a network of tunnels used during WWII. The entrance – now bricked up – is located under the turf of the north-east side. The fascinating **41** **Hunterian Museum** is located on the south side of the square inside **the Royal College of Surgeons** at numbers 35-43.

It is named after John Hunter (1728-1793), regarded as the founder of 'scientific surgery'. An apparently difficult and blunt man, he died in 1793 after suffering a fit during an argument at St George's Hospital over the acceptance of students for training. In 1799 the government purchased his collection of around 15,000 specimens, many of which are

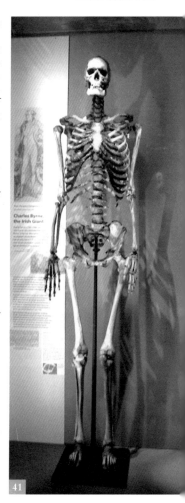

on display today. The museum has recently undergone a multi-million pound refurbishment transforming the formerly old fashioned displays. A glittering 'Crystal Gallery' now houses over 3,000 of John Hunter's original 18th-century specimens. They include teeth retrieved from soldiers on the battlefield of Waterloo, a necklace of human teeth brought from the Congo by the explorer Henry Morton Stanley and a denture belonging to Sir Winston Churchill.

The skeleton of the 'Irish giant' Charles Byrne (1761-1783) is also on display. Byrne was thought to be over 8 feet tall, although he was actually more like 7ft 7ins. He was so afraid that doctors would dissect his corpse that he requested to be buried at sea, but John Hunter, ever determined, bought Byrne's corpse for £500. The Hunterian Museum is open Tuesday to Saturday, 10am-5pm.

Leave the square on the south-west corner and walk down Portsmouth Street. At number 13-14 is ㊷ **The Old Curiosity Shop**, which dates from the 1560s but which, despite its claims, is unlikely to have been the inspiration of

Dickens's book. In any event it is a rare example of an Elizabethan building in London, and one of the oldest shops in the capital.

Follow the map that takes you through ㊸ **Clement's Inn**, where the now defunct Inn of Chancery once stood before its demolition in 1891. Continue south until you come back onto the Strand where you can see Wren's fine church of ㊹ **St Clement Danes**, once used by the lawyers of Clement's Inn. Nicknamed the 'island church', it appears stranded in the middle of the road, a result of the widening of the old lanes. It claims to be the church referred to in the opening line of the nursery rhyme *Oranges and Lemons* ('Oranges and lemons, say the bells of St. Clement's').

The walk ends here and just to the south is Temple underground station (closed Sundays). You are also within a few minutes walk of Covent Garden, Charing Cross and other stations. ●

VISIT...

Temple Church (see p.128)
Temple, EC4Y
www.templechurch.com

Middle Temple Hall (see p.131)
2 Plowden Buildings, EC4Y
www.middletemple.org.uk

Sir John Soane's Museum
(see p.144)
13 Lincoln's Inn Fields, WC2A
www.soane.org

Hunterian Museum (see p.145)
35-43 Lincoln's Inn Fields, WC2
www.rcseng.ac.uk/museums/

EAT, DRINK...

Seven Stars pub (see p.136)
53 Carey Street, WC2A

Cittie of Yorke pub (see p.141)
22 High Holborn, WC1V

SHOP...

Leather Lane Market
Leather Lane, EC1N
www.leatherlanemarket.co.uk

Hatton Gardens
Hatton Gardens, EC1N
www.hatton-garden.net

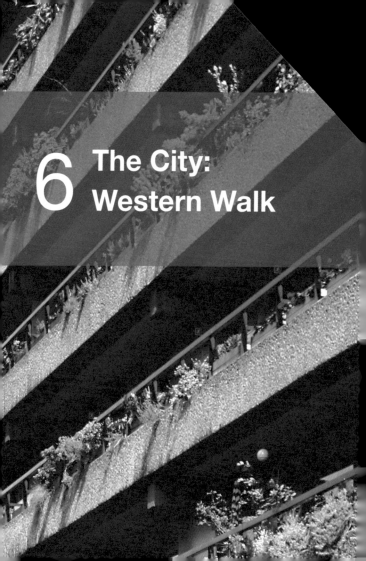

6 The City:
Western Walk

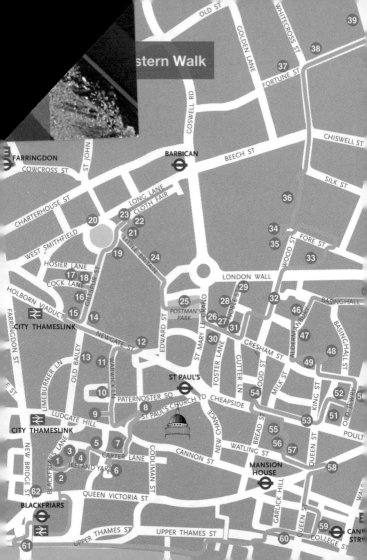

stern Walk

OLD ST
WHITECROSS ST
39
GOLDEN LANE
38
37 FORTUNE ST
COSWELL RD
CHISWELL ST
FARRINGDON
COWCROSS ST
BARBICAN
BEECH ST
SILK ST
ST JOHN
CHARTERHOUSE ST
LONG LANE
36
CLOTH FAIR
23
WEST SMITHFIELD
22
34
21
35
FORE ST
WOOD ST
HOSIER LANE
19
24
33
17 18
LONDON WALL
COCK LANE
16
29
BASINGHALL
32
HOLBORN VIADUCT
15
14
28
25
46
POSTMAN'S
PARK
26
CITY THAMESLINK
NEWGATE ST
12
27
47
31
FARRINGDON ST
13
11
30
GRESHAM ST
48
EDWARD ST
OLD BAILEY
WARWICK
FOSTER LANE
GUTTER LN
WOOD ST
49
10
ST PAUL'S
54
MILK ST
LIMEBURNER LN
PATERNOSTER SQ
CHEAPSIDE
KING ST
52
8
ST PAUL'S CHURCH YD
NEW CHANGE
53
51
9
LUDGATE HILL
BREAD ST
55
OLD JEWRY
POULT
CITY THAMESLINK
5
7
WATLING ST
56
57
QUEEN ST
BLACKFRIARS LANE
1
3
CARTER LANE
CANNON ST
58
NEW BRIDGE
4
2
IRELAND YARD
6
GODLIMAN ST
MANSION
HOUSE
62
QUEEN VICTORIA ST
GARLICK HILL
BLACKFRIARS
59
60
CAN
61
UPPER THAMES ST
UPPER THAMES ST
COLLEGE HILL
STR

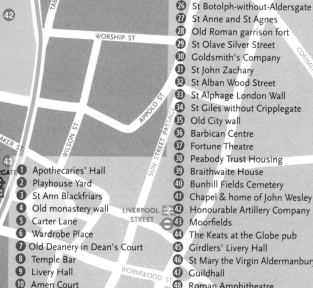

25 Postman's Park
26 St Botolph-without-Aldersgate
27 St Anne and St Agnes
28 Old Roman garrison fort
29 St Olave Silver Street
30 Goldsmith's Company
31 St John Zachary
32 St Alban Wood Street
33 St Alphage London Wall
34 St Giles without Cripplegate
35 Old City wall
36 Barbican Centre
37 Fortune Theatre
38 Peabody Trust Housing
39 Braithwaite House
40 Bunhill Fields Cemetery
41 Chapel & home of John Wesley
42 Honourable Artillery Company
43 Moorfields
44 The Keats at the Globe pub
45 Girdlers' Livery Hall
46 St Mary the Virgin Aldermanbury
47 Guildhall
48 Roman Amphitheatre
49 St Lawrence Jewry
50 Great Synagogue
51 Frederick's Place
52 St Olave Jewry
53 Cheapside
54 St Peter Westcheap
55 St Mary le Bow
56 Bow Church Yard
57 St Mary Aldermary
58 Roman Temple of Mithras
59 St Michael Paternoster Royal
60 St James Garlickhythe
61 Blackfriars Bridge
62 Black Friar pub

1 Apothecaries' Hall
2 Playhouse Yard
3 St Ann Blackfriars
4 Old monastery wall
5 Carter Lane
6 Wardrobe Place
7 Old Deanery in Dean's Court
8 Temple Bar
9 Livery Hall
10 Amen Court
11 Cutlers' Hall
12 Christ Church Newgate
13 Old Bailey
14 Viaduct Tavern
15 St Sepulchre without Newgate
16 Old watch house
17 Cock Lane
18 Fat golden cherub
19 St Bartholomew's Hospital
20 West Smithfield
21 13th-century gatehouse
22 St Bartholomew-the-Great
23 No. 41 Cloth Fair
24 Little Britain

The City: Western Walk

Start/Finish: Blackfriars underground/rail station
Distance: 5.5 miles

From Blackfriars station cross over Queen Victoria Street and walk up Black Friars Lane. Pass Playhouse Yard and continue up the Lane, looking out on the right for **❶ Apothecaries' Hall**, home to the Apothecaries' Livery Company. If you are visiting during the week you can walk through the small entrance into a beautiful courtyard. The Livery Companies have their origins in medieval times, when trade associations or guilds were formed with the aim of protecting the economic interests of their members and maintaining proper standards within each trade or profession.

In 1515 the 48 Livery Companies of the time were ranked in order of precedence. This practice continues in respect of the 108 Companies that currently exist, around 38 of which have their headquarters in the City.

From the 18th century, trade and commerce became increasingly liberalised and the Livery Companies could no longer control the trades and professions they had originally monopolised. They survived by gradually transforming themselves into primarily charitable and social institutions. However, a few still have an active involvement in regulating their professions, and many control substantial assets that have been accumulated over the centuries. The Worshipful Society of Apothecaries of London was incorporated

① Apothecaries' Hall Courtyard

as a Livery Company in 1617. It once controlled the production and distribution of medicines and regulated parts of the medical profession. The Society moved to this site in 1632, and the current hall was rebuilt on the ruins of the original, which was destroyed during the Great Fire of 1666. The hall once contained an 'Elaboratory' in which the first large-scale production of medicines in England took place, this function only ending in 1922. In 1673 the society also founded one of London's greatest treasures – the Chelsea Physic Garden – which can still be visited today. The society remains involved in examinations and educational diplomas connected to its profession.

Return to ❷ **Playhouse Yard**. Blackfriars is named after the black cappa (cloaks) worn by the friars of the vast Dominican monastery that dominated this area from 1275. It was in this monastery that a court conducted the divorce proceedings of Henry VIII and Catherine of Aragon in 1529, something of an own goal given this ultimately led to the King's break with Rome and the subsequent dissolution of Blackfriars in 1538. Following this, the former monastery buildings were demolished or taken over for other purposes.

In the 1590s the Elizabethan theatrical manager James Burbage (1531-1597) converted the former refectory building of the monastery into a playhouse, today the site of Playhouse Yard. It was originally used by the Children of the Chapel, a company of child actors whose productions rivalled those of adult theatrical troupes. It is thought William Shakespeare's reference in *Hamlet* to 'little eyasses' was intended as a dig at these youthful competitors for London's theatre audiences.

From 1608 the playhouse was used by the King's Men led by Burbage's son, Richard (1568-1619). Shakespeare was a leading member of this troupe, both as an actor and its star writer, and some of his later works written around this time include *Cymbeline*, *The Winter's Tale* and *The Tempest*.

Unlike most other London theatres, the Blackfriars playhouse had a roof, and was used by the King's Men as an alternative to the more famous Globe in Southwark during the winter months. Up to 700 people could be accommodated within the playhouse, and the revenue it received from each performance has been estimated to have been double that of the Globe. It was eventually closed by the Puritans in 1642 and demolished in 1655.

Continue eastwards and walk up Church Entry on the left. This contains a small garden with some old gravestones, which occupies the site of **❸ St Ann Blackfriars**. This church was built after the monastery had been shut down and was used by a mainly Puritan congregation who spent many decades protesting about the disruption to their services caused by the playhouse next door. As mentioned above, the Puritans had the last laugh (if they did ever laugh). Along with 88 other City churches, St Ann's was destroyed in the Great Fire of 1666, but was not one of the 51 chosen by the City authorities to be rebuilt.

Re-trace your steps and walk into **Ireland Yard.** In 1613 Shakespeare bought a dwelling here, located within the old monastery gate house, for £140. When he died the property was left to his daughter Susanna Hall.

Continue east, looking out on the left for another small garden that incorporates the old graveyard of St Ann Blackfriars. This was used for burials until 1849, and by the entrance you can see the ruins of the **❹ old monastery wall**.

155

Follow the map up Friar Street then along **5** **Carter Lane**, where to your right you will find **6** **Wardrobe Place**. Enter the courtyard that stands on the former garden of the King's Wardrobe, a grand 14th-century house first used by Edward III to store royal ceremonial robes. In 1604 Shakespeare came here to collect 4 1/2 yards of cloth for a costume he wore as a participant, along with the rest of the King's Men, in the ceremonial procession of James I. The King's Wardrobe was destroyed in the Great Fire of 1666.

Follow the map to reach the south side of St Paul's Cathedral, passing **7** **The Old Deanery in Dean's Court** on the left. Designed by Wren and dating from 1670, today this serves as the London palace of the Bishop of London. Just to the right along St Paul's Churchyard is the circular City information office. The staff here can help arrange visits to the City's Livery Halls which are normally closed to the public.

The churchyard of St Paul's, and nearby Paternoster Square, was an important place for London's publishers and second-hand booksellers from the late medieval period until the mid 20th century. This was also a site for public executions, the most notable victim being Guy Fawkes in 1606.

St Paul's Cathedral was founded by Ethelbert, King of Kent (c.560-616 AD) in 604 AD and the current building was famously built by Sir Christopher Wren after the Great Fire of London. You may wish to visit the Cathedral at this point, and if you do, make sure to look out for the shrouded statue of John Donne (1572-1630), the great Elizabethan poet and a former Dean of St Paul's. Donne was buried in the crypt and his effigy was the only monument from Old St Paul's to survive the fire (the scorch marks are still visible). It bears Donne's typically witty epitaph, 'John Donne, Undone'.

On the north-west corner of the Cathedral precinct stands ❽ **Temple Bar** – a City gateway built by Sir Christopher Wren in the late 17th century which originally stood on Fleet Street. In 1878 it was dismantled due to traffic congestion. It was re-assembled in the grounds of a country house outside London, and only recently returned to the City as part of the redevelopment of Paternoster Square. There is a useful information board beside it that tells you about Temple Bar's history, including how its spikes once held the severed heads of executed traitors.

Follow the map to Ave Maria Lane where immediately on the left is a small lane that leads to Stationers Hall, the ❾ **Livery Hall of the Worshipful Company of Stationers and Newspaper Makers**. This has been their home since 1611 (the

current building dates from after the Great Fire). Until 1911 a copy of every publication had to be registered here, although this obligation was largely ignored by publishers after about 1700. Many of Shakespeare's plays and sonnets were registered here.

Continue along the Lane and almost immediately on your you will see ⑩ **Amen Court** (private road). Containing a number of 17th and 18th-century houses, this quiet area is where many of the Cathedral's clergy and other staff live and work. John Collins (1905-1982), a former canon at the Cathedral, lived in the court and it was in his flat in November 1957 that the Campaign for Nuclear Disarmament (CND) was formed, with politicians Denis Healey and Michael Foot among those in attendance. The wall along the edge of the court was built deliberately high to prevent prisoners in the neighbouring Newgate Prison escaping, and it is said the court is haunted by the ghosts of some of the men executed at Newgate during its 800 year history.

Continue north up Warwick Lane, looking out on the left for ⑪ **Cutlers' Hall**, home to the Cutlers' Livery Company since 1887. This trade association traces its origins back to 1389, and once controlled the making of swords and surgical instruments.

Follow the map to reach Newgate Street. Just to the right over the road are the tower and outer walls of ⑫ **Christ Church Newgate**. This church, and Christ's Hospital School that stood nearby, were both built on the site of Greyfriars monastery, which was dissolved by Henry VIII in 1538. The Great Fire destroyed the church and school, both of which were rebuilt by Wren. The school moved out of London to Horsham in the early 20th century, and the church was gutted during the Blitz. The walls and tower you can see are all that remain of the church, the former nave converted into a pleasant rose garden and the tower now a private residence.

Head west along Newgate Street with the **⑬ Central Criminal Court at Old Bailey** on your left. You can watch criminal cases in progress from the public galleries when the courts are in session (the galleries are open 10am-1pm and 2pm-5pm; no children). The court complex was built in 1902 on the site of the recently demolished Newgate Prison, the most feared institution in London for many centuries and named after the City wall gatehouse in which it was originally located.

Over the centuries the prison had many famous inmates including Ben Jonson, Christopher Marlowe, John Milton, Oscar Wilde and Daniel Defoe. In the latter's *Moll Flanders* (1722), the title character is born inside Newgate itself. The open space at the junction with Old Bailey was London's main site for public executions in the late 18th century after the original execution site at Tyburn (near today's Marble Arch) fell out of favour. Thousands would turn up to watch the executions and in 1807 a stampede resulted in 28 people being killed.

Christian Murphy was the last person to be burnt at the stake in England at Newgate in 1789 (although she had been strangled to death beforehand), whilst in 1820 the Cato Street conspirators were the last prisoners to suffer the fate of being beheaded. After

15

the Irish Fenian leader Michael Barrett was publicly hanged outside Newgate in 1868, executions were carried out privately within the prison.

Facing Old Bailey is the **14** **Viaduct Tavern**, which dates from around 1870. One of the most atmospheric Victorian 'gin palaces' to survive in London, it features a wonderfully ornate interior and is worth a stop for lunch and a pint (although it is closed at the weekends). Its cellars are thought to have originally been part of Newgate Prison and can be visited by appointment.

Opposite the Tavern is the enormous church of **15** **St Sepulchre without Newgate**, the largest parish church in the City. First recorded in 1137, it was later rebuilt after having been destroyed in the Great Fire. Unlike many churches destroyed in 1666, the parishioners were responsible for organising the restoration. Originally dedicated to St Edmund, in medieval times it was renamed after the Holy Sepulchre in Jerusalem because both churches stood outside the western side of their respective cities. It became the symbolic embarkation point for

Crusaders leaving London for the Holy Land. One of the notable people buried here, and remembered by a memorial inside, is Captain John Smith (1580-1631). He was the founder of the early American colony of Jamestown in Virginia, his life was famously saved by the Indian Princess Pocahontas (c.1595-1617).

Inside you can also see a hand bell once rung by the church sexton as he walked at midnight through an underground tunnel – now blocked up – that was linked to Newgate Prison. This ceremony would take place the night before an execution, with the sexton urging the condemned prisoners to repent and ending his journey outside their cell shouting the ominous words 'And when St Sepulchre's bell in the morning tolls, The Lord have mercy on your souls!'. The main church bells are also those referred to in the famous rhyme *Oranges and Lemons* in the line '"When will you pay me?" say the bells of Old Bailey'.

Continue up Giltspur Street, looking out on the left for the ⑯ **old watch house** of 1791 (later rebuilt). It was used to guard against body-snatchers who took corpses from the graveyard and sold them to anatomists at St Bartholomew's Hospital nearby.

⑰ **Cock Lane** is on the left, so-named because of the sordid goings on that took place here when it was the only licensed street for prostitutes in the medieval City. It was later the location of a famous public scandal in 1762 concerning the *Cock Lane Ghost*. The main characters were William Kent and his mistress Fanny Lynes, sister of his dead wife, who lodged in a house at number 33 belonging to William Parsons. Kent and Parsons fell out over money the latter had borrowed but refused to re-pay. Later whilst Kent was away Fanny claimed the ghost of her sister was haunting

the room she shared with Parsons' daughter Elizabeth and trying to warn Fanny of her impending death by scratching on the walls.

Kent and his mistress understandably soon moved out, and Fanny died soon after of smallpox. Parsons claimed the haunting of the room continued and that now Fanny's own ghost was accusing William of murdering her. Parsons charged thousands of fascinated visitors a fee to listen and communicate with 'scratching Fanny of Cock Lane'. Given the accusations against Kent, some of London's most prominent people investigated the case, including Samuel Johnson. It was discovered that Parsons's daughter was making the noises using a wooden clapper hidden under her clothes and Parsons was imprisoned for his deception. Johnson later published *An Account of the Detection of the Imposture in Cock Lane*. Cock Lane was also where John Bunyan (b. 1628), author of *The Pilgrim's Progress*, died in 1688.

On the corner facing Giltspur Street look up to see the figure of a ⑱ **fat golden cherub**, which marks the furthest western extent of the Great Fire. Some people believed that the fact the fire started in Pudding Lane and stopped at what was originally known as Pye (or Pie) Corner was a sign from God that Londoners were being punished for their gluttony.

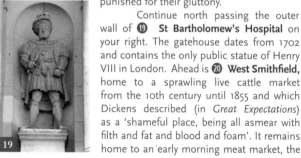

Continue north passing the outer wall of ⑲ **St Bartholomew's Hospital** on your right. The gatehouse dates from 1702 and contains the only public statue of Henry VIII in London. Ahead is ⑳ **West Smithfield**, home to a sprawling live cattle market from the 10th century until 1855 and which Dickens described (in *Great Expectations*) as a 'shameful place, being all asmear with filth and fat and blood and foam'. It remains home to an early morning meat market, the last of London's ancient markets to remain in its original location.

'Smithfield' is a corruption of the medieval 'smooth field', and is today a pleasant open area surrounded by shops, restaurants and bars. However, in the past it was a place of jousting tournaments and public executions. Plaques on the wall of the hospital just past the gatehouse recall that William Wallace (b. 1270), Scotland's 'Braveheart', was hanged, drawn and quartered here in 1305. During the reign of Queen Mary (1516-1558) in the 1550s many protestants were martyred here. It is said Mary watched the burnings inside the half-timbered gatehouse of St Bartholomew's church nearby.

Later, during the Great Plague of 1664-5, Smithfield was used as a burial pit for victims. It was also where medieval horse and cloth fairs were held every August around St Bartholomew's Day. The festivities surrounding the fairs developed into the famous St Bartholomew Fair which was held from 1133 until 1855 when the City authorities banned it on account of the immorality it encouraged. This was beautifully described in a penny ballad from 1641:

163

Cutpurses and Cheaters, and
Bawdy House Keepers
Punks, Aye! and Panders and
casheered Commanders...
Alchemists and Pedlars,
Whores, Bawds and Beggars
In Bartholomew Fair.

St Bartholomew's Hospital
(more commonly known as Barts)
is the oldest hospital in London
and was originally part of the priory
dedicated to the eponymous Saint.
The priory was founded on this site
in 1123 by Rahere (d. 1144), once
a jester to Henry I, who vowed
to open a church here after his
apparently miraculous recovery
from an illness contracted during
a pilgrimage to Rome. After the
priory was dissolved in 1539 the
hospital was forced to close,
however it was re-founded on a
secular basis in 1546.

The hospital is a parish in
its own right and contains its
own church of St Bartholomew-
the-Less. It also contains an
interesting museum covering
the history of the priory and the
hospital. Visitors to the museum
can also see the Grand Staircase
flanked with paintings by William
Hogarth (1697–1764). Hogarth,
born in nearby Bartholomew Close
and baptised in St Bartholomew-

the-Great, offered his services to the hospital when he heard they might commission a foreign painter instead. The museum is open Tuesday to Friday 10am-4pm and tours are available (tel: 020 7601 8152).

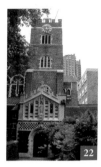

Next to Wallace's plaque, and behind the **㉑ 13th-century gatehouse** with its half-timbered house of 1595 on top, is the church of **㉒ St Bartholomew-the-Great**, the finest Norman church left in London. It was allowed to continue as a parish church within the half-demolished remnants of the dissolved priory, and has undergone many alterations since the 1540s. The atmospheric Norman choir, near to the tomb of Rahere, may be familiar to visitors as it has been used for scenes in many recent films including *Four Weddings and a Funeral*, *Shakespeare in Love*, *The Other Boleyn Girl* and Guy Richie's *Sherlock Holmes*.

Benjamin Franklin, one of America's greatest statesmen and scientists, worked in 1725 for a printer based in the Lady Chapel inside the church, and whilst here he lodged in nearby Little Britain.

Walk up Cloth Fair where, at number 44, Betjeman's Bar pays homage to the area's most famous resident of recent years, the much-loved Poet Laureate John Betjeman (1906-1984). A plaque in neighbouring Cloth Court commemorates his actual home, where he lived between 1955-77, eventually moving out because of his frustration with traffic congestion. Just ahead at **㉓ number 41** is a very rare example of an early 17th-century merchant's house that survived the Great Fire. It remains a private residence to this day.

Return to West Smithfield and walk down **㉔ Little Britain**. In Dickens' *Great Expectations* it is here Pip comes to visit the lawyer Jaggers, and is described as a 'gloomy street'. It is named after the medieval Dukes of Brittany who once owned a house here.

25 Postman's Park

At the end of the road cross over and bear right, and then turn left through some gates into **25** **Postman's Park**. This is named after the postmen who worked nearby in the former Post Office headquarters in King Edward Street. It contains on the left-hand side a unique memorial wall to heroic ordinary men and women, which was created in 1900 by the Victorian painter and sculptor George Frederic Watts (1817-1904). Each hand-painted tile contains the details of a particular hero, including Alice Ayres, 'daughter of a bricklayers labourer, who by intrepid conduct saved three children from a burning house in Union Street, Borough at the cost of her own young life'.

It was Ayres's story that most inspired Watts, and it also inspired playwright Patrick Marber whose play *Closer* features a character who visits the park and decides to adopt the name Alice Ayres. The play was made into a film in 2004 starring Jude Law, Julia Roberts, Clive Owen and Natalie Portman (who played Alice). Ayres Street in Borough was also re-named in Alice's memory in 1936.

Carry on through the Park passing by the side of **26** **St Botolph-without-Aldersgate**. Probably founded in the late Saxon period, the church stood outside the Aldersgate entrance in the City wall. It is one of three churches in the City dedicated to the Saxon patron saint of travellers, all symbolically founded beside a City gate because that is where people would begin or end their journeys. The current structure was built in 1789-1791 by Nathaniel Wright.

The City gate of Aldersgate stood nearby until it was demolished in 1761. Samuel Pepys (1633-1703), the great diarist, passed by in 1660 recording in his diary entry for 20 October 'This afternoon, going through London... I saw the limbs of some of our new traitors set upon Aldersgate, which is a sad sight to see; and a bloody week this and the last have been, there being ten hanged, drawn and quartered'.

Cross straight over St Martin's le Grand, named after a medieval monastery that once stood in this area. Look out for a useful

27

28

29

information board opposite the church, which shows how this road follows the route of the 2nd century AD Roman wall that once skirted the City, and also features a drawing of what Aldersgate looked like.

Follow the map into Gresham Street, passing the church of **27** **St Anne and St Agnes** on the left. Founded in the 13th century, it is the only City church with a double dedication. It was badly damaged in the Great Fire of London and was restored by Wren. It was later gutted during the Blitz and rebuilt according to Wren's original design. It is currently used by the Lutheran church. If visiting during the week be sure to look out for the excellent lunchtime concerts.

Walk past the church and take a small detour down Noble Street on the left. You pass the substantial remains of the **28** **old Roman garrison fort** (which originally covered 12 acres) and the City wall. At the end of Noble Street is a small garden that stands on the site of the now lost City church of **29** **St Olave Silver Street**.

First recorded in 1181, the church was destroyed during the Great Fire and never rebuilt. It was almost certainly attended by William Shakespeare, who is known to have lodged in Silver Street – a thoroughfare that has long since disappeared – between 1603 and 1605. Then aged around 40, he probably wrote plays such as *Othello*, *Measure for Measure*, *All's Well that Ends Well*, *Timon of Athens* and *King Lear* whilst living in the house that was situated a stone's throw away on the other side of today's London Wall road.

The fact that he lived in Silver Street is known because in 1612 he was required to give evidence at the Court of Requests in Westminster in connection with legal proceedings brought by a Stephen Belott against his Huguenot father-in-law Christopher Mountjoy. Belott argued Mountjoy, Shakespeare's landlord in Silver Street, had promised but failed to pay a dowry of £60 when Belott had married Mountjoy's daughter in 1604.

Shakespeare was required to present a deposition covering his recollection of what was or was not promised by his former landlord, and the evidence suggests the playwright was even asked by his landlord to try and help encourage the couple to get married. The deposition is the only time that Shakespeare's spoken words were ever recorded. Charles Nicholl's excellent book *The Lodger: Shakespeare on Silver Street* (2007) is worth reading if you would like to find out more.

Return to Gresham Street and walk eastwards. On the right-hand side on the corner with Foster Lane is the Livery Hall of the ㉚ **Goldsmith's Company**. It received its Royal Charter in 1327 and for

centuries London's craftsmen had to bring their gold and silver items to the Hall for assaying and marking. This gave rise to the phrase 'hallmark'. The current hall dates from 1835 and its grand drawing room doubled up for Buckingham Palace in the scene from the Oscar winning film *The Queen* in which Helen Mirren (playing the title role) reads out a televised tribute to Diana, Princess of Wales.

On the left-hand side of Gresham Street you pass the small garden that stands on the site of another lost City church that was not rebuilt

33 City Wall by St Alphage

after the Great Fire, **③①** **St John Zachary.**
This church was first recorded in the 12th
century and was closely associated with the
Wax Chandlers whose livery hall can be seen
opposite on Gresham Street. The Chandlers
once controlled the trade in the wax used for
candles and embalming, and the current
hall is the sixth on the site – the first dating
from 1501.

Head left down Staining Lane to see at
the end a small garden that occupies the site
of St Mary Staining, a church first recorded
in 1189 and lost during the Great Fire.

Take the small pathway to the right of the garden that leads
you through St Alban's Court into Wood Street. The view ahead is
dominated by the free-standing Wren tower in the middle of the
road, which was once part of the church of **③②** **St Alban Wood
Street.** This church's origins may date as far back as the 8th century
AD, and the medieval church was later rebuilt after the Great Fire in
a Gothic design by Wren. However, it was badly damaged during the
Blitz and was not rebuilt. The tower is today a private residence.

On the other side of the tower is Love Lane, its name recalling
its past as a notorious red light area in medieval times. Continue
north up Wood Street going up the escalator into the Barbican
complex, and follow the map to the right
along Alban Highwalk.

Shortly you reach the remains of
another lost City church – **③③** **St Alphage
London Wall.** You first pass the crumbled
tower that overlooks London Wall itself, and
then over to the left you will see some steps
leading down to a garden that is dominated
by a substantial section of the old Roman
and medieval City wall. This might be a
good place for a picnic if you would like
somewhere peaceful to sit.

The church was dedicated to St Alphage, an Archbishop of Canterbury murdered by the Danes in 1012. St Alphage's was probably founded not long after this, although by the 16th century it was in a poor state of repair. The congregation decided to re-found their church amongst the abandoned buildings of Elsing Spital, a medieval priory and hospital for the blind that had been dissolved during the reign of Henry VIII. This church had to be rebuilt in the 18th century and was finally demolished, with the exception of the tower, in the 1920s.

Walk back up the steps and continue north, shortly bearing left to cross over Willoughby Walk. Bear left and head for the clearly visible church tower of **34 St Giles without Cripplegate**.

Descend some steps to visit St Giles, one of the very few medieval churches left in the City to have survived the Great Fire. It was founded around 1100 AD, with much of the current structure dating from the mid 16th century.

The writer Daniel Defoe (1660-1731) was baptised in St Giles, and the poet John Milton (1608-1674) was buried here in 1674. In 1793 workmen broke open Milton's grave, some taking his teeth as souvenirs. An enterprising local also charged curious visitors to see his remains. William Shakespeare attended the christening of his brother Edmund's son in the church, although sadly this nephew – Edward Shakespeare – died not long after and was buried here. Oliver Cromwell was married in St Giles in 1620.

At the rear of the church is another superb section of the **❸❺ old City wall** with an accompanying information board. The entrance in the wall known as Cripplegate was located near here, first built by the Romans in around 120 AD and finally demolished in 1760. The Jews' Garden – until 1177 the only place in medieval England where Jews could be buried – was also once located near the church. During this period when a death occurred in Jewish communities based in places such as Exeter or York the body had to be brought here.

Walk back up the steps and continue right into the **❸❻ Barbican Centre**, keeping straight ahead. As you begin to enter the main building follow the signs for the Guildhall School of Music and the exit onto Silk Street. Alternatively, if you need a refreshment stop, the Barbican has a good café on the ground floor, which overlooks both the water features at the heart of the complex and St Giles.

Once on Silk Street continue north, walking up Whitecross Street. This is a gritty, old-fashioned working class thoroughfare where a debtors' prison once stood in the 19th century. Only in the last few years has the street become more gentrified, a process that has slowly spread from the southern tip, whose City offices spill out workers at lunchtimes in search of sushi bars and Waitrose sandwiches.

Stop at the junction of Dufferin Street on the right and Fortune Street on the left. Just down Fortune Street on the right is a plaque that recalls this was once the site of the **❸❼ Fortune Theatre** that was built in 1599 for the actor Edward Alleyn (1566-1626) and impresario Phillip Henslowe (d. 1616). Alleyn, a contemporary of Shakespeare and arguably the greatest actor of his era, played the lead in a number of plays by Christopher Marlowe and made enough money during his career to found the prestigious Dulwich College. In the 1998 film *Shakespeare in Love* he is portrayed by actor Ben Affleck. The theatre was square in shape and constructed by Peter Street, also responsible for the more famous Globe theatre south of the river.

Signs of the area's poverty-stricken past become readily apparent as you turn right at Dufferin Street. This street is home

NEAR BY LIE THE REMAINS OF
THE POET-PAINTER
WILLIAM BLAKE
IT...
AND O...
CATHERI...SOPHIA
17... ...1831

40

41

to the distinctively designed **㊳ Peabody Trust housing association buildings**, and Dufferin Court, just off Dufferin Street, contains houses originally designed for costermongers, including special sheds to house their barrows. The Trust was founded in 1862 by American philanthropist George Peabody (1795-1869) to help London's poorer classes, and today owns and manages 18,500 properties across the capital.

Head left at Bunhill Row. On the left is **㊴ Braithwaite House** where the Kray twins were arrested in their mother's flat by the police on 8 May 1968. They were convicted of separate murders and imprisoned the following year. Enter the historic **㊵ Bunhill Fields cemetery** on the right-hand side.

Originally called 'bone hill', it is thought to have served as a burial ground for around 1,000 years. When it closed in 1854 about 123,000 corpses had been interred here. It is best known as the burial place for London's non-conformists from the late 17th century to the mid 19th century, including great artists and writers such as John Milton, Daniel Defoe, William Blake, and

John Bunyan. Milton lived nearby at the now demolished number 125 Bunhill Row between 1662 and 1674, and it was here that he completed *Paradise Lost* and wrote all of *Paradise Regained*. The hut in the centre of the burial ground contains a useful guide to where the most notable tombs are located.

Walk through to exit on City Road. Opposite is the former **41** **chapel and home of John Wesley** (1703-1791), founder of the Methodist movement. The chapel was opened in 1778 and designed by the eminent architect George Dance the Younger (1741-1825). Wesley lived in the house next to the chapel for the last 11 years of his life and his tomb is located in the garden to the rear. The Chapel is normally open Monday to Saturday 10am-4pm and Sunday 12.30pm-1.45pm.

Continue south along City Road passing on the right-hand side the massive site occupied by the **42** **Honourable Artillery Company (HAC)**, which lies between Bunhill Fields to the north and Chiswell Street to the south. The HAC is the oldest surviving regiment in the British Army and is able to trace its origins back to 1296. From 1538 to 1658 it was based in Spitalfields, originally practising archery on the open grounds there before changing over to cannons.

Shortly you pass the rather soulless Finsbury Square on the left, laid out in the late 18th century by George Dance the Younger. Continue across the junction into what becomes Moorgate, named after another entrance in the City wall originally founded by the Romans. You pass Ropemaker Street on the right, named after the rope-walks laid out here. Daniel Defoe died in this street in 1731.

Look out also on the right for the parallel street **43** **Moorfields**, named after the marshy moor that lay outside the City walls and which was only drained in the 1520s. After the Great Fire thousands of homeless Londoners set up makeshift camps on Moorfields. During this period it was also notorious as a haunt of prostitutes and highwaymen.

Continue on to pass **44** **The Keats at the Globe** public house on the right, dedicated to poet John Keats (1795-1821). Keats was born in his father's public house that once stood on this site, and he lived here until 1804.

Follow the map across London Wall. If you carried on down Moorgate you would pass at number 49 an anonymous office block that once housed the 'All Russian Co-Operative Society', or '**Arcos**', in the 1920s. The office was a front for a Soviet espionage mission that attempted to de-stabilise the British government and was closed down in May 1927. Diplomatic relations with the USSR were ended shortly after the closure.

However, on this walk follow the map and pass the **45** **Girdlers' Livery Hall** on the right-hand side along Basinghall Avenue. Founded in the early 14th century, this guild controlled the medieval trade in girdles – then an important item of clothing. Whilst the current hall is a modern building, the Girdlers have been based on this site since 1431.

Shortly you reach the garden that sits on the ruins of **46** **St Mary the Virgin Aldermanbury**, first recorded in 1181. The medieval church was destroyed in the Great Fire and later rebuilt by Wren. However, it was gutted during the Blitz and at the end of the war the substantial remains were, amazingly, moved to America. The rebuilt church can now be found in the campus of Westminster College in Fulton, Missouri as a memorial to Winston Churchill, who made his 'Iron Curtain' speech there. The bust of Shakespeare in the garden is there to remember the playwright's great friends, and former parishioners of St Mary's, John Heminges and Henry Condell. Seven years after Shakespeare's death, they gathered his plays together for the first time and published them in the famous *First Folio* of 1623.

Follow the map to walk alongside **47** **Guildhall**, home of the Corporation of London, and the centre of local government in the City for the past 800 years. Its name originates from the money – or *geld* – collected here as taxes. Parts of the current building date back to the 1400s and the whole site stands roughly on top of the Roman amphitheatre. It also contains a medieval crypt (rarely open unfortunately). Guildhall was once a venue for major trials, including those of Lady Jane Grey in 1553, and some of Guy Fawkes's fellow Gunpowder Plot conspirators in 1606. It was also where the fictional trial of *Bardell vs Pickwick* took place in Charles Dickens' *The Pickwick Papers* (1837).

Cross over Guildhall Yard to visit the Guildhall Art Gallery. This contains an interesting selection of art works, particularly paintings that show how the City looked in past centuries. However, the real attraction is the excavated remains of the **48** **Roman amphitheatre** underneath, cleverly supplemented by graphics to show how it would have originally appeared when it could hold around 6,000 spectators – not far off the capacity of the Royal Albert Hall. The gallery and amphitheatre are open Monday to Saturday 10am-5pm, and Sunday 12 noon-4pm (admission is also free on Friday and after 3.30pm on other days).

The church of **49** **St Lawrence Jewry** – the official church of the Corporation of London – stands beside Guildhall, and was first built in 1136. It was later rebuilt by Wren after the Great Fire, and its name recalls that

this part of the City was once inhabited by a sizeable Jewish community. The Jews had originally arrived from Rouen after William the Conqueror (1027-1087) realised he needed their money-lending services. They were expelled from England in 1290 after persecution and this country was sadly the first in Europe to enforce such a wholesale expulsion.

Follow the map down Old Jewry, looking out on the left-hand side for a plaque that recalls where the **50** **Great Synagogue** stood until being closed in 1272. Old Jewry was also the address for Lemuel Gulliver, the hero of Jonathan Swift's *Gulliver's Travels* (1726). Almost at the end of Old Jewry turn right into **51** **Frederick's Place**, a charming old City street.

You will see a plaque outside number six commemorating Benjamin Disraeli (1804-1881) who worked here as an articled clerk for a firm of lawyers from 1821 to 1824. It was clear to everyone that the flamboyant Disraeli was not destined for a career in the dusty courts of Chancery and he went on instead to become a famous novelist and twice served as Prime Minister. Opposite is a plaque that remembers where accountant Edwin Waterhouse (1841-1917) used to work. The firm he founded continues to this day as part of the global accountancy giant PriceWaterhouseCoopers.

You can also see the Eastern side of **Mercers Hall**, the headquarters of the Mercers Livery Company. The vast Hall occupies the area from here westwards to Ironmonger Lane where its main entrance is located. Headquartered in this part of London since the 16th century, the Mercers' origins date even further back to the mid 14th century. The trade of 'mercery' covered many types of merchandise, although this Company was mainly concerned with luxury goods. In the official ranking of Livery Companies – based loosely on the date of foundation and economic importance – the Mercers are officially number one. They control a portfolio of assets valued at around £450 million with extensive property holdings in the City and Covent Garden. Sir Richard Whittington (1354-1423), four times Mayor of London, and inspiration for the pantomime hero Dick Whittington, is the most famous former Mercer. Other past members include William Caxton, Sir Thomas More, Sir Rowland Hill and Lord Baden Powell.

Retrace your steps slightly and walk down narrow St Olave's Court, on the west side of Old Jewry, which leads onto Ironmonger Lane. On the right behind the iron fence is an office block that incorporates Wren's tower from his church of ❷ **St Olave Jewry**. The medieval church was rebuilt by Wren after the Great Fire but closed in 1888, with only the tower surviving the subsequent clearance for a new office development.

Walk up Ironmonger Lane to reach ❸ **Cheapside**, once the busiest street in the Saxon and Medieval City. Its name is derived

Ironmonger Lane

from 'ceap' or 'cheap', an old English word for market, and the grid-system of streets running off Cheapside dates from the rebuilding of the City after it was reoccupied during the reign of Alfred the Great. This was also where Londoners put up a bitter fight against William the Conqueror in December 1066, several weeks after the Norman army had triumphed at the more famous Battle of Hastings.

As you turn right and head westwards you will notice many of the streets are named after the trades or goods with which they were once associated. Examples include Ironmonger Lane (where Thomas a Beckett was born in 1118), Poultry, Honey Lane, Milk Street (where Thomas More was born in 1478) and Bread Street (where the poets John Donne (1571) and John Milton (1608) were both born).

Walk westwards as far as Wood Street, stopping to look at the small garden at its entrance which occupies the site of **54** **St Peter Westcheap**. St Peter's was first mentioned in 1196 but destroyed in the Great Fire and not rebuilt. In 1559 Elizabeth I passed through Cheapside and stopped at the door of St Peter's to receive a gift of a Bible from the parishioners.

The huge plane tree in the former churchyard is thought to have inspired Wordsworth when he wrote his 1797 poem *The Reverie of Poor Susan;*

At the corner of Wood Street, when daylight appears,
Hangs a thrush that sings loud, it has sung for three years:
Poor Susan has passed by the spot, and has heard
In the silence of morning, the song of the Bird.
Tis a note of enchantment; what ails her? She sees
A mountain ascending, a vision of trees;

The three small shops on the corner of Wood Street and Cheapside date from 1687. They give you a rare glimpse of what the rest of Cheapside would have looked like following the rebuilding of the City after the Great Fire.

In 1290 Edward I's wife Queen Eleanor died near Lincoln, and her slow funeral procession to Westminster Abbey stopped twelve times along the way. The King later ordered a stone monument (called a 'cross') to be erected at each stopping place, including Charing Cross in London. Less well known is that there was also an **'Eleanor Cross'** in Cheapside, and for many centuries this stood at the junction with Wood Street. However, it was demolished by the Puritan parliamentary Committee for the Demolition of Monuments of Superstition and Idolatry in 1643, and today only three original 'Eleanor Crosses' survive. Parts of the Cheapside Cross can be seen in the Museum of London, on London Wall (www.museumoflondon.org.uk)

Cross over to visit the church of **55 St Mary le Bow** whose famous Wren tower dominates Cheapside. By tradition only those born within the sound of Bow bells can be considered a true 'cockney', although in the days before car traffic the bells would have been heard much further away than is possible today. The church was first recorded in the 11th century, and is named after the arches, or 'bows', in the Norman crypt. Its famous bells, immortalised in the children's rhyme *Oranges*

54

55

and Lemons ('"I do not know", says the great bell of Bow'), once rang out the City curfew at 9pm every evening. Wren designed the current church after the Great Fire destroyed the medieval building.

Walk into **56** **Bow Church Yard** on the west side of the church where you can find a small entrance that leads down some steps to the surviving Norman crypt, thought to be the oldest church room in London. There is also an excellent vegetarian restaurant down in the crypt (accessible through the main entrance, Café Below see p.185), which is a good place for a stop if visiting mid-week.

Continue south down narrow Bow Lane, one of best places to provide a sense of the 'old' City. Just to the east used to be a red light area named – in typically forthright medieval fashion – 'Gropecunt Lane'. At the bottom of Bow Lane you pass **57** **St Mary Aldermary** (meaning 'older Mary' as distinct from younger churches with the same dedication). It was first recorded in around 1080 and rebuilt in an unusual Gothic style by Wren after the Great Fire. It contains an impressive fan-vaulted plaster ceiling of a type normally found only in cathedrals.

Cross over both Watling Street, originally part of the old Roman road that ran between London and Dover, and Queen Victoria Street. Shortly on the right you reach the ruins of the 2,000 year old **58** **Roman Temple of Mithras**. This was dedicated to the Persian god of light and the sun and was originally a subterranean place of worship. The temple may have been built here by detachments of the Roman army that had served in Persia before being stationed in London.

The sacrifice of a bull was an important part of the Mithratic cult, and by tradition this happened during the main annual festival on 25th December. When Emperor Constantine made Christianity the official Roman religion in the 4th century AD he tried to stamp out rival religions and cults, whilst cleverly absorbing some of their more popular features into Christianity – hence the date allocated for Christmas. This temple may

also have been converted for use by the early Christian church in London. Some items discovered during excavations are displayed at the Museum of London.

Follow the map, crossing over Cannon Street and reaching College Hill. Sir Richard Whittington used to live in this street (look for the plaque) and was buried in the neighbouring church of **59** **St Michael Paternoster Royal** in 1423. The current church was built by Wren after the Great Fire.

Walk along Skinners Lane, passing another superb Wren church **60** **St James Garlickhythe**. It is nicknamed 'Wren's lantern' on account of its high ceiling and large windows that flood the interior with light. The last part of the church's name refers to a medieval landing place (or 'hythe') that once stood nearby.

Cross over busy Upper Thames Street and follow the signs for the Millennium Bridge. If these are not obvious, just aim for the Thames path, which runs alongside the river. You pass Queenhythe, once an important dock that operated here for around 800 years up until the 16th century. It was named after Queen Matilda, daughter of Henry I, who built the country's first public toilet nearby in the early 12th century.

Walk beside the Thames, looking out on the right for the City of London School that can trace its origins back to 1442. Former pupils include authors Kingsley Amis and Julian Barnes, Prime Minister H. H. Asquith, and actor Daniel Radcliffe. Pass under the Millennium Bridge with the Tate Modern and the modern Globe reconstruction visible on the opposite bank. Ahead is Blackfriars Railway Bridge followed by **61 Blackfriars Bridge**, both built by the Victorians. In June 1982 the Italian Roberto Calvi (b.1920), nicknamed 'God's Banker' because of his connections to the Vatican, was found hanging from a rope underneath the arches of Blackfriars Bridge. Probably murdered, the true circumstances of his death have never been properly explained, giving rise to countless conspiracy theories involving the Mafia, the Catholic church and the mysterious Masonic lodge, P2.

In the wall of the north bank immediately under Blackfriars Bridge is a small hole through which the outflow of the 'lost' River Fleet joins the Thames. Beginning in Hampstead, the Fleet runs

Millennium Bridge (foreground), **61** *Blackfriars Bridge (background)*

south-easterly underneath King's Cross, Clerkenwell and Farringdon before reaching the Thames. As London developed, the once open river became increasingly polluted and was gradually covered over between the 1730s and 1870s.

Head up the stairs on the west side of the bridge and head northwards to return to Blackfriars station. Just opposite the station is the ❻❷ **Black Friar public house**, built in 1873 and later transformed by members of the Arts & Crafts movement in 1905. The mosaics and reliefs on the outside, together with the art noveau interior depicting jolly monks at work, make this one of London's most unusual public houses and worth a stop after a long walk. When finished cross to the station and the end of the walk. ●

VISIT...

Guildhall Art Gallery (see p.177)
Guildhall Yard, EC2V
www.cityoflondon.gov.uk

Postman's Park (see p.167)
Little Britain, EC1A

Barbican Centre (see p.173)
Silk Street, EC2Y
www.barbican.org.uk

Smithfield Market (see p.162)
225 London Central Mkts, EC1A
www.smithfieldmarket.com

EAT, DRINK...

Viaduct Tavern (see p.160)
126 Newgate Street, EC1A

Keats at the Globe (see p.176)
199 Moorgate, EC2M

Black Friar public house (above)
174, Queen Victoria St, EC4V

Café Below (see p.182)
Cheapside, EC2V
www.cafebelow.co.uk
Vegetarian café in the crypt of
St Mary-le-Bow.

Smiths of Smithfield
67-77 Charterhouse St, EC1M

7 Hampstead Walk

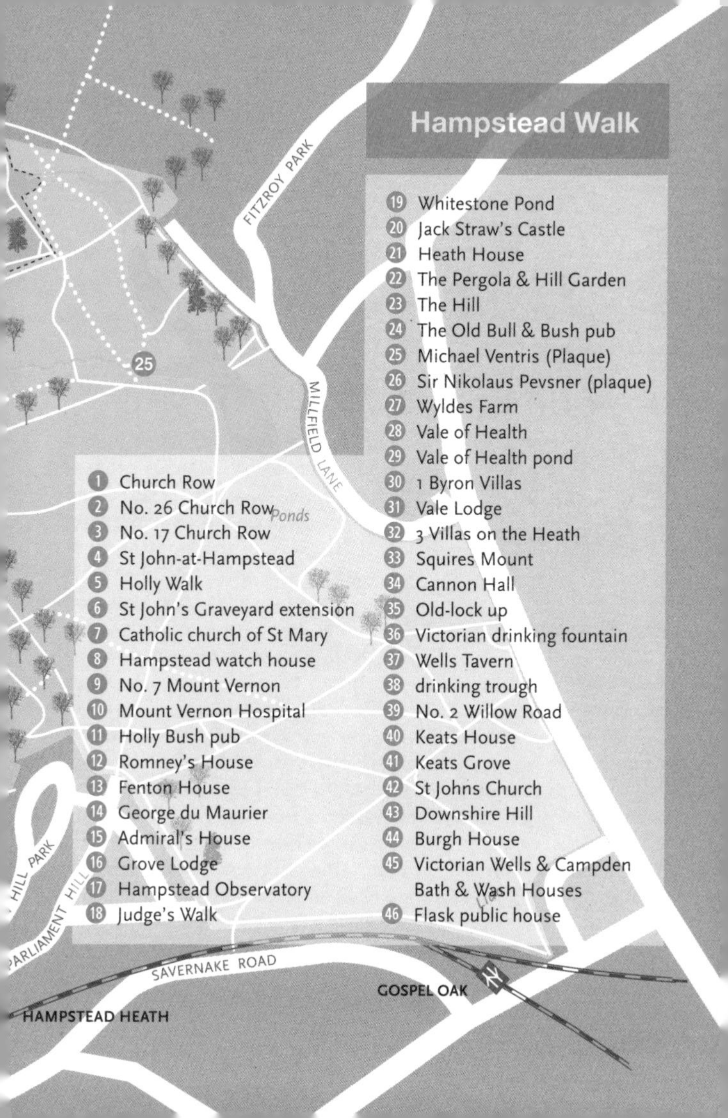
Hampstead Walk
19 Whitestone Pond
20 Jack Straw's Castle
21 Heath House
22 The Pergola & Hill Garden
23 The Hill
24 The Old Bull & Bush pub
25 Michael Ventris (Plaque)
26 Sir Nikolaus Pevsner (plaque)
27 Wyldes Farm
28 Vale of Health
29 Vale of Health pond
30 1 Byron Villas
31 Vale Lodge
32 3 Villas on the Heath
33 Squires Mount
34 Cannon Hall
35 Old-lock up
36 Victorian drinking fountain
37 Wells Tavern
38 drinking trough
39 No. 2 Willow Road
40 Keats House
41 Keats Grove
42 St Johns Church
43 Downshire Hill
44 Burgh House
45 Victorian Wells & Campden Bath & Wash Houses
46 Flask public house
1 Church Row
2 No. 26 Church Row
3 No. 17 Church Row
4 St John-at-Hampstead
5 Holly Walk
6 St John's Graveyard extension
7 Catholic church of St Mary
8 Hampstead watch house
9 No. 7 Mount Vernon
10 Mount Vernon Hospital
11 Holly Bush pub
12 Romney's House
13 Fenton House
14 George du Maurier
15 Admiral's House
16 Grove Lodge
17 Hampstead Observatory
18 Judge's Walk
FITZROY PARK
MILLFIELD LANE
Ponds
25
HILL PARK
PARLIAMENT HILL
SAVERNAKE ROAD
GOSPEL OAK
HAMPSTEAD HEATH

Hampstead Walk

Start/finish: Hampstead underground station
Distance: 4.7 miles

From the underground station turn left down Hampstead High Street and cross over to head up Oriel Place. The red-brick buildings on the left used to be owned by the Hampstead Wells and Campden Trust, a charity founded over 300 years ago to help the local poor. The Trust originated from a 1698 bequest of six acres of then-undeveloped Hampstead land which contained a natural spring of chalybeate (or iron-enriched) water. The well was the basis of Hampstead's transformation during the 18th century from a sleepy village into a popular spa resort and evidence of this legacy can be seen at various places along the walk.

At the top of Oriel Place cross over Heath Street to enter **1 Church Row**. Hampstead is the highest spot in London, and until the mid 17th century was a village of around 600 inhabitants that existed almost completely independently from overcrowded London down below. However, in the days when tuberculosis, smallpox and cholera were common in London, the attraction of Hampstead's healthy hill air attracted the wealthier classes and grand houses began to be built from the 1680s. The later growth of Hampstead as a spa resort from about 1700 also drew developers and by 1800 it had become a suburban town.

Hampstead is undeniably pretty and, although as expensive as Kensington or Mayfair, it possesses a more individualistic character.

It is particularly known for its many innovative house designs which regularly feature in architectural textbooks (see the Goldfinger house towards the end of the walk).

Hampstead's proximity to almost 800 acres of heathland also marks it out as special, offering the nearest thing to open countryside that exists within a suburb so close to the centre of London. Church Row is a good place to properly start the walk as it is arguably the finest street in Hampstead, and certainly one of the best preserved Georgian streets in London. It was built in the early 1700s in the Dutch style made fashionable by William of Orange. Walking here on a Sunday morning when the church bells of St John are ringing feels like being in a quaint country town, with only the cars giving a clue as to what century you are in.

Hampstead is said to have more blue plaques than any other London suburb, and is known for the number of literary, artistic and intellectual figures that have long colonised it. Many lived in Church Row including poet Lord Alfred Douglas (or 'Bosie') (1870-1945) who lived at ➋ **number 26** in 1913-14.

His relationship in the 1890s with the writer and playwright Oscar Wilde (1854-1900) led ultimately to Wilde's conviction and imprisonment for gross indecency. Wilde died a broken man just a few years after being released, and was never fully reconciled with his younger lover. Douglas was a complicated man, who abandoned his preference for male lovers of the younger kind to marry soon after Wilde's death, later becoming a father. In later life he bitterly regretted ever having met Wilde, and spent much of his life pursuing feuds with others. One resulted in his imprisonment in 1924 after being convicted of criminal libel against Winston Churchill.

H. G. Wells (1866-1946), author of *The Time Machine* and *War of the Worlds*, lived at ➌ **number 17** from 1909-1912. Another Hampstead resident and author, D. H. Lawrence (1885-1930), was invited to Wells's home one evening only to complain bitterly about his host's insistence that he borrow a dinner jacket before sitting down to eat with the other guests. The comedian and satirist Peter Cook (1937-1995) also lived at number 17.

4 *St-John-at-Hampstead*

Halfway down Church Row is the parish church of ❹ **St John-at-Hampstead**. Dating from 1745 and consecrated two years later, it was preceded on this site by a number of earlier churches built from the late Saxon period onwards. In the medieval period much of Hampstead – a name derived from the Saxon word for 'homestead' – was owned by the monks of Westminster Abbey. In 1349 the Abbott and twenty six other monks from Westminster came to Hampstead in a desperate attempt to escape the Black Death that was devastating London, however they were all already infected with the plague and soon died.

The churchyard is fantastically atmospheric, full of dark corners and narrow paths and worth a good walk around. Bram Stoker (1847-1912) was almost certainly thinking of this churchyard when he wrote his famous novel *Dracula* (1897), part of which is set around Hampstead. In the book two of the main characters – Dr Van Helsing and Dr Seward – eat a meal at Jack Straw's Castle (seen later on in the walk) before setting off to examine Lucy's tomb. Dr Seward records that 'About ten o'clock we started from the inn. It was then very dark, and the scattered lamps made the darkness greater... At last we reached the wall of the churchyard, which we climbed over. With some little difficulty, for it was very dark, and the whole place seemed so strange to us, we found the Westenra tomb'.

John Constable (1776-1837), the English Romantic painter, lived in Hampstead for many years and was buried here along with six of his children and his wife (there is a sign to the tomb). You can also see the tomb of John Harrison (1693-1776), inventor of the marine chronometer that for the first time allowed sailors to establish accurately their longitude whilst navigating the high seas.

Others buried here include Labour leader Hugh Gaitskell, Jane Austen's aunt, Samuel Taylor Coleridge's grandchildren, Evelyn Waugh's parents and several members of the du Maurier family. The latter include Sylvia Llewelyn Davies (1866-1910) and two of her

five sons, Michaël and George. J. M. Barrie (1860-1937) met George and his brothers Jack and Peter by chance in Kensington Gardens one day in 1897, and his subsequent friendship with the Llewelyn family inspired Barrie to write *Peter Pan*. After Sylvia died of cancer Barrie became guardian to the five Llewelyn boys, but their lives were no fairy tale. Michael, the brother considered to have been the main inspiration for Peter Pan, drowned in mysterious circumstances aged only 21. George died fighting in WWI and Peter committed suicide at Sloane Square tube station in 1960.

Inside the surprisingly spacious and elegant interior of the church is a memorial to another former Hampstead resident, the poet John Keats (1795-1821), more of whom later.

Leave the church and continue down Church Row, said to be haunted by the ghost of a red-haired woman who worked as a maid in a house on the street and who killed a child, smuggling out the dismembered body inside a carpet bag. Some people claim to have seen the ghost, and others have reported a strange presence – most often described as a sudden drop in temperature – along this part of the road.

Head right at Frognal, following a small loop on the map that takes you around Frognal Gardens and back to Church Row. Charles De Gaulle (1890-1970) lived at number 99 Frognal from 1940 to 1942 while directing the efforts of the Free French forces during WWII, although today it is hard to imagine him in this leafy middle-class suburb as war raged throughout Europe. Sting – otherwise known as Gordon Sumner – lived at 108 Frognal in the 1980s, and the former Labour leader Hugh Gaitskell resided at number 18 Frognal Gardens in the early 1960s.

When back on Church Row return to St John's and head up the narrow ❺ **Holly Walk**, just opposite. This takes you past the ❻ **extension of St John's graveyard** on the right-hand side, which dates from 1811. This is worth a wander around as the old gravestones surrounded by wild flowers make this one of the most picturesque graveyards in London. Many of the gravestones record the profession of the deceased and, unsurprisingly given this is Hampstead, it is not hard to find an actor, philosopher or painter among them.

Up the hill on the right is the unobtrusive ❼ **Catholic church of St Mary** dating from 1816 and originally used by French émigrés to London in an age when being openly Catholic was still frowned upon by the authorities. Just past the church on the same side is a building which once served as the ❽ **Hampstead watch house** in the 1830s. The parish constables were based here and they formed Hampstead's first police force. Dame Judi Dench lived at number 4 Prospect Place on the right hand side between 1968 and 2001.

At the top of the hill you reach Mount Vernon and ⑨ **number 7** on the corner is where writer Robert Louis Stevenson (1850-94) stayed at various times in the 1870s. Best remembered for *Treasure Island*, *The Strange Case of Dr Jekyll and Mr Hyde*, and *Kidnapped*, he was one of many consumptives who came to Hampstead to try to restore their health. He later moved to Samoa and died aged just 44.

Bear right along Mount Vernon as it bends around to the left, and down the slope. On the left is the imposing site of the former ⑩ **Mount Vernon hospital**, a vast infirmary block dating from 1896. The hospital was dedicated to the treatment of 'Consumption and Diseases of the Chest', but closed for its original purpose in the early 20th century. In recent years it has been converted into expensive flats housing a number of celebrities including at least one member of the Spice Girls.

Follow the map downhill to Holly Mount on the left. This contains the ⑪ **Holly Bush**, one of Hampstead's most charming and old-fashioned public houses. Given this is a long walk, this is an ideal place for a stop and a good pub meal. The building dates from the 1640s when Holly Mount was built, and it originally served as the stables and outbuildings of the grand house behind it, later owned in the 1790s by the noted society painter George Romney (1734-1802). In the 18th century Dr Johnson and James Boswell both drank here and its nooks and crannies make for a great atmosphere.

Head back up Holly Hill looking out on the right for number 6, which was **⑫ Romney's House**. At the top of the triangle of grass to the left are the magnificent iron gates of **⑬ Fenton House**. Named after the Baltic merchant who once owned it, the house is now run by the National Trust. One of the oldest houses in Hampstead, it contains fine collections of paintings, European and Oriental porcelain and early keyboard instruments. However, its finest feature is the orchard and gardens to the rear which you can visit on a cheaper ticket if you are short of time.

American visitors might be interested to know that one of the earliest owners of the house was Joshua Gee (1667-1730), who dealt in silk, iron and other commodities. He bought Fenton House in 1706, and was a founding partner with US President George Washington's father of a company that produced pig iron in the United States. The initials of Gee and his wife Anna can still be seen intertwined on the fine wrought iron gates. Fenton House is open on March weekends only and from Wednesday to Sunday from April to November.

15 *View of Admiral's House from Fenton House Garden.*

When finished walk up Hampstead Grove by the side of Fenton House. The large house at number 28 was owned between 1874 and 1895 by writer and Punch cartoonist  **George du Maurier** (1834-1896) and is currently occupied by a famous Hollywood director. George Du Maurier is today largely forgotten; however, he originated some terms that are now part of the English language. In his gothic horror book *Trilby* (1894) the behaviour of Svengali – a scheming musician and hypnotist – resulted in the character's name entering the dictionary as a term for a person who exercises a sinister influence on another. The style of hat known as a 'trilby' also originated from a design used in the original London stage adaptation of his book of the same name.

George's son was the prominent actor-manager Sir Gerald du Maurier (1873-1934), and his daughter was Sylvia Llewelyn Davies, mother of the five boys mentioned earlier who inspired Barrie's *Peter Pan*. Sir Gerald was the first actor to portray the dual role of George Darling and Captain Hook in the original stage performance of *Peter Pan* in 1904, and the well-known cigarette brand 'Du Maurier' was named after him. His daughter, the novelist Daphne du Maurier (1907-1989), is probably the best known member of the family. Movie versions of her books *Rebecca, Jamaica Inn* and *The Birds* were all directed by Alfred Hitchcock.

Continue uphill and on the left you will see a distinctive street sign, which shows hands pointing towards Admiral's House and Grove Lodge. Follow the sign until you reach a white clapboard giant on the right, known as **Admiral's House** and built in around 1700. It was once owned by an eccentric naval lieutenant called Fountain North (d. 1811) who had the roof built to look like the deck of a ship and fired cannon from the terraces on the King's birthday or after naval victories. The *Mary Poppins* books, written by another Hampstead resident P. L. Travers (1899-1996), feature an eccentric Admiral Boon who lives in a house shaped like a ship from which he fires cannon.

Sir George Gilbert Scott (1811-1878), architect of St Pancras station and the Albert Memorial in Hyde Park, lived at Admiral's House between 1856 and 1864. The painter John Constable once lived nearby (see below) and in the 1820s painted Admiral's House three times. The paintings can be seen today in the Tate Modern, the V&A and the Alte Nationalgalerie in Berlin. It is also thought that tunnels were built under the garden connecting the house to the Heath, and legend has it they were used by the infamous 18th century highwayman Dick Turpin as an escape route when he was being hunted down by the authorities.

The neighbouring house, ⑯ **Grove Lodge**, was once the home to John Galsworthy (1867-1933) who wrote much of *The Forsyte Saga* and its sequels whilst living here. Galsworthy won the Nobel Prize for Literature in 1932, but by this time he was so ill that he was unable to attend the awards ceremony and his medal was sent to him here.

Continue up Hampstead Grove looking out on the left for the site of ⑰ **Hampstead Observatory**. The observatory and the weather station alongside it were opened by the Hampstead Scientific Society in 1910. The weather station has been checked daily since then and has produced the longest continuous record of meteorological readings of any similar station in Britain. The observatory is open to the public on certain winter evenings; however these can vary so check the Society's website at www.hampsteadscience.ac.uk.

If you are interested in John Constable's links with Hampstead you may wish to make a small detour along Lower Terrace (in front of the Observatory) to **⑱ Judge's Walk**. Constable lived at number 2 with his family during the summer months of 1821 and 1822 and it was his favourite viewpoint in Hampstead, although it is hard to imagine now what inspired him as the land has been developed over the centuries. Judge's Walk is said to have been named after the lawyers who fled to this area from the City during the Great Plague of London in 1665. Unable to find accommodation because of the other Londoners who were sheltering here, they were forced to conduct their business in makeshift tents and under the shelter of trees.

Continue up Hampstead Grove to reach **⑲ Whitestone Pond**, one of the highest spots in London at 134 metres above sea level and named after an old mile marker that can still be found in the bushes on the right-hand side. This prominent position made it a natural choice as a site for an Armada Beacon, marked today by a large flagpole. In 1588 when the Spanish Armada was first sited off the Hampshire coast a series of beacons were lit across the country to warn the Navy; the signal took two days to make its way as far as Hampstead before moving onto the east coast.

Continue along the left-hand side of the pond and past the clapboard **⑳ Jack Straw's Castle**, a former public house named after one of the leaders of the 14th-century Peasants' Revolt who, legend has it, stayed in the vicinity. The current structure is largely a modern rebuild that was recently converted into flats, but the Castle was once one of the most popular pubs in

London and was frequented by Karl Marx, Charles Dickens, Wilkie Collins and William Thackeray. Dickens wrote to his friend John Forster inviting him to 'muffle yourself up and start off with me for a good brisk walk over Hampstead Heath. I knows a good 'ous there where we can have a red-hot chop... and a glass of good wine...'. In Forster's biography of the writer he wrote how this 'led to our first experience of Jack Straw's Castle, memorable for many happy meetings in coming years'.

Just opposite is **21** **Heath House** (stranded in the middle of the junction of North End Way and Spaniards Road). This mansion dates from the early 18th century and was owned in the 1790s by Samuel Hoare Jr (1751-1825), a Quaker banker and philanthropist. He entertained prominent men of his day here including the poet William Wordsworth and the anti-slavery campaigner William Wilberforce. His grandson John Guerney Hoare was prominent in a long and bitter fight by the residents of Hampstead in the 19th century to stop the Heath being built over by developers, a battle won in the 1870s when it finally became a public park.

22

Walk past Jack Straw's Castle and then head left down Heath Brow and past a car park before reaching the Heath. Take the woodland path to the right and shortly you come upon the most hidden delight of Hampstead Heath, **22** **the Pergola and Hill Garden**. On the right is a small path that leads to a gate: head through this to go up a spiral staircase that leads into the upper storey of the Pergola. Walk along the Pergola, a decadent, rambling mass of a structure covered in plants and vines and unlike anything else to be found in London.

22 The Pergola and Hill Garden

It was built by the industrialist and philanthropist Lord Leverhulme (1851-1925) in the early 1900s. His fortune, much of it derived from the manufacture of soap, also paid for the purchase of **The Hill** – the massive house you can see to the right of the Pergola. It is now called Inverforth House after Baron Inverforth who bought it after Leverhulme's death, and it has since been converted into expensive apartments.

Walk right to the end of the Pergola and then head down to walk around Hill Garden. When finished take the path on the other side of the house that leads into Inverforth Close and re-joins North End Way.

Head left down this busy road until after a few minutes you see 24 **The Old Bull and Bush** public house on the right hand side. This historic pub was immortalised in the song *Down at the Old Bull and Bush* sung by the Australian-born music hall star Florrie Forde (1875-1940). The pub can trace its history back to the mid 17th century when it was originally a farm. After getting a drinks licence it was frequented by artists such as William Hogarth who, according to legend, planted a tree in the pub garden that still stands today. It later became popular with Cockneys – hence the song – spending a day in Hampstead away from the smog of London.

Near the pub is the site of the part-built North End (or 'Bull and Bush') tube station on the Northern Line, which would have been the deepest London Underground station at 221 feet below ground. The platforms were excavated before the construction was cancelled in around 1906. During WWII Winston Churchill apparently spent time here examining the half-finished tunnels. He was inspecting potential sites that could be used to house the cabinet should the main Cabinet War Rooms in Whitehall be damaged during German bombing. The back up site finally selected was the Paddock – an underground base in Dollis Hill whose existence was only confirmed in 1973. During the Cold War, some parts of the abandoned tube station were designated as part of the Underground's civil defence headquarters, to be used in the event of a nuclear war. Today the platforms and lower passageways still exist, though they are mostly bricked off and not accessible to the public. However, the surface entrance can be seen at the corner of North End and Wildwood Terrace. Visit www.underground-history.co.uk if you wish to see some photos of the site.

Walk up North End beside the pub and bear left along what becomes a gravel track. Suddenly you are back into the countryside of the Heath. On the right at ㉕ **number 19** is a plaque to former resident Michael Ventris (1922-56), an architect and scholar who helped decipher Linear B, an ancient Greek language. This breakthrough was crucial in establishing links between early Cretan civilisation and Mycenaean Greece.

Shortly on the left is Wildwood Terrace, where outside ㉖ **number 2** is a plaque to the renowned historian of art and architecture Sir Nikolaus Pevsner (1902-1983). He lived here from 1936 until his death and his books remain standard texts on English architecture.

Track to Wyldes Farm

Continue along the track and shortly you can see a dark weather-boarded house on the left which used to form part of ㉗ **Wyldes Farm** in the 17th century. Artist and poet William Blake (1757-1827) used to stay at the farm whilst visiting his friend John Linnell (1792-1882), a noted landscape painter who lived here in the 1820s. Later Charles Dickens stayed for two weeks with his wife Catherine in 1837 as they recovered from the shock of the sudden death of Mary Hogarth, Dickens's beloved sister-in-law.

He described it as 'a cottage of our own, with large gardens, and everything on a small but comfortable scale'.

Continue on along the path which bears left until you reach Wildwood Road and then head right. Ignore the smaller paths on the right-hand side that lead onto the Heath until you reach a bend in the road that veers left. There is a bigger path heading sharp right (just before Wildwood Rise), which you take, following it uphill through woodland.

This leads you out onto Spaniards Road and straight ahead on the other side is an entrance to Kenwood House, the beautiful 18th-century mansion that contains a first-rate art collection (including works by Gainsborough, Rembrandt and Vermeer) and café, all set in lush grounds. If you have time it is worth a visit and you can return to the walk route. However, on this walk we cross over and head down Spaniards Road, shortly passing some buildings and immediately afterwards taking the left-hand path leading to the Heath (the sign says 'Access to horse ride for permit holders only').

The next destination is the ㉘ **Vale of Health** to the south. To reach it walk past the gate on the left and bear right. This takes you through a secluded part of the Heath,

where you walk down a small hill. Continue to bear right and you will soon come out onto a wide open area from where you head to the path on the far right-hand corner which takes you down to the Vale of Health itself.

As you are leaving the main part of the Heath it is worth noting that it has long been a place of refuge for Londoners. As mentioned earlier, the monks of Westminster fled here to escape the Black Death, and many more came to Hampstead to camp out during the Great Plague of 1665 and the Great Fire the following year.

A less well-known crisis that prompted Londoners to shelter in Hampstead, took place in 1524 when astrologers convinced much of the capital's population that a great flood was about to submerge the city. Around 20,000 people abandoned their homes in panic and many came here to watch the predicted devastation. However, on the day predicted it did not even rain and astrologers excused themselves by 'discovering' their calculations had been one hundred years out.

The political philosopher and revolutionary Karl Marx (1818-83) used to bring his family to the Heath most Sundays to escape their cramped and grimy living quarters in Soho. There is even a photo of the Marx family on the Heath taken in May 1864 with a 'mighty roast veal' as the centrepiece of their picnic.

In Bram Stoker's *Dracula* the Heath is where a number of attacks by a sinister 'bloofer lady' take place on children. In the book the 'Westminster Gazette' reports 'several cases have occurred of young children straying from home or neglecting to return from their playing on the Heath. In all these cases the children were too young to give any properly intelligible account of themselves... all who have been missed at night, have been slightly torn or wounded in the throat'.

Walk down the path, passing the caravan park on the right, to reach the picturesque  **29 Vale of Health pond** that is flanked by some of the nicest houses in Hampstead. The Vale covers around six acres and in the late 18th century was a notorious mosquito-infested marshland known as Hatchett's Bottom.

The Hampstead Water Company changed all that by draining the land in the 1770s, and by 1802 the area had become known by its current name – adopted by the developers building new houses here to bolster its appeal to potential purchasers. The Water Company was responsible for many of the ponds found to this day on the Heath, which were used to supply drinking water to Londoners. The ponds were filled by the 'lost' River Fleet which still has its source on the Heath and runs underground through London to exit into the Thames near Blackfriars Bridge.

Retrace your steps from the pond and take the first left uphill

with the caravan park to your right. At the top on the left is **30** **1 Byron Villas** where D. H. Lawrence (another Hampstead consumptive) and his wife Frieda lived in 1915. During this time they would walk onto the Heath at night and watch the German Zeppelin bombers dropping their loads on London below. Lawrence was visited in Hampstead by other well-known figures such as Aldous Huxley, W. B. Yeats, and Bertrand Russell.

Even today, the Vale remains isolated from the rest of Hampstead village, and artists and writers have been drawn to its secluded charms from the time it was first developed. Just past Byron Villas on the right-hand side is **31** **Vale Lodge**, thought to have been the home of the romantic poet and political radical Leigh Hunt (1784-1859). He moved to the Vale in around 1815, and poets John Keats and Percy Shelley regularly stayed with him here.

Head back down the other way along the Vale of Health road (passing Byron Villas to your left) and continue past some beautifully-proportioned 19th-century houses which today tend to sell for at least £2 million. On your right you pass number **32** **3 Villas on the Heath**, home in 1912 to Rabindranath Tagore (1861-1941), the Bengali poet and first Asian recipient of the Nobel Prize for Literature.

At the top cross over East Heath Road and down **33** **Squires Mount** lined on the left by elegant early 18th-century cottages. At the end stop to look at the majestic **34** **Cannon Hall** directly ahead, which was built in 1730. Originally used by the magistrates in Hampstead, between 1916 and 1934 it served as the home of Sir Gerald du Maurier and was where his daughter Daphne spent much of her childhood. Bear left of the house down Cannon Lane, where on the right about halfway down you can see the remains of the **35** **old-lock up**. This was also built in around 1730, and was used by the magistrates in Cannon Hall to imprison offenders. It remained in use until the watch-house on Holly Walk (see earlier) was opened in the 1830s.

Follow the map across Well Road (The Logs at numbers 17-20 is home to singer Boy George) and then down some stairs to reach Well Walk, looking out for the **36** **Victorian drinking fountain** straight ahead. Both roads are named after Hampstead's spring waters that first became popular in the mid-17th century. In 1698 the Hon Susanna Noel, mother and guardian of the infant Earl of Gainsborough, Lord of the Manor of Hampstead, donated six acres in this part of Hampstead for the benefit of the local poor.

The result was the Hampstead Wells and Campden Trust mentioned at the start

37

of the walk. In around 1700 the Trust decided to advertise the medicinal virtues of the chalybeate waters that sprang up at the original well in the hope that sales of the water would increase the Trust's revenues.

The Trust was helped by the enthusiastic pronouncement by respected local physician Dr William Gibbons that the 'Hampstead waters were full as efficacious in all cases where ferruginous waters are advised as any chalybeate waters in England, unless Scarborough Spa, which is purgative'.

Whilst difficult for us to understand today, such endorsements were important in an age when most people had to make do with drinking water that had been taken from the polluted Thames or collected from rainwater. Within a few years, commercially savvy operators such as John Duffield had leased the land from the trust and developed this part of Hampstead into a popular spa town – one of many such resorts in England.

The water was taken from the now-closed Head Spring in Well Road and then bottled and sold throughout London. A main distributor and bottler was the Lower Flask Tavern (now the Flask public house encountered later on). A Long Room and Pump Room were built (just opposite where the fountain is found today) for visitors, allowing them to take the water and socialise at the organised dances and dinners.

However, within a few years Hampstead became known as much for the drunken debauchery that took place in these new venues and the gambling houses that grew up alongside them as for the medicinal qualities of its waters. From the 1730s the trust decided to take action and began to take back control from the developers. From then until the end of the 18th century, when the national craze for spa resorts had largely declined, Hampstead spa was a more upmarket affair and only those thought sufficiently respectable were allowed to take the waters. By the 19th century Hampstead was firmly established as a favourite location for London's middle classes, and the decline of the spa resort was not of any great consequence.

Head along Well Walk and at the corner of Christ Church Hill you will find the **37** **Wells Tavern**, formerly the Green Man and once closely associated with the Hampstead Spa. Walk down Christchurch Hill and bear left as it continues into Willow Road. At the junction with Willow Road look out for the low **38** **drinking trough**, one of around 800 set up in London by the Metropolitan Drinking Fountain and Cattle Trough Association that was founded in 1859. Within a few years it was estimated that around 300,000 people were using the fountains during the summer, and that a single trough could supply the needs of 1,800 horses in a day.

You pass **39** **number 2** on the right-hand side. This house was designed by the architect Ernö Goldfinger (1902-1987) who also lived here with his family. Although it looks like it was built in the 1960s, it actually dates from 1939 and is one of the best examples of Modernist architecture in the country. The Hungarian-born Goldfinger, said to be the inspiration for Ian Fleming's James Bond villain, is best known as the architect of The Trellick Tower in North Kensington. Number 2 is now owned by the National Trust, and visits are by tour only – check the Trust's website for details (www.nationaltrust.org. uk) or call 01494 755570.

Follow the map around the edge of the Heath and then up Keat's Grove. On the left-hand side is ㊵ **Keats House** where the poet John Keats lived for 14 months between 1818 and 1820. A year before Keats came to the house he had moved with his two brothers to another property just beside the Wells Tavern. Here he had tried to nurse his consumptive brother Tom, however his efforts were in vain and Tom died shortly after they arrived. John Keats was almost certainly fatally infected himself during this period of close proximity to his brother.

After Keats moved to Wentworth Place (now Keats House) he met Fanny Brawne. Despite now suffering from consumption, Keats became engaged to Fanny, and his creative energies blossomed. It was in this garden whilst sitting under a plum tree that he wrote *An Ode to a Nightingale*. As his illness worsened he left for the better climate of Italy where he died in 1821 aged only 25. The neighbouring houses were later turned into a museum, and a visit here inspired Thomas Hardy to write his own poem *At a House in Hampstead* (1920). Keats House is open to visitors Friday to Sunday 1pm-5pm.

At the top of ④ **Keats Grove** turn right into Downshire Hill in front of the striking church of ㊷ **St John** that dates from the 1820s. ㊸ **Downshire Hill** contains some of the finest houses in Hampstead, and has been home to many notable residents including photographer Lee Miller (number 21 in the 1930-40s), John Constable (number 25 in 1826-7), and Jim Henson, creator of the Muppets (number 50 in the 1980s). At the end you pass the picturesque Freemason's Arms public house, which has a lovely garden and good food if you need a break.

Head back up Willow Road and keep left to reach Well Walk again. Literary figures associated with this street include J. B. Priestley (1894-1984), who lived at number 27 from 1929 to 1931 and wrote part of his classic novel *The Good Companions* here. John Constable lived at number 40 after moving here in 1827; however, a year later his wife died of tuberculosis leaving him to look after their seven children. D. H. Lawrence and his wife lived briefly at number 32 during 1917.

Cross over and head up New End Square to find the entrance to ㊹ **Burgh House** on the right hand side. The house dates from 1703 and was built for a wealthy Quaker family, before being inhabited in 1720 by Dr William Gibbons, the physician mentioned earlier who did much to promote Hampstead's waters. Now an excellent small museum covering the history of Hampstead, it contains a pleasant café, a useful selection of local history books and an art gallery. In the 1930s it was home to Rudyard Kipling's

daughter, Elsie Bambridge. Kipling, author of *Kim*, *The Jungle Book* and *Gunga Din*, used to come here regularly to see her, including a last visit just a few days before his death in 1936. The house is open Wednesday to Sunday 12noon-5pm.

Leave the house and walk up Flask Walk. On your right you pass the **45** **Victorian Wells and Campden Bath and Wash Houses** (1888), one of the initiatives by the Hampstead Wells and Campden Trust to help Hampstead's poorer inhabitants. Amazingly, the trust still survives today, with capital of £12 million and annual expenditure of around £500,000.

Continue up Flask Walk passing the **46** **Flask** public house, one of the best pubs in North London and where you can often spot an old actor or local celebrity having a quiet pint. The bottles – or flasks – used to distribute the local spa waters were filled here in the 18th century. The pub is said to be haunted by the ghost of a 19th-century landlord called Monty who likes to move tables and rattle windows. Ahead is Hampstead High Street and the end of the walk. ●

VISIT...

Fenton House (see p.197)
Hampstead Grove, NW3
www.nationaltrust.org.uk

Hampstead Observatory
Lower Terrace, nr Whitestone
Pond, NW3 (see p.200)
www.hampsteadscience.ac.uk

Keats House (see p.214)
2 Keats Grove, NW3
Tel: 020 7332 3868

Burgh House (see p.215)
1 New End Square, NW3
www.burghhouse.org.uk

EAT, DRINK...

Holly Bush (see p.196)
22 Hollymount, NW3
www.hollybushpub.com

Old Bull & Bush (see p.204)
Northend Road, NW3
www.thebullandbush.co.uk

Wells Tavern (see p.213)
30 Well Walk, NW3
www.thewellshampstead.co.uk

No 2 Willow Road (see p.213)
www.nationaltrust.org.uk

Flask public house (see above)
14 Flask Walk, NW3
www.theflaskhampstead.co.uk

Flask public house

8 Notting Hill Walk

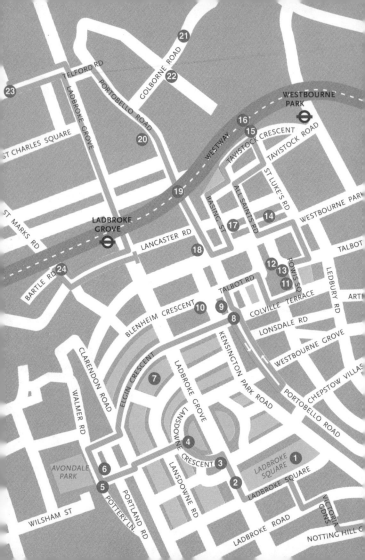

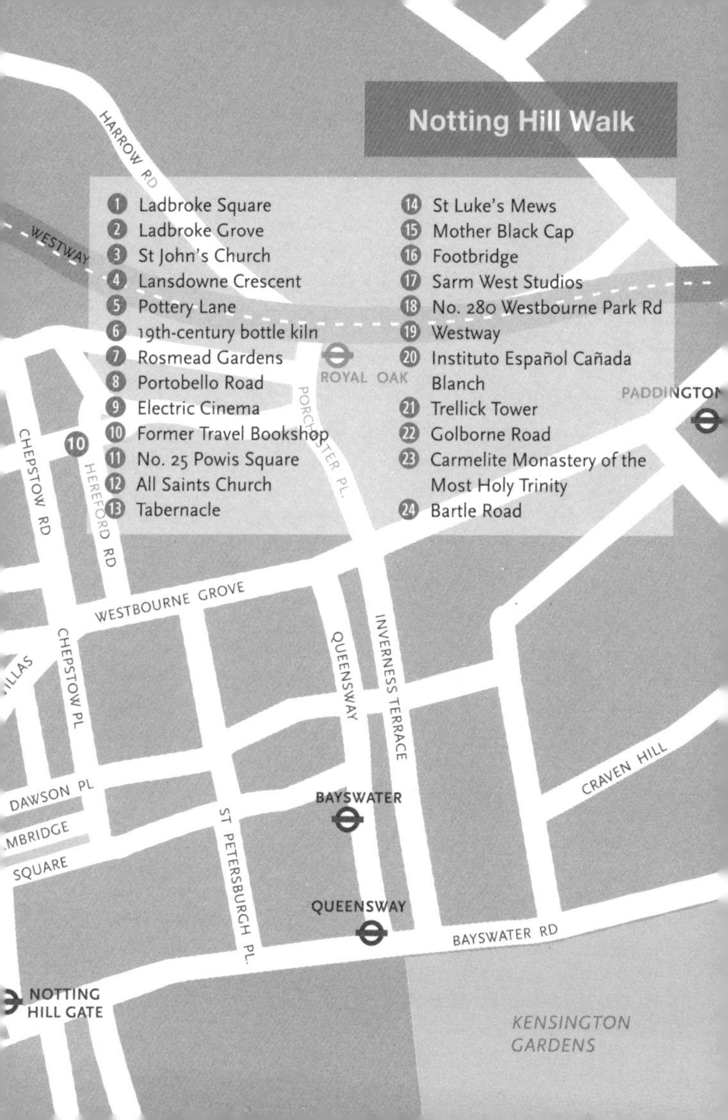

Notting Hill Walk

HARROW RD

WESTWAY

ROYAL OAK

PORCHESTER PL.

PADDINGTON

CHEPSTOW RD

HEREFORD RD

CHEPSTOW PL

WESTBOURNE GROVE

QUEENSWAY

INVERNESS TERRACE

VILLAS

DAWSON PL.

MBRIDGE

SQUARE

ST PETERSBURGH PL.

BAYSWATER

CRAVEN HILL

QUEENSWAY

BAYSWATER RD

NOTTING HILL GATE

KENSINGTON GARDENS

Notting Hill Walk

Start/finish: Notting Hill Gate underground station
Distance: 4 miles

From Notting Hill Gate underground station head west along Notting Hill Gate itself, staying on the north side. The origins of the place name 'Notting Hill' are unclear, although an early derivation – 'Knottynghull' – was recorded in 1356. The 'gate' comes from the road tollgate that operated here between 1769 and 1864.

Shortly on the right-hand side there is a small passageway that you take to reach Victoria Gardens. Here you get a first glimpse of the superb houses found in this area, many of which date from the 19th century and are often immaculately kept. Follow the map along Ladbroke Road and up Ladbroke Terrace to reach the south side of ❶ **Ladbroke Square**.

The centre of the square contains the largest private communal garden in London, just one of thirteen dotted around Notting Hill. Sadly very few of the gardens passed on the walk are open to the public, so for most people the only option is to peer through the railings. The London Parks and Gardens Trust does, however, run the Open Garden Squares Weekend every year (normally in June), providing the opportunity to visit some of Notting Hill's – and London's – most exclusive private spaces (visit the trust's website at www.opensquares.org for details).

Continue along the south side of the square. The Notting Hill district remained largely rural until the westward expansion of London reached Bayswater in the early 19th century. The main landowner then was the Ladbroke family and from the 1820s they began to lay out residential streets to meet the housing needs of the capital's growing middle class. This explains why so many of the streets around here bear the Ladbroke family name.

At the end of the square you reach ❷ **Ladbroke Grove**, a long, busy road that runs from Holland Park north towards Kensal Green. Walk up the hill, stopping at the church of ❸ **St John** on the left. The church dates from 1845 and was built in an early neo-Gothic style. Beside it is a plaque recalling that this was once the heart of the old **Hippodrome racecourse**, which originated in 1836 when local entrepreneur John Whyte leased 200 acres of land from James Weller Ladbroke to create 'a racing emporium more extensive than Ascot or Epsom'.

Spectators would have stood at the summit of Notting Hill looking down on the horses racing below, but the enterprise was short lived as the course was blighted by waterlogging that caused the horses to suffer terrible injuries. This problem, combined with the hostility Whyte faced from local residents whose rights of way had been impaired, ensured the Hippodrome was a commercial failure and by 1841 it had closed.

After the racecourse closed the land was used for the development of new housing. However, the Hippodrome's

outline can still be traced today in the crescent-shaped roads that circumnavigate the hill (Blenheim Crescent, Elgin Crescent, Stanley Crescent, Cornwall Crescent and Lansdowne Crescent).

Walk up ❹ **Lansdowne Crescent** on the other side of the church. Fans of Jimi Hendrix (1942-1970) may wish to continue along the crescent to **numbers 21-22**. This was once the site of the **Samarkand Hotel** where Hendrix was found unconscious on the morning of 18th September, 1970 by his girlfriend Monika Danneman. He was certified dead on arrival at hospital, the official cause of death given as inhalation of vomit and barbiturate intoxication.

Walk down Lansdowne Rise on the left of the crescent (retracing your steps if you visited the Hendrix site). At the bottom follow the map down Clarendon Cross and Hippodrome Place to reach Walmer Road. South of Walmer Road is ❺ **Pottery Lane**, which recalls this area's old nickname – '**the Potteries**'. In the 19th century this was a slum, and also a centre for the manufacture of bricks and tiles. The industry exploited the heavy clay deposits found in the area, the bricks and tiles produced being fired in a series of local specialist kilns. Walk up Walmer Road and on the right-hand side you will see a rare example of a ❻ **19th-century bottle kiln**. Pass this and take the next right past **Hippodrome Mews**, one of the few places in the area that provides any obvious link with the old racecourse.

This area was also known as the 'Piggeries' after the pig farmers who moved here in the early 19th century, having been forced out by the development of the land around Marble Arch. By 1830 the ratio of pigs to humans was judged to be three to one. Number 77 Pottery Lane was used for the exterior shots of the photographic studio used by the lead character (played by David Hemmings) in Michelangelo Antonioni's cult film *Blowup* (1966).

Continue up to cross Clarendon Road to enter Elgin Crescent, where the vast houses often sell for more than £5 million. Shortly on the right are Rosmead Road and ❼ **Rosmead Gardens**. Whilst the romantic comedy film *Notting Hill* (1999) grates with its representation of an all-too-perfect London, it made the area world famous. In the film the two main characters, bookshop owner William Thacker (Hugh Grant) and film star Anna Scott (Julia Roberts) sneak into the private Rosmead Gardens. Other locations from the film are seen later on in the walk. Continue along Elgin Crescent looking out for **number 60** on the left-hand side where India's first Prime Minister Jawaharlal Nehru (1889-1964) lived between 1910 and 1912.

8 Portobello Road

After a few minutes you reach the vibrant  **8** **Portobello Road**, Notting Hill's most famous street. It was originally a rural lane leading to Portobello Farm in the north of Notting Hill, and the origins of its famous market began in the mid 19th century when local gypsies congregated here to trade herbs and horses. A more general market developed over time; however, it only became well known to Londoners after its trading hours were extended from Monday to Saturday in 1927. On Saturdays the market is in full swing. Antiques and collectables are found at the southern end of Portobello Road, giving way to fruit and vegetables about halfway up. The north end is dominated by second-hand goods, as is the Portobello Green section of the market, which sets up shop beneath the roar of the Westway.

Portobello Road – originally 'Porto Bello Lane' – was named after Puerto Bello, a port in the Gulf of Mexico that exported treasure to Spain. The British Navy under Admiral Sir Edward Vernon captured the port in 1739, and subsequently many pubs, streets and districts throughout the British Empire were named after Vernon and Puerto Bello.

Turn right to head south down Portobello Road. Shortly on the left you pass number 142, known in the 1990s as Nicholls Arcade, and home to an antiques business. It was in the Arcade that the scenes depicting the interior of Thacker's bookshop in the film *Notting Hill* were filmed, and where the two main characters first meet. The travel bookshop that actually inspired director Richard Curtis will be seen shortly on the walk.

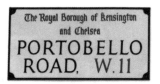

This part of Portobello Road is where the antiques

shops are found. Continue south, crossing over Westbourne Grove, and on the left you pass Denbigh Terrace where at different times comedian Peter Cook and Virgin boss Richard Branson lived at number 19. Just ahead on the same side is Denbigh Close. The house at number 18 featured in the film *The Italian Job* (1969).

Re-trace your steps north up Portobello Road, full of cafés and restaurants if you need a refreshment break. On the left at number 191 is the **9** **Electric**. Dating from 1911, this was England's first purpose-built cinema and was originally named the Imperial Playhouse. During WWI the cinema was stoned by locals who suspected its German manager of using lights to direct Zeppelins on their bombing runs. The serial killer John Reginald Christie, who lived at 10 Rillington Place nearby, worked as a projectionist here during WWII. You can read more about Christie and Rillington Place later on in the walk.

Continue up Portobello Road and shortly you see Blenheim Crescent on the left. *Notting Hill*'s scriptwriter Richard Curtis carried out research for the film at the former ⑩ **Travel Bookshop** at 13-15 Blenheim Crescent on the left-hand side.

Head down Talbot Road almost opposite Blenheim Crescent and follow the map along Colville Gardens and Colville Terrace into **Powis Square**. This area is an important part of Notting Hill's legacy as a centre for alternative culture – something now hard to imagine given its current reputation as the location of choice for the rich and famous.

Walk up the left hand (west) side of the Square until you reach the junction with Talbot Road. On the corner is ⑪ **Number 25 Powis Square** which was used for the exterior shots of the main house portrayed in Donald Cammell's and Nic Roeg's influential 1970 film *Performance*. Starring Mick Jagger as a jaded rock star, the film is infamous for the erotic scenes between Jagger and Anita Pallenberg, filmed while Keith Richards, Pallenberg's boyfriend of the time, reportedly sat outside in his Rolls Royce fuming with jealousy.

From the junction you can see on the left ⑫ **All Saints Church** (just off the north-west side of the square) which was at the epicentre of London's 'underground' scene in the late 1960s. During 1966 the **London Free School** – a loose collective of idealists organising events for local people – hosted various 'social nights'.

The events featured the so-called 'Sound/ Light Workshop' of Pink Floyd, some of that band's very first appearances. The flyers of the time put out by John 'Hoppy' Hopkins – London Free School co-founder and leader of the underground movement – referred to a 'pop dance featuring London's farthest out group The Pink Floyd in interstellar overdrive stoned alone astronomy domini – an astral chant and other numbers from their space-age book'. The gigs took place in the church hall, now demolished, just by the Square.

The Pink Floyd drummer Nick Mason later recalled how the gigs attracted 'the local hip fraternity... students or college dropouts, proud of being freaks... often in a chemically altered state'. Money from the gigs went to help finance the *International Times* – the underground paper of 60s London.

It was during this period in Notting Hill that Pink Floyd's original member Syd Barrett is said to have written the band's early hit *See Emily Play* (1967) after meeting Emily Young. Young is now regarded as one of England's greatest sculptors; however, in 1966 she was the 'aristocratic flower child' who 'tries but misunderstands, dressed in a gown that touches the ground'. Young was then at Holland Park School nearby and was part of the London Free School scene along with her school friend, the future actress Anjelica Huston.

You will notice the centre of Powis Square – known as Powis Square Gardens – is open to the public, unlike many of the exclusive squares you have passed so far on the walk. The reason for this goes back to 1968 when local residents and hippy activists protested about children being at risk from traffic whilst playing in the streets, forcing the authorities to open the gardens to the public.

Also, on the north side of the square is the **13** **Tabernacle**, today a community arts centre but also where in the past The Rolling Stones and Pink Floyd held rehearsals and The Clash played gigs. This Grade II listed building was originally a Christian evangelical place of worship when it was built in the 1880s and was called the Talbot Tabernacle after the Talbot family who owned the freehold of nearby Portobello Farm.

The London Free School was also involved in the

transformation of the Notting Hill Carnival from what was still a small-scale celebration in the early 1960s into the massive world-famous event it is today, attended by over one million people every August bank holiday. The origins of the carnival date back to the 1950s when large parts of Notting Hill suffered from social deprivation, and the infamous slum landlord Peter Rachman (1919-1962) owned a number of properties in the area.

Rachman crowded thousands of newly-arrived immigrants from the West Indies in his slums, using violence and intimidation to exploit his tenants. Many of the West Indians had little choice in an era when it was still common to see signs outside lodging houses warning 'no blacks, dogs or Irish'. Rachman's original properties were around Powis Square, and 'Rachmanism' has now entered the English language – meaning exploitation by an unscrupulous landlord.

The immigrants also had to face a campaign of racist intimidation by local white 'Teddy Boys' who were backed by the fascist British Union. Racial tensions finally erupted in the Notting Hill Riots in the autumn of 1958, at the time the worst in living memory. The carnival developed largely as a response to the riots, although few people realise it was originally held in 1959 in St Pancras Town Hall (now Camden Town Hall). By 1965 the carnival had moved outside, but was still a lot smaller than it is today.

Continue north across Westbourne Park Road and into All Saints Road. Now fairly genteel, this was formerly the front line of the local black community's struggle with the police. From 1968 to 1991 the Mangrove restaurant stood at number eight. Owned by Frank Crichlow, this Caribbean restaurant and community centre was the hippest place in Notting Hill and where 'turn on West Indian and English feasts' were served to celebrities such as Jimi Hendrix, Sammy Davis Jr, Marvin Gaye, Nina Simone and Vanessa Redgrave. The Mangrove was the subject of a number of police raids over the years – usually drug related – and became symbolic of the poor relationship between the police and the local community.

In 1976 another riot broke out in this part of Notting Hill after confrontations between locals and the police during the carnival. Rock legend has it that the Clash's song *White Riot* (1977)

14 St Luke's Mews

was inspired by Joe Strummer's and Paul Simonon's participation in the disturbance. The band's spiritual home is often described as being at the north end of the Portobello Road and under the Westway. It was here in the 1970s that they would meet up and where they played their early gigs in locations such as Acklam Hall beside the Westway. The band took every opportunity at the start of their career to be photographed under the elevated motorway, and in their song *London's Burning* (1977) they include the lines: 'Up and down the Westway, in and out the lights, what a great traffic system, it's so bright, I can't think of a better way to spend the night than speeding around underneath the yellow lights...'. Other bands who emerged out of the alternative scene that was once so evident in Notting Hill and Ladbroke Grove during the 60s and 70s include Hawkwind, The Deviants and the Pink Fairies.

On the right off All Saints Road is ⑭ **St Luke's Mews**. Paula Yates, the television presenter and one-time wife of Bob Geldof and girlfriend of INXS's Michael Hutchence, died at number four on 17th September, 2000 aged just 41. The coroner decided she died accidentally of a heroin overdose.

At the end of All Saints Road turn right down Tavistock Road and then left (north) up St Luke's Road. At number 41 (recently demolished) once stood the fictitious ⑮ **Mother Black Cap** — supposedly located in Camden — that featured in the cult 1987 film *Withnail and I*. In the film Withnail and Marwood (the 'I' of the title) enter the pub and the alcoholic Withnail orders 'Two large gins. Two pints of cider. Ice in the cider'. The two out-of-work actors (played by Richard E. Grant and Paul McGann) receive a frosty reception from the Irish regulars and are seen being chased towards the ⑯ **footbridge** beside the pub that crosses over the Westway, with the distinctive Trellick Tower in the background. Some artistic licence was clearly taken in this scene as in 1969 — when the film is set — neither the Westway nor The Trellick Tower had been completed.

Follow Tavistock Crescent westwards. The crescent once contained the home (now demolished) of Rhaune Laslett, an early founder of the carnival, and a key gathering place for the London Free School in the 1960s. When you reach Basing Street head south to reach the ⑰ **Sarm West Recording Studios** at the far end (number 19).

This was once home to Chris Blackwell's Island Records. Bob Marley recorded here, and it was here too that Led Zeppelin recorded *Stairway to Heaven*, featuring Jimmy Page's famous guitar solo. Trevor Horn later based his ZTT label here, and recorded many hit records at the studios in the 1980s, including those by Frankie Goes to Hollywood. You may recognise the outside of the studios from the Band Aid video for *Do They Know It's Christmas?*. Bob Geldof and Midge Ure hosted the all-star recording session here in November 1984, which included artists such as Bono, Sting, Wham!, and Boy George. Recent clients of the studio include Madonna, Paul McCartney, Roger Waters and Radiohead.

At the end of Basing Street head west down **Westbourne Park Road** to return to Portobello Road. ⑱ **Number 280** Westbourne Park Road – found as it continues on the other side of Portobello Road – was used to film the exterior of Thacker's home in *Notting Hill*. In real life it was owned by the film's scriptwriter Richard Curtis, although he sold it shortly after the film was released. The new owner became so irritated with people knocking on the famous blue door that she sold it, the proceeds going to charity. However it does not appear to have stopped tourists trying their luck, and the replacement door is currently painted an obstinate black.

Continue north along Portobello Road under the roaring ⑲ **Westway**, which opened in 1970. The Westway has inspired many artists and writers over the years, most notably the late J. G. Ballard in his tale of modern alienation *Concrete Island* (1974). In the book an architect breaks down on the two-mile elevated motorway but is unable to stop any cars to assist him. Injured, he is forced to survive in a desolate slip-way, tormented by a strange woman and her simple giant of a companion who together thwart his attempts to escape.

The area ahead is often referred to as North Kensington and compared to Notting Hill Gate has comparatively high levels of poverty and unemployment. Waves of immigrants have settled here for at least a century including, but certainly not limited to, the Irish, Jews, West Indians, Spanish, Moroccans, and many from the Horn of Africa and Eastern Europe. This constant renewal of the population makes the area one of the most cosmopolitan in the world.

Continue north along Portobello Road, looking out for number 293 on the left hand side. In the 60s this was home to a famous fashion boutique named 'I was Lord Kitchener's Valet'. Its old military style jackets were popular with rock stars such as Jimi Hendrix, Eric Clapton and members of The Beatles and The Who. Robert Orbach, director of the boutique, later recalled his amazement one day when John Lennon, his wife Cynthia and Mick Jagger came into the shop and the latter bought a red Grenadier guardsman jacket for £5. The boutique is also thought to have inspired Peter Blake when he was designing the military-style costumes worn by The Beatles for the iconic album cover of *Sgt. Pepper's Lonely Hearts Club Band* (1967).

Continue north and you will shortly see the impressive-looking Spanish School – ⑳ **Instituto Español Cañada Blanch** housed in a former Franciscan convent built in 1862. The school relocated from Greenwich in 1982 although the Spanish connection with this area began in the 1930s when the Spanish Civil War ended. Spanish refugees and political exiles settled in the west of the city along Portobello Road, Ladbroke Grove, Bayswater and Queensway. One of the most notable Spanish shops is R Garcia & Sons – a fantastic deli at number 248-250 Portobello Road established in 1957.

Continue along Portobello Road, stopping on the north side of Golborne Road to get the best view of the intimidating **㉑ Trellick Tower** on the eastern side. This 31 storey, 322-feet-high Brutalist slab was designed by the Modernist architect Ernö Goldfinger (1902-1987) – a Hungarian often described as having been the inspiration for the famous James Bond villain of the same surname. Others have suggested that Ian Fleming's inspiration was Charles W. Engelhard, Jr, an American mining and metal tycoon who Fleming knew personally. In any event the tower opened in 1972, and for many years was nicknamed the 'Terror Tower'. It came to symbolise all that was wrong with inner-city high-rise living, with drug-dealing prevalent on abandoned stairwells and residents often feeling imprisoned in their flats due to high levels of crime.

However, the tower's reputation has since undergone a renaissance, and the building is now a Grade II* listed style icon. It is very similar to Goldfinger's earlier, but no less distinctive, Balfron Tower in Poplar, east London. Trellick

Tower's 217 flats were all originally let as council homes, but many are now privately owned and a flat can cost more than £300,000.

㉒ **Golborne Road** and its surrounding streets are home to a vibrant international community, and is an excellent place for a wander with lots of interesting cafés. On market days it evokes the spirit of Portobello Road before the latter was invaded by coffee chains and more commercial ventures. If you want to see how people lived here just a few decades ago look out for the work of Roger Mayne (b. 1929) (www.rogermayne.com). He spent the period between 1956 and 1961 in Southam Street – just east of Golborne Road – taking a seminal series of photographs of every-day life that are considered to be among the best images of London ever recorded. The singer Morrissey has used a number of Mayne's photographs for the front covers of his records.

Continue along Portobello Road and take a left down Telford Road to reach Ladbroke Grove. If you want to see a rare example of an inner-city monastery then cross over to walk down St Charles Square. At the end is the ㉓ **Carmelite Monastery of the Most Holy Trinity** (see following page), situated in a beautiful three acre garden. It was founded in 1878 by seven sisters from a monastery in Paris. Although the public cannot visit the monastery, the website (www.carmelitesnottinghill.org.uk) contains photos and information about the way of life of the sisters within. When finished return to Ladbroke Grove.

Continue south down Ladbroke Grove to Ladbroke Grove tube station just south of the Westway. This station was originally called Notting Hill when it opened in 1864; however, the name was changed in 1919 to avoid confusion with the new Notting Hill Gate station.

Just to the west of Ladbroke Grove is ㉔ **Bartle Road**, reached by walking down the eastern part of Lancaster Road, which runs off Ladbroke Grove. This was formerly Rillington Place where the murderer **John Reginald Christie** lived at number 10 between 1943 and 1953. One of Britain's most notorious serial killers, Christie killed at least six women at the house, including his wife. His crimes were only discovered after a tenant at Rillington Place, Timothy John Evans, had already been hanged in connection with the deaths of Evans's wife and child. It is now generally thought Christie was the real killer, and he even had the gall to provide testimony that helped secure Evans's conviction. Whilst the miscarriage of justice suffered by Evans was tragic, it did bolster the cause of opponents to the death penalty and helped hasten its final abolition in 1969.

In 1961 Ludovic Kennedy wrote a book about the murders entitled, *Ten Rillington Place*, which was made into a film by Richard Fleischer in 1971. Local residents, sick of ghoulish tourists, forced the street to be renamed, and number 10 was demolished to make way for the Westway. The site of the house now lies beneath a small garden along Bartle Road.

The walk ends at Ladbroke Grove station. If you wish to return to Notting Hill Gate then walk west up Lancaster Road off Ladbroke Grove to reach Portobello Road. Keep walking south until you reach Pembridge Road and then Notting Hill Gate underground station. ●

㉓ *Carmelite Monastery*

SHOP...

Portobello Market (see p.227)
Portobello Rd, W11
www.portobellomarket.org

Books for Cooks
4 Blenheim Crescent, W11
www.booksforcooks.com

VISIT...

Electric Cinema (see p.228)
191 Portobello Road, W11
www.electriccinema.co.uk

EAT, DRINK...

Falafel King
274 Portobello Rd, W11

Uncles
305 Portobello Rd, W11

Santo
299 Portobello Rd, W11
www.santovillage.com

The Hummingbird Bakery
133 Portobello Road, London
www.hummingbirdbakery.com

9 Southwark & Bankside Walk

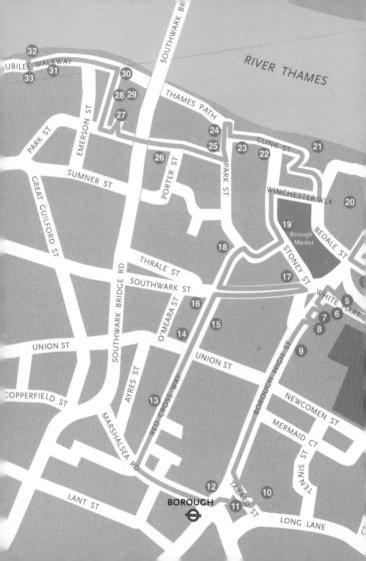

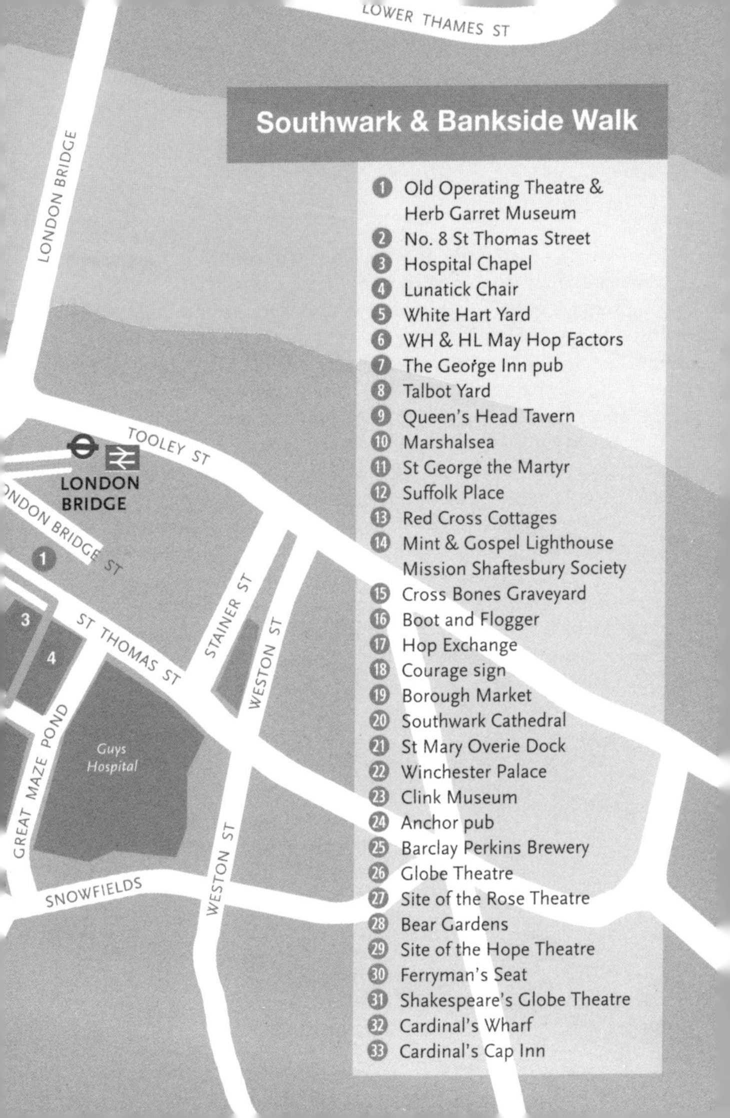
Southwark & Bankside Walk
1 Old Operating Theatre & Herb Garret Museum
2 No. 8 St Thomas Street
3 Hospital Chapel
4 Lunatick Chair
5 White Hart Yard
6 WH & HL May Hop Factors
7 The George Inn pub
8 Talbot Yard
9 Queen's Head Tavern
10 Marshalsea
11 St George the Martyr
12 Suffolk Place
13 Red Cross Cottages
14 Mint & Gospel Lighthouse Mission Shaftesbury Society
15 Cross Bones Graveyard
16 Boot and Flogger
17 Hop Exchange
18 Courage sign
19 Borough Market
20 Southwark Cathedral
21 St Mary Overie Dock
22 Winchester Palace
23 Clink Museum
24 Anchor pub
25 Barclay Perkins Brewery
26 Globe Theatre
27 Site of the Rose Theatre
28 Bear Gardens
29 Site of the Hope Theatre
30 Ferryman's Seat
31 Shakespeare's Globe Theatre
32 Cardinal's Wharf
33 Cardinal's Cap Inn
LOWER THAMES ST
LONDON BRIDGE
TOOLEY ST
LONDON BRIDGE
LONDON BRIDGE ST
ST THOMAS ST
STAINER ST
WESTON ST
GREAT MAZE POND
Guys Hospital
WESTON ST
SNOWFIELDS
1
3
4

Southwark & Bankside Walk

Start: London Bridge underground/rail station
Finish: London Bridge/Waterloo underground/rail station
Distance: 2 miles

From London Bridge station follow the map to reach Borough High Street and then walk up St Thomas Street.

This area has long been associated with medical institutions: the oldest – St Thomas' Hospital, which was founded in the early 12th century – was connected to the Priory of St Mary Overie, which once stood nearby. St Thomas' Hospital survived the closing of the priory during Henry VIII's Dissolution of the 1530s, but in the 19th century it was forced to leave the area to make way for the development of London Bridge station. St Thomas' re-opened in the 1860s at its current site south of Westminster Bridge.

Guy's Hospital, the second major hospital associated with this area, was founded in 1721 and is still based here. It was named after Sir Thomas Guy (1644-1724), a locally-born printer and publisher who made a fortune investing in the South Sea Company before the bubble famously burst. Much of the South Sea Company's revenues came from slave trading, so this indirectly funded the creation of Guy's Hospital. The original purpose of Guy's was to accept patients that St Thomas' Hospital had already decided were 'incurable'.

On the left as you head up St Thomas Street you will see St Thomas' Church, which dates from 1703 and houses the fascinating ❶ **Old Operating Theatre and Herb Garret Museum**. The attic of the church was originally used as an apothecary for St Thomas' Hospital, and housed medicinal herbs. In 1815 part of the roof was converted into an operating theatre, where female patients of St Thomas' Hospital were operated upon, without anaesthetic, under the gaze of a large audience of medical students. Horrific as this sounds, it was certainly an improvement on the previous arrangement under which operations were performed within the ward itself and in front of fellow patients. The theatre remained in use until 1862 when it was bricked up and forgotten about after St Thomas' Hospital moved away from Southwark. The rooms were re-discovered in 1956 and carefully restored, the result being the country's only surviving 19th-century operating theatre. The museum is open 10.30am-5pm daily.

At ❷ **number 8** St Thomas Street (just opposite the Old Operating Theatre) is a plaque recording that the poet **John Keats** (1795-1821) lived at the site whilst a student at Guy's and St Thomas' Hospitals in 1815-16. Keats quickly abandoned his medical career to concentrate on his poetry, although not before contracting venereal disease from a local prostitute.

On the right you see the large metal gates of Guy's Hospital, which you enter. On the right-hand side of the courtyard is the small but elegant 18th-century ❸ **Hospital Chapel**, which is worth a visit to see a 1779 statue depicting Sir Thomas Guy holding the hand of one of the 'incurables' the hospital was originally designed to help.

Otherwise continue straight ahead through the courtyard, passing a statue of Sir Thomas Guy dating from 1734. You come out onto a path between two courtyards where, on the left-hand side, is found a stone alcove known as the ❹ **Lunatick**

Chair. The alcove is a rare relic of the old London Bridge that spanned the Thames for 600 years until it was replaced by John Rennie's design in 1831 (itself demolished in 1968). The old bridge contained fourteen alcoves, which were added between 1757-62; another surviving alcove resides in Victoria Park in Hackney. The alcove was bought by Guy's for ten guineas and put into the wall of the old 'Lunatick House' that once stood here to provide some outdoor shelter for convalescing patients.

Continue along the path straight ahead which takes you into the King's College campus, and head sharply right to follow the map into **⑤ White Hart Yard**, a small alleyway.

A plaque commemorates this as the site of **The White Hart Inn**, immortalised by Shakespeare in *Henry VI Part II*, and mentioned by Charles Dickens in *The Pickwick Papers*. In Shakespeare's play, as in the actual events of 1450, a rebel army led by Jack Cade threatens to conquer London. Cade based himself in the yard as his army fought for control of London Bridge and the heart of the City, but his forces were pushed back and began to melt away after the King offered a general amnesty.

The amnesty did not benefit Cade and as his position begins

to collapse in the play he laments 'Hath my sword therefore broke through London gates, that you should leave me at the White Hart in Southwark?'. He was killed soon after: legend has it that his body was officially identified by the landlady of the White Hart before it was dismembered and Cade's head displayed on a spike on nearby London Bridge. The White Hart was also the scene of the meeting between Mr Pickwick and Sam Weller in Dickens's *The Pickwick Papers*. Sadly the Inn was demolished in 1889.

In the Yard you can also see one of the 19th-century entrances to ❻ **WH & HL May Hop Factors**, a legacy of the brewing and hop trading industries that were important to Southwark for many centuries. Follow the map out onto Borough High Street and turn left, looking out on the east side for the distinctive ornate frontage of the old WH & HL May building overlooking the road.

Walk down Borough High Street where on the left-hand side you shortly come across another yard containing ❼ **The George Inn** public house, the only surviving original galleried coaching inn in London. The yards off Borough High Street were once full of such coaching inns, where travellers would stay the night before setting off at dawn on trips south of London and to the continent. Until the advent of the railways in the 19th century, coaching inns like this were common throughout the country, often spaced ten miles apart so the horses pulling the mail and stage coaches could be regularly changed.

The George dates from 1677, replacing an earlier inn that was destroyed by fire. There has almost certainly been an inn on the site since medieval

times. During Shakespeare's era plays were staged in the courtyard, originally galleried on all sides. Charles Dickens mentions the George in *Little Dorrit* (1857) and a copy of the author's original life assurance policy is kept on a wall beside the main bar. This is a good place for a break if you want some lunch before continuing on the walk.

Just along from the George is ⑧ **Talbot Yard**, the site of another historic inn, the Tabard. Long demolished, the Tabard was where the pilgrims gathered before setting off for Canterbury in Geoffrey Chaucer's great work of the 1380s *The Canterbury Tales*. In the Prologue Chaucer writes:

> *In Southwark, at the Tabard, as I lay*
> *Ready to go on pilgrimage and start*
> *To Canterbury, full devout at heart,*
> *There came at nightfall to that hostelry*
> *Some nine and twenty in a company*
> *Of sundry persons who had chanced to fall*
> *In fellowship, and pilgrims were they all*
> *That toward Canterbury town would ride.*

Continue along Borough High Street and look on the left for number 103 where a plaque recalls that this was once the site of the ⑨ **Queen's Head Tavern**, and also where one of Southwark's most influential inhabitants was born. John Harvard (1607-1638) was one of nine children born in Southwark to the Harvard family, headed by his father Robert who was a local butcher, publican and official. John was baptised in St Saviour's Church (now Southwark Cathedral), educated at the church's grammar school, and later at Cambridge. Sadly he had a fairly tragic life. His father and a number of his siblings died in an outbreak of the plague, and shortly after John escaped England to settle in Massachusetts, where he died of tuberculosis aged only 30.

John Harvard left a bequest in his will of around £750 and 400 books to a local college, derived partly from the proceeds of the sale of the Queen's Head Tavern. The college was re-named in his honour and developed into the prestigious Harvard University, the oldest institution of its kind in the United States. The bequest was evidently well managed as today the University controls a fund of around $35 billion.

Continue south passing Newcomen Street and Mermaid Court, the location for four Southwark prisons between the 18th and 19th centuries. Shortly you will see the grand spire of **St George the Martyr**. Just before reaching the church on the left is a small public garden where on the far side are the remains of the high wall of another Southwark prison, the now demolished  **Marshalsea**. This prison is notable as it was where Charles Dickens's father John – the inspiration for Micawber in *Great Expectations* – was imprisoned in 1824 for failing to pay a debt of £10.

The Dickens family had been very respectable, but the whole family, except 12-year-old

Charles and his sister Fanny, moved into the Marshalsea alongside John Dickens. The shock to the sensitive Charles was immense, and in later life he recalled that 'even now, famous and caressed and happy, I often forget in my dreams that I have a dear wife and children... and wander desolately to that time in my life'.

Many of his works were directly influenced by the experience, particularly *Little Dorrit* in which the heroine is born inside Marshalsea, where she lives with her father. The prison was notorious amongst Londoners for its terrible conditions, being singled out for attack by Wat Tyler's rebels in 1381 and described by John Wesley in 1753 as 'a picture of hell on earth'. By Dickens's time Marshalsea had become largely a debtor's prison and it was closed in 1849. Standing here you are re-tracing the steps of Dickens, as in 1856 whilst writing *Little Dorrit* he returned to the site of so much childhood sadness for him to 'find any ruins of the Marshalsea'.

Leave the gardens to walk past the imposing church of ⓫ **St George the Martyr**. The current building is the third on the site and was built in a Classical style between 1734 and 1736. It is often referred to as 'Little Dorrit's Church' as the heroine of the novel was christened here, and later spends a night in the vestry after being locked out of the prison. It is also where Little Dorrit marries Arthur Clenman – the east window of the church contains a depiction of Little Dorrit kneeling down and wearing a bonnet.

Opposite the church follow the map along Marshalsea Road where on the right is a plaque recalling that this was once the site of ⑫ **Suffolk Place**, the London home of the Dukes of Suffolk during the 15th and 16th centuries. Henry VIII set up a mint here in around 1543 after his sister married into the Suffolk family, and money continued to be produced here until Suffolk Place was demolished in 1557.

As a result the surrounding area became known as the 'Mint' and was notorious in Georgian and Victorian London as a dangerous slum or 'rookery'. As the Mint lay within one of the areas of London known as a 'liberty' – a manor outside the jurisdiction of the City authorities, and often untouched by the forces of law and order – it became a sanctuary for thieves and debtors. The latter would often flee into the Mint where they could not be arrested, though this special status was finally removed by statute in 1723.

In 1824 the 12-year-old Charles Dickens stayed in lodgings in nearby Lant Street (just south of Marshalsea Road) whilst his family lived inside Marshalsea Prison, and the author would have been familiar with the awful conditions of the area that were later described in the 1890s by a researcher for social reformer Charles Booth as 'a set of courts and small streets which for number, viciousness, poverty and crowding, is unrivalled in anything I have hitherto seen in London'.

Head up Redcross Way where, on the left, is a row of pretty cottages beside a communal garden that look out of place in inner-city London. ⑬ **The Red Cross Cottages** and garden were founded by Victorian reformer and social housing pioneer, Octavia Hill (1838-1912), who was determined to help London's poor by giving them decent and affordable housing. The land was developed in the

1880s, and tenants seeking an escape from the surrounding slums had to be careful in their behavior as swearing or drinking could lead to eviction. Hill later went on to help found both the Army Cadet Force and the National Trust.

Continue north and just on the left at the junction with Union Street is the 1907 building that once housed ⑭ **The Mint & Gospel Lighthouse Mission Shaftesbury Society**, the signage still visible. The Shaftesbury Society's first president was the 7th Earl of Shaftesbury (1801-1885), the great Victorian philanthropist and social reformer. It had its roots in the Ragged School Union, which offered basic education facilities in many of London's 19th-century slums.

Cross over and continue north up Redcross Way where just on the right hand side is the site of the ⑮ **Cross Bones Graveyard**, one of the strangest places in London. For many centuries Southwark was infamous for its brothels (or 'stews') near the Thames, many licensed by the Bishops of Winchester who were the major landowners in the area. The prostitutes – nicknamed the 'Winchester Geese' – had to pay part of their earnings in rent and fines to the Bishops of Winchester. However, despite

having added to the church's coffers, when they died they were not able to receive a normal burial because of their lowly status and instead were interred here on unconsecrated ground.

John Stow (1525–1605) described the place in his guide *A Survey of London* (1598) as being where 'single women were forbidden the rites of the church, so long as they continued that sinful life, and were excluded from Christian burial, if they were not reconciled before their death. And

⓭ *Red Cross Cottages and Garden*

therefore there was a plot of ground called the Single Woman's churchyard, appointed for them far from the parish church'.

Today the graveyard belongs to Transport for London and there is no public access. However, local people have created a unique shrine at the gates celebrating 'The Outcast Dead', attaching hundreds of ribbons and trinkets to remember those unfortunate enough to have warranted burial here. By the late 18th century the brothels were less common, and the graveyard was used for pauper burials. Around 15,000 people are thought to have been interred in unmarked graves here over the centuries before the graveyard was shut in 1853 due to overcrowding.

Just opposite the graveyard is an isolated and atmospheric bar called the **16** **Boot and Flogger**. It is the only premises in the country allowed to sell wine without a licence, a privilege awarded to certain 'Free Vintners' dating from Elizabethan times. The pub's name refers to a corking device in which a leather boot holds the bottle whilst the wooden flogger 'flogs' in the cork. It is worth a visit if you would prefer to take a break before being enveloped in the bustle around the cafés and bars of Borough Market and Bankside that lie further ahead.

Continue north under one of the many railway bridges that snake their way around the area and cross over Southwark Road bearing right. On the left-hand side you soon come to the elegant Victorian building that once housed the **17** **Hop Exchange**. Southwark had close connections with the brewing industry from the 17th century until the early 20th century and the Exchange was opened in 1867. The hops bought and sold there were a crop that had originally been introduced into England from the Netherlands, and were added to beer to give a distinctive bitter taste and act as a preservative.

Working-class Cockney families would often travel en masse down to Kent to get seasonal work in the hop fields, and when transported to London the hops were stored in the many warehouses that were once dotted around Southwark. Today the exchange has been converted into private offices, but during normal business hours you can look around the huge atrium where the hop traders once worked. The excellent natural light is a deliberate feature of the Victorian design, allowing the traders to examine the quality of the hops being marketed.

Head back slightly on yourself and continue north up Redcross Way and then head right into Park Street, noting the old ⑱ **Courage** sign on the wall of a building on the left-hand side, one of the few remaining physical reminders of the breweries that were once based here. Just before you reach the entrance to ⑲ **Borough Market** you may recognise some of the buildings on the right – used as the backdrop for a number of scenes in Guy Ritchie's film *Lock, Stock and Two Smoking Barrels* (1998) – see following page.

The market is arguably the most atmospheric in London, and is also the capital's oldest fruit and vegetable market with its origins in the 13th century when the boisterous Southwark Fair was held just south of London

Park St, Borough Market
(featured in the film Lock, Stock & Two Smoking Barrells)

Bridge. The current market buildings date from the mid 19th century and, despite a controversial recent redevelopment, there are still plenty of cafés and food stalls in the area for a refreshment break. The market opens to retail customers each Thursday (11am-5pm), Friday (12pm-6pm) and Saturday (9am-4pm). The more adventurous may wish to see the wholesale traders at work, any night except Saturday (2am-8am).

Follow the map along Stoney Street then into Winchester Walk to reach ⑳ **Southwark Cathedral**. The oldest Gothic church in London, it was founded in the 9th century AD by St Swithun, Bishop of Winchester, as a college for priests, and in 1106 the church of St Mary Overie (or 'over the river') was built on the site as part of the Priory of St Mary Overie. Benefiting from the patronage of the Bishops of Winchester who lived nearby, the priory church was rebuilt between 1220 and 1420. After the Dissolution of the Monasteries in the 1530s the church was taken over by local worshippers, and was eventually renamed St Saviour's.

In the 16th century Southwark and Bankside, being outside the jurisdiction of the City authorities, became the location of choice for those setting up entertainments that were banned within the City itself. This included a number of Elizabethan theatres such as the famous Globe, and many actors lived in the parish of St Saviour's including William Shakespeare. Around half of those actors listed on the front of the *First Folio* (1623) – the first collected edition of Shakespeare's plays – are mentioned in the church's registers.

The cathedral contains a memorial to Shakespeare, and also to his brother and fellow actor Edmund (1580-1607) who was buried here. Little is known about Edmund, although he died just a month after his infant son had been buried north of the Thames at St. Giles' Cripplegate. It is thought that William arranged Edmund's burial at St Saviour's, the church records showing that a premium price was paid for a morning service (presumably to allow the

actors attending the service to be available to perform later that afternoon), and the ringing of the great church bell.

Relations between the local actors (or 'players') and the clergy were not always easy given the perceived immorality of the theatrical profession. In 1616 the chaplain of St Saviour's preached a sermon criticising those 'who dishonour God... by penning and acting of plays'.

John Harvard was baptised here in 1607 and the cathedral contains a Harvard Chapel. There are also a great number of impressive tombs and monuments including that of writer John Gower (d. 1408) who was a friend of Geoffrey Chaucer and who has been described as the first 'English poet' because he wrote in the native language as well as the more customary Latin or French. Surprisingly, this grand building has only been a cathedral since 1905, and its official name of the Cathedral and Collegiate Church of St Saviour and St Mary Overie recalls its ancient past. If you find Borough Market too crowded, the cathedral contains an excellent café at the rear, with outside seating when the weather is good.

20

Follow the map to reach the edge of the Thames passing the medieval **㉑ St Mary Overie Dock**, which currently contains a full-size modern replica of the *Golden Hinde*, the galleon in which Sir Francis Drake sailed around the world between 1577 and 1580. Walk down Clink Street – named after the Liberty of the Clink, a medieval manor outside the jurisdiction of the City authorities – and on the left you can see the remains of **㉒ Winchester Palace**. The Bishops of Winchester lived in the palace between 1140 and 1626 whilst attending to matters in London. Winchester was the old Saxon capital of the country, and the Bishops of Winchester traditionally had a powerful position both politically and economically in medieval England.

Only the west side of the 12th-century Great Hall with its unusual 14th century Rose Window remains. The palace was used until the 17th century. It was later converted into warehouses and the building largely destroyed by a fire in 1814. Many royal visitors were entertained in the Hall, including James I of Scotland on his wedding to Joan Beaufort in 1424.

The Bishops of Winchester once owned vast tracts of land in London and elsewhere and this included about 20 'stews' or brothels that lay along the riverside. The stews were licensed by the church, much of the regulation set out under Ordinances of 1161 signed by Thomas à Becket – ironic given he later became a saint following his martyrdom in Canterbury Cathedral.

The Ordinances were strict, including the imposition of a fine of twenty shillings should any 'woman of the bordello... draw any man by his gown or by his hood or by any other thing...'. However the prostitutes were also given some protection and provided they paid their rent to the 'stewholder' they were given 'free licence and liberty to come and go, without any interruption'. These church-owned and regulated brothels operated for about 500 years until the Puritans put an end to many of them – along with the local theatres and animal baiting pits – in the mid 17th century.

Beside the remains of the Palace you pass the ㉓ **Clink Museum**, situated in the old Clink prison whose notoriety gave birth to the well-known phrase about being 'in the clink'. The prison was founded in the 12th century and was connected by underground tunnels to Winchester Palace. Originally designed to hold troublesome priests, the Clink became a useful place to imprison troublemakers from the nearby theatres, inns and brothels. Whilst conditions were brutal, the relationship between jailer and prison was a complicated one and local prostitutes held in the Clink might be allowed to ply their trade from within the prison in return for paying an appropriate bribe.

During the reign of Elizabeth I many Puritans were harshly treated, under suspicion of plotting to overthrow the Queen. Some were thrown into the Clink, often being starved to death; however, some survived and later travelled on *The Mayflower* to America in 1620. The Clink was burned down in the anti-Catholic Gordon Riots of 1780 and never re-opened. The Museum is open Monday to Friday 10am-6pm, Saturday and Sunday 10am-9pm. It is fairly honest in its depiction of conditions inside the Clink, so young children may find it a little frightening.

At the end of Clink Street you can see the Thames on your right. On the corner is the ㉔ **Anchor** public house which dates from the 18th century, and contains cubby holes originally used by those hiding from the threat of imprisonment in the Clink. Both the Anchor, and its 15th-century predecessor on the site, the Castle and Hoop inn, were once used as brothels.

The Castle and Hoop would have certainly been known to Shakespeare, while Samuel Pepys visited the Anchor on 2 September 1666 to watch the Great Fire, recording: 'When we could endure no more upon the water, we to a little alehouse on the Bankside... and there staid till it was dark almost, and saw the fire grow... it made me weep to see it. The churches, houses and all on fire, and flaming at once; and a horrid noise the flames made, and the cracking of houses at their ruine'.

Head away from the Thames down Park Street, looking out for a plaque on the left recalling this was once the location of a number of breweries over the years. These included the ㉕ **Barclay Perkins Brewery**, which during its heyday in the 19th century claimed to be the largest brewery in the world, and was certainly one of the largest employers in the area. The brewery, which had been founded in 1781, was taken over by Courage in 1955 and finally closed in the 1980s.

Further along Park Street on the left you come to the site of the ㉖ **Globe Theatre.** There are some information boards worth reading, and the tiles on the open space in front indicate the curve of the famous 'O' shaped theatre. The Globe was built in 1599 by the Burbage family and became one of Southwark's best-known playhouses until it was destroyed in 1613 by a fire caused by a spark from a theatrical cannon during the premiere of Shakespeare's *Henry VIII*. The playhouse was rebuilt on the same site, but the Puritans finally closed it in 1642 and it was demolished soon after.

Continue along Park Street to pass a plaque near the entrance of Rose Alley indicating the site of another famous Elizabethan theatre, ㉗ **the Rose**. This was built in 1587 by Philip Henslowe, the great rival to the Burbage family, and was the first theatre constructed in the area. Edward Alleyn (1566-1626), regarded as one of the greatest actors of his generation, was closely associated with Henslowe and the Rose, but the theatre's small size compared to the Globe meant it was never as popular and was demolished in around 1606. Famous plays first performed at the Rose include Christopher Marlowe's *Doctor Faustus*, *The Jew of Malta* and *Tamburlaine the Great*; Thomas Kyd's *The Spanish Tragedy*; and Shakespeare's *Henry VI Part I* and *Titus Andronicus*.

In 1989 excavations revealed the foundation of the Rose (they lie behind the window of the modern building on the right-hand side of Rose Alley); it is possible to visit them as part of the modern Globe's tours to the Rose (telephone the Globe Exhibition on 020 7902 1500, email exhibit@ shakespearesglobe.com or visit www.shakespeares-globe.org).

Continue along Park Street and head north up ㉘ **Bear Gardens**, thought by some to be the place Shakespeare lived when he worked at the Globe. On the right is a plaque recalling that this was the site of another great Elizabethan theatre, ㉙ **the Hope**. This theatre was built, again by Henslowe, in 1614 on the site of the Bear Garden, a bear-baiting venue. Even after the Hope was opened, bear baiting continued within the building, which was constructed to allow animals to be safely secured. It was finally demolished in the 1650s and replaced by another building which was visited by Samuel Pepys in August 1666. He recorded in his dairy how 'after dinner with my wife and Mercer to the Beare garden, where I have not been I think of many years and saw some good sport of the bull's tossing of the dogs – one into the very boxes. But it is a very rude and nasty pleasure'. At the end of the Bear Gardens is the ㉚ **Ferryman's Seat**, inserted in a modern building on the right just before you reach the Thames. The date of the seat is unknown, but it was taken from an earlier building and is thought to have been used for centuries by the ferrymen who once worked on the Thames. Until 1750, London Bridge was the only major crossing point in central London, so the ferrymen were an essential service for Londoners wanting an alternative.

Continue west along the Thames path to reach ㉛ **Shakespeare's Globe Theatre**, a faithful reconstruction of the original Elizabethan playhouse. Apart from putting on plays, it contains an excellent exhibition on Shakespeare and the theatre's history, and tours are also available. Visit the Globe's website for more details (www.shakespeares-globe.org).

To the west of the Globe and facing the Thames is ㉜ **Cardinal's Wharf**, containing a few tall 18th-century houses that are the oldest in the area. Number 49 was built in around 1710 and stands on the site of the ㉝ **Cardinal's Cap Inn**. This Inn was popular with Elizabethan ferrymen, and once housed a brothel. The narrow Cardinal Cap Alley runs alongside and would have been known to Shakespeare. Gillian Tindall's recent book *The House by the Thames* is a good read for those interested in finding out more about number 49 and the history of the area. A plaque records that Sir Christopher Wren lived here while St Paul's was being built, and that in 1502 Catherine of Aragon, later married to Henry VIII, took shelter here on her first landing in London. Sadly both connections are thought today to be untrue.

The walk ends here and you can return along the riverside to London Bridge station, or alternatively continue past Tate Modern and the Southbank Centre to London Waterloo. ●

SHOP...

Borough Market (see p.255)
8 Southwark Street, SE1 1TL
www.boroughmarket.org.uk

VISIT...

Clink Museum (see p.260)
1 Clink Street, SE1
www.clink.co.uk

Old Operating Theatre & Herb Garret Museum (see p.244)
9a St. Thomas Street, SE1
www.thegarret.org.uk

Shakespeare's Globe Theatre
21 New Globe Walk, SE1
www.shakespeares-globe.org

Tate Modern
53 Bankside, SE1
www.tate.org.uk

Vinopolis
No.1 Bank End, SE1
www.vinopolis.co.uk

EAT, DRINK...

Anchor public house
(see p.261)
34 Park Street, Southwark, SE1

Boot and Flogger (see p.254)
10 Redcross Way, SE1

The George Inn (see p.247)
77 Borough High St, SE1
www.nationaltrust.org.uk

10 East Rotherhithe Walk

CANADA WATER

SURREY QUAYS ROAD

QUEBEC WAY

① Canada Dock

CANADA WATER

REDRIFF ROAD

ELGAR ST

TEREDO ST

③ James Walker

FINLAND ST

④

⑤ GREENLAND PIER

BRUNSWICK QUAY

GREENLAND DOCK

②

ROPE ST

⑥

SOUTHWARK PARK

SURREY QUAYS

REDRIFF ROAD

GREENLAND QUAY

SOUTH DOCK

⑦

HAWKSTONE RD

LOWER RD

PLOUGH WAY

YEOMAN ST

GROVE ST

DEPTFORD WHARF DE

⑧

CROFT ST

BUSH RD

LONGSHORE

⑨

CONCORDE WAY

⑩ FORESHORE

SILWOOD ST

EVELYN ST

OXESTALLS RD

BOWDITCH

PEPYS PARK

⑫

TRUNDLEY'S RD

DEPTFORD PARK

GROVE ST

⑬ SAYES COURT DA

EVELYN

KERRY RD

EDWARD ST

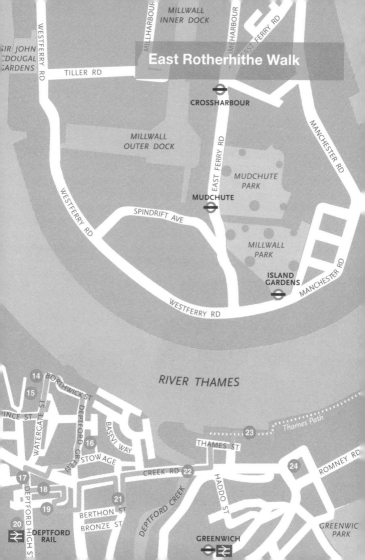

MILLWALL
INNER DOCK

MILLHARBOUR

INNER HARBOUR

WEST FERRY RD

WESTFERRY RD

SIR JOHN
MCDOUGAL
GARDENS

TILLER RD

East Rotherhithe Walk

CROSSHARBOUR

MANCHESTER RD

MILLWALL
OUTER DOCK

EAST FERRY RD

MUDCHUTE
PARK

MUDCHUTE

WESTFERRY RD

SPINDRIFT AVE

MILLWALL
PARK

ISLAND
GARDENS

MANCHESTER RD

WESTFERRY RD

RIVER THAMES

14

15

BORTHWICK ST

WATERGATE ST

DEPTFORD GREEN

BASEVI WAY

Thames Path

23

INCE ST

16

STOWAGE

THAMES ST

24

ROMNEY RD

17

CREEK RD

22

HADDO ST

18

DEPTFORD HIGH ST

21

DEPTFORD CREEK

19

BERTHON ST

BRONZE ST

20

DEPTFORD
RAIL

GREENWICH

GREENWICH
PARK

East Rotherhithe Walk

Distance 4.5 miles
Start: Canada Water underground station
Finish: Greenwich (various options)

The walk begins at Canada Water underground station in Rotherhithe. From the station follow the map along the north side of Canada Water, formerly known as ❶ **Canada Dock**. Canada Dock was opened in 1876 to hold grain and timber, much of it originating from Canada, and was one of 10 docks in this area owned by the Surrey Commercial Docks Company until the company's closure in 1970. At the north-east corner head through the car park onto Surrey Quays Road and bear right. You pass a retail park on the left and head straight over to Brunswick Quay.

The Quay lies on the north side of the huge ❷ **Greenland Dock**, originally called the Howland Great Wet Dock when it opened

in 1696. This is the oldest dock south of the Thames and it was also once the largest commercial dock in the world. It was originally used to refit the ships of the East India Company and from the 1720s was used by whaling ships from Greenland, hence the name. Blubber boiling houses used to line the south side of the dock, the end product being whale oil. From 1807 the dock was used principally for timber and grain imports

Greenland Dock is a relatively rare survivor of the old Surrey docks complex that collectively covered over 150 acres of water, making this part of Rotherhithe resemble a giant lake on 19th-century maps. Sadly, many of the neighbouring docks were filled in after the Surrey Docks closed, unable to cope with competition from larger docks outside London and the introduction of containerisation.

Greenland Dock covers 22.5 acres and is surrounded by a number of residential developments built on and named after the old timber warehouses that once stood here. Brunswick Yard became Brunswick Quay, Swedish Yard became Swedish Quay, and

2 *Greenland Dock*

so on. The dock is now used extensively for water sports – look out for the cormorants, Canada geese and swans that like to visit.

Skirt around the north side of the dock, passing a bust of ❸ **James Walker** on the left. Walker (1781-1862) worked as the chief engineer on many of the great docks that were built in London during the 19th century, and also designed a number of bridges and lighthouses around the country.

Cross over a couple of mid ❹ **19th-century swing bridges** to stand by the old lock-gates facing the Thames on the south-east corner. Just beside here is the 19th-century ❺ **Tide Gauge House** facing the river, which was used to work out the state of the tide so the lock-gates onto the Thames could be operated efficiently.

Continue along the Thames Path, passing the Greenland Pier river bus stop. Shortly you pass over another narrow bridge which crosses the entrance to ❻ **South Dock**. This dock was originally called the East Country Dock and was built in 1807-11 and connected to Greenland Dock by the Greenland Cut. South Dock is about one third of the length of Greenland Dock and is now London's largest marina. During WWII it was emptied of shipping and used for the building of the Mulberry floating harbours that were invaluable to the Allies after D-Day in June 1944.

The docks you have visited were once connected to the now-closed **Grand Surrey Canal.** This canal was opened in 1809 and ran for three miles down to Camberwell, with

two small offshoots forming the Croydon Canal and the Peckham Branch. Because of competition from the railways the Grand Surrey Canal eventually became uneconomical and closed in the 1940s, with most of the canal being filled in during the 1960s. However, if you ever look at an old map of London (there are plenty free to view on the internet) it is fascinating to see how prominent on the landscape the old canal and docks were. Today often the only trace of them is a municipal park lying on top of a filled in dock-basin, or a road running along the line of what was once a canal.

Continue along the Thames Path where shortly on the right is a ⑦ **stone** marking the parish boundary of St Mary's Rotherhithe and St Paul's Deptford. Until 1899 it also marked the boundary of Kent and Surrey.

You are now in Deptford, an area sandwiched between Southwark to the west and Greenwich to the east. For many centuries Deptford was really two places – the tiny fishing village of Deptford Strand by the Thames, and Deptford itself. The latter was surrounded by Kent countryside and was

based around the 'deep ford' (hence 'Deptford') across the River Ravensbourne. Today's Deptford Bridge, just south of Deptford High Street, stands on the same location as the old ford.

Deptford's fortunes changed forever in 1513 when Henry VIII (1491-1547) decided to base first a royal naval storehouse and then later a dockyard here. Henry was attracted to the area as it was near his favourite palace at Greenwich and also his London-based Royal Armouries. Before 1513 munitions and cannon from the Royal Armouries had to be transported all the way to Portsmouth where the original naval dockyard was based. Henry also founded the naval dockyard at Woolwich around the same time.

. The foundation of the royal dockyards meant Deptford grew rapidly and it became an important town. Over 350 navy ships were built in Deptford's yards over the centuries, and many more were supplied (or 'victualled') and repaired here. One notable example was HMS *Neptune* which was launched here in 1797, and was one of the main battleships at the Battle of Trafalgar in 1805. After the battle, the *Neptune* helped tow the crippled HMS *Victory*, which was carrying Nelson's body, back to Gibraltar.

Gradually the waters in Deptford began to silt up eventually becoming too shallow to launch the larger vessels the Navy needed. The shipbuilding yards finally closed in 1869 and the 27 acre site was subsequently used as a foreign cattle market until 1912. Deptford remained the victualling yard for the Navy for another 100 years; but increasingly had to rely on other industries and began to sink into obscurity compared to Greenwich, its more upmarket neighbour.

Continue down ❽ **Deptford Wharf** which formerly contained a wet dock used for convict transport ships en route to Australia. Pass the Aragon Tower and the **Pepys Estate** to the right. The latter is named after Samuel Pepys (1633-1703), the famous English diarist, who was a regular visitor to the Deptford shipbuilding yards in his role as a senior Naval official. He recounts these visits in detail in his diary, as well as his more clandestine trips to see his lover Mrs Bagwell. Mr Bagwell was a carpenter in the dockyard who sacrificed his wife to Pepys in order to benefit from Pepys's patronage.

In his entry for 20 February 1665 Pepys recorded how he found 'Bagwells wife, whom I directed to go home and I would do her business; which was to write a letter to my Lord Sandwich for her husband's advance into a better ship as there should be occasion – which I did; and by and by did go down by water to Deptford yard, and then down further and so landed at the lower end of the town; and it being dark, did privately enter en la maison de la femme Bagwell, and there I had sa compagnie, though with a great difficulty; neanmoins, enfin je avais ma volonte [eventually I had my way] it being now near 9 a-clock; and there I did drink some strong waters and eat some bread and cheese'.

Deptford Wharf becomes ⑨ **Deptford Strand**, scene of one of the most notorious murders in literary history. On 20 May 1593 the playwright Christopher Marlowe (1564-1593) was arrested on a charge of atheism, at a time when such a heresy could lead to being burnt at the stake. Surprisingly he was granted bail but ten days later was murdered in a lodging house on Deptford Strand. The official coroner's report, only rediscovered in 1925, records his murder by Ingram Frizer as being an act of self-defence after Marlowe flew into one of his characteristically violent rages. However, his companions in the house were also agents of the Elizabethan secret service under the great 'Spymaster' Sir Francis Walsingham, and Marlowe is known to have carried out spying activities himself.

The official report (originally in Latin) records how Marlowe and his three companions met in 'Detford [sic] Strand... in a room in the house of a certain Eleanor Bull... after supper the said Ingram and Christopher Morley [a.k.a Marlowe] were in speech and uttered one to the other divers malicious words for the reason that they could not be at one nor agree about the payment of the sum of pence, that is le recknynge... [Marlowe] gave the aforesaid Ingram two wounds on his head... in defence of his life... [Ingram] gave the said Christopher... a mortal wound over his right eye of the depth of two inches... of which mortal wound [Marlowe]... there instantly died'.

Officially therefore Marlowe died in a fight over a bill. However his murderer was soon pardoned and many think the playwright was assassinated on Walsingham's orders.

Marlowe, who in his short life penned *Tamburlaine*, *The Jew of Malta*, *Doctor Faustus*, *Edward II* and *The Massacre at Paris*, was buried in Deptford's parish church of St Nicholas – seen later. Shakespeare paid tribute to Marlowe in his play *As You Like It* (c.1599) quoting some of Marlowe's own poetry, and including the lines 'When a man's verses cannot be understood, nor a man's good wit seconded with the forward child, understanding, it strikes a man more dead than a great reckoning in a little room', a reference to the alleged murder over the 'reckoning' in Deptford Strand.

If you walk down Longshore on the right, and then back along the Thames Path, you will see a number of older buildings which are all that remain of the Navy's extensive  **victualling yards**, which kept ships and their crew supplied with provisions. The houses along Longshore known as the 'Terrace' were used by Naval officers and date from the 1780s. The buildings facing the Thames (behind the cannon) were used to store rum and have now been converted for residential use.

Other warehouses stored everything required for sea journeys including biscuits, mustard and chocolate. There were also slaughterhouses within the complex, with the butchered meat being salted in order to preserve it. The area was renamed the Royal Victoria Yard after Queen Victoria's visit in 1858, and the 35 acre site remained in use until around 1961 after which most of the land was used for the construction of the Pepys Estate.

Walk past the storehouses and ahead you can see, behind a fence, a number of commercial buildings (not accessible to the public) that occupy the site of the old Navy shipyards. At this point you have to head inland to walk around the site but before doing so look out for the **11 plaque** on the front of the storehouse building that recalls how Sir Francis Drake (1540-1595) was requested by Queen Elizabeth I to permanently berth his famous ship the *Golden Hinde* in Deptford Creek in 1581 as a memorial to his having 'circuited round the whole earth'. On 4 April of that year she dined on the ship and knighted the great explorer, and the *Hinde* remained in Deptford Creek for a 100 more years until it eventually fell apart.

Deptford was also where many great early voyages of discovery began, including those under the leadership of Sir Walter Raleigh, Martin Frobisher, and Captain James Cook. This spirit of exploration was well-captured by Joseph Conrad (1857-1924) in his classic book *The Heart of Darkness* (1902). Conrad was a seasoned sailor himself, and knew the area well, writing of how 'They had sailed from Deptford... the adventurers and the settlers... Hunters for gold or pursuers of fame, they all had gone out on that stream... The dreams of men, the seed of commonwealths, the germs of empires'. Perhaps unsurprisingly he named the main character of his book 'Marlow'.

An information board facing the Thames also recalls how whales were commonly seen in the river in past centuries, and on June 2 1658 the diarist John Evelyn (1620-1706) recorded seeing one that was 58 feet long, and which was killed by Deptford residents 'after a long conflict... with the harping irons'.

Follow the map past the playground into ⑫ **Pepys Park** and then right along Foreshore and left at Bowditch to re-join Pepys Park. Head diagonally across the grass in the shadow of some of Deptford's tower blocks. Head left along Grove Street looking out on the left-hand side for some old naval dockyard gates, and continue until you see the entrance to the secluded ⑬ **Sayes Court garden**.

This stands on the site of the house where John Evelyn lived from 1652. Evelyn's diary is an important record of 17th-century life as he interacted with some of the great men of his age including Sir Christopher Wren, Samuel Pepys and Charles II. He recorded his day to day experiences during great events such as the Great Plague and Great Fire of London, and the death of Charles I. A gifted amateur architect and landscaper – he proposed a grand plan to Charles II for the rebuilding of the City after the Great Fire – Evelyn laid out a beautiful garden here on the 100 empty acres that originally surrounded his house.

Grinling Gibbons (1648-1721), the famous wood carver, lived in a 'poor solitary thatched house in a field' within Evelyn's grounds. Gibbons came to England from Rotterdam to work as a carpenter in the Royal dockyard; however, in 1671 Evelyn discovered his tenant's remarkable talents as a carver and recommended him to Wren. Wren subsequently employed Gibbons to carve many of the furnishings that still adorn some of London's finest churches and palaces.

Samuel Pepys was a regular visitor here, recording in his own diary on October 4 1665 that Evelyn 'showed me his gardens, which are for variety of evergreens, and hedge of holly, the finest things I ever saw in my life'. Charles II also visited Evelyn here in February 1663, the diarist recording 'came his Majestie to honor my poore Villa with his prescence, viewing the Gardens and even every roome of the house'.

The house and its then famous gardens were later wrecked by Deptford's most surprising resident, Tsar Peter the Great of Russia (1672-1725). Peter lived in Deptford for three months in 1698 to learn the art of shipbuilding, staying at Sayes Court which was rented from Evelyn. The Tsar pretended to be an ordinary carpenter in the nearby dockyard; however, his great stature (he was six foot seven inches tall), Russian accent and wildly extrovert personality probably meant no one was fooled. Peter's time in London was part of a long European tour whose purpose was to learn Western ideas and techniques that could be taken back to modernise feudal Russia.

Peter enjoyed a drink with his party-loving entourage, the latter described by Evelyn's disgusted estate steward as being full of 'right nasty' people. The Russians wrecked Evelyn's house and garden – the carpets were soiled and ruined, his paintings used for target practice, and fifty chairs destroyed. For Evelyn the worst calamity was the destruction of his prized holly bush after it was rammed through by a wheelbarrow with the drunken Tsar of Russia sitting inside.

In three months the Russians inflicted £350 of damage – then a substantial sum – which Sir Christopher Wren on behalf of the Treasury repaid to a very annoyed Evelyn. The diarist recorded in an entry on June 9 1698 that he went to Deptford to 'view how miserably the Tzar of Muscovy had left the house'.

Sayes Court was demolished in 1728-1729 and a workhouse was built on the site before it became part of the Royal Victoria Yard. The fenced-in tree at the centre of the park is thought to be a survivor from Evelyn's garden.

On the other side of the park exit onto Sayes Court Street and walk down it before heading left into Prince Street. Head left at Watergate Street which leads you back towards the Thames. This becomes Borthwick Street, and at the end behind the wall on the left-hand corner you see the ⑭ **Master Shipwright's House** of 1708 built for Joseph Allin. It is also known ironically as the 'Shipwright's Palace' on account of the scandal that erupted about how much public money was being used to fund the construction. The old warehouses facing the Thames are currently being redeveloped, and **⑮ the wall** of the former dockyard runs alongside this street.

Continue down Deptford Green to reach the church of **⑯ St Nicholas** on the left. The church was founded at the latest in the 12th century and its ragstone tower is largely 14th-century. The remainder of the church dates principally from a reconstruction in 1697, with further work carried out after damage was inflicted during the Blitz. The main gate contains two distinctive 17th-century skull and cross bone carvings, typical of the *memento mori* designs of the era, which were designed to remind the congregation of the inevitability of death.

The old charnel house lies opposite the entrance to the church. The church contains a fine reredos and a panel depicting *Ezekiel in the Valley of the Dry Bones*, which is thought to be the work of Grinling Gibbons. There is also a memorial on the west wall to Richard and Mary Evelyn, children of John Evelyn.

283

16 St Nicholas Church

The north-east corner of the churchyard contains a memorial to Christopher Marlowe who was buried here in an unmarked grave after his murder in Deptford Strand, and whose death was recorded in the surviving church register for 1 June 1593 as 'slaine by Francis Frezer'. The vicar's misspelling of the murderer Ingram Frizer's name in this official record unfortunately caused historians much confusion in later years. The memorial contains the poignant line (from Marlowe's *Doctor Faustus*), 'Cut is the branch that might have grown full straight', a reminder that had he lived longer the playwright could have rivalled Shakespeare in terms of world-wide reputation. Perhaps those who laid the memorial thought it fit not to quote Marlowe's infamous remark (attributed to him by a government spy) that 'All they that love not tobacco and boys are fools'. The church opening times may vary so it best to ring (020 8692 8848) to check.

On the north-east side of the church is an exit that leads to an area near the Thames used by the East India Company between 1600 and 1782, and which was later the site of the world's first high voltage electric power station. The station was opened in 1891 and designed by Sebastian Ziani de Ferranti. It remained in use until 1983, later being demolished and built over to create the Fairview Housing development (which today con-tains a modern statue of Peter the Great).

However, on this walk continue south down Deptford Green and head right at McMillan Street. Cross over busy Creek Road to walk down ⑰ **Deptford High Street**. The High Street has a vibrant atmosphere, and hosts a great street market each Wednesday,

Friday and Saturday. In recent years some have described Deptford as the 'new Shoreditch' because of its popularity with artists, students and musicians. The High Street contains a number of old artisan buildings built in the late 18th century (see numbers 32-34, 62-66, 150, 203 and 205 and 227).

Number 34 was once the Chapman's Oil and Colour Shop, and it was here that Mr and Mrs Farrow were murdered by the Stratton brothers in 1905. The case is notable because it was the first time a murder conviction was secured in this country using fingerprint evidence, and the Strattons were hanged as a result.

Number 146 was the site of an old Quaker Meeting House that was demolished in 1907. Peter the Great attended meetings in the old building during his stay in Deptford, discussing religion with William Penn (1644-1718), the founder of the American State of Pennsylvania.

Just to the south of the High Street (although I do not suggest you walk down this far) is Deptford Bridge, once an important crossing point over the River Ravensbourne as mentioned earlier. Medieval pilgrims to Canterbury would pass along this route when leaving London, and in Chaucer's *The Canterbury Tales* Deptford is mentioned in following lines from *The Reeve's Prologue*:

> Tell forth your tale, and do not waste the time.
> Here's Deptford! And it is half way to prime.
> There's Greenwich town that many a scoundrel's in;
> It is high time your story should begin.

Take the second left along the High Street into ⑱ **Albury Street**. This contains a number of fine houses built by a local bricklayer named Thomas Lucas from 1705, and which are particularly notable for their elaborately carved doorcases. They were originally used as houses for sea captains and shipwrights connected to the naval ship yards, and legend has it that Nelson's mistress Lady Hamilton once lived here.

Follow Albury Street to the end and bear right, which leads you through a small playground and gardens to the north gate of

19

⑲ St Paul's church. One of the finest Baroque churches in London, it was built in 1713-30 by Wren's pupil Thomas Archer (1668-1743) in Portland stone and contains a distinctive semi-circular portico. At the time the church was built Deptford had become a substantial town in its own right, and was known for attracting religious and political dissenters.

In 1710 the newly-elected Tory Government felt it necessary to re-affirm the power of the Church of England in London's newer towns and suburbs, and embarked on a programme to build 'fifty new churches'. While far less than fifty were actually built, St Paul's was typical of those that were as it has a grandeur designed to remind the local population that the Church of England was still at the heart of the country's religious life. Archer was also responsible for another Baroque masterpiece, the church of St. John in Smith Square, Westminster.

Just south of the church is **⑳ Deptford Station**, one of the original stopping points on the Greenwich to London Bridge railway that was constructed from 1836. This was London's first passenger railway line.

Exit the church on the east side to reach Deptford Church Street and head north before turning right into Creek Road. Shortly on your right walk up Creekside to visit one of London's most extraordinary recent buildings, the **㉑ Laban dance studio**. Whilst the studio is principally for the use of dancers, the public can attend performances and visit parts of the building such as the café, Monday to Friday 9am-5pm. The building was designed by Herzog & De Meuron, architects of Tate Modern, and won the

prestigious Stirling Prize for architecture in 2003. If you visit Laban's website (laban. org) you can also find out how to book a guided tour of one of the architectural triumphs of south-east London, despite the deep-green gardens to the front that resemble the set of *Teletubbies*. The studio also looks fantastic at night when the lime, magenta and turquoise colours shine out spectacularly.

Continue along ㉒ **Creek Road** to see on either side of the bridge the creek itself. This is actually part of the River Ravensbourne which rises at Caesar's Well in Keston before flowing into the Thames eleven miles later. Like many of the docks and canals mentioned above, the creek has faded away and been built over in the last few decades.

Just after the bridge head left down Norway Street and follow the map to take you out onto the ㉓ **riverfront** at Greenwich which is the end of this walk. Ahead is the domed building that covers the Greenwich entrance of the Thames foot-tunnel built in 1902 which takes you to the Isle of Dogs.

The well-known tourist attractions of ㉔ **Greenwich** lie ahead, including the Cutty Sark (constructed in 1869 and currently being restored after fire damage in 2007), Greenwich's fine markets, the Royal Observatory, Greenwich Park, and Greenwich Hospital. Once finished in Greenwich you can return to central London from Greenwich station (overland or DLR). ●

SHOP...

Deptford Market
Deptford High St, SE8

Greenwich Market
Greenwich Church St &
Greenwich High Rd, SE10
www.greenwichmarket.net

VISIT...

National Maritime Museum
Romney Rd, SE10
www.nmm.ac.uk

Royal Observatory
Blackheath Av, SE10
www.nmm.ac.uk

EAT, DRINK...

Laban Centre (see p.288)
Creekside, SE8
Tel: 020 8691 8600

Yellow House
126 Lower Rd,
Surrey Quays, SE16
Tel: 020 7231 8777

Wibbly Wobbly
Greenland Dock, off Rope St,
Surrey Quays, SE16
Tel: 08721 077 077

Trafalgar Tavern
Park Row, Greenwich, SE10
Tel: 08721 077 077

24   *Greenwich riverfront*

11 Docklands Walk
Part 1

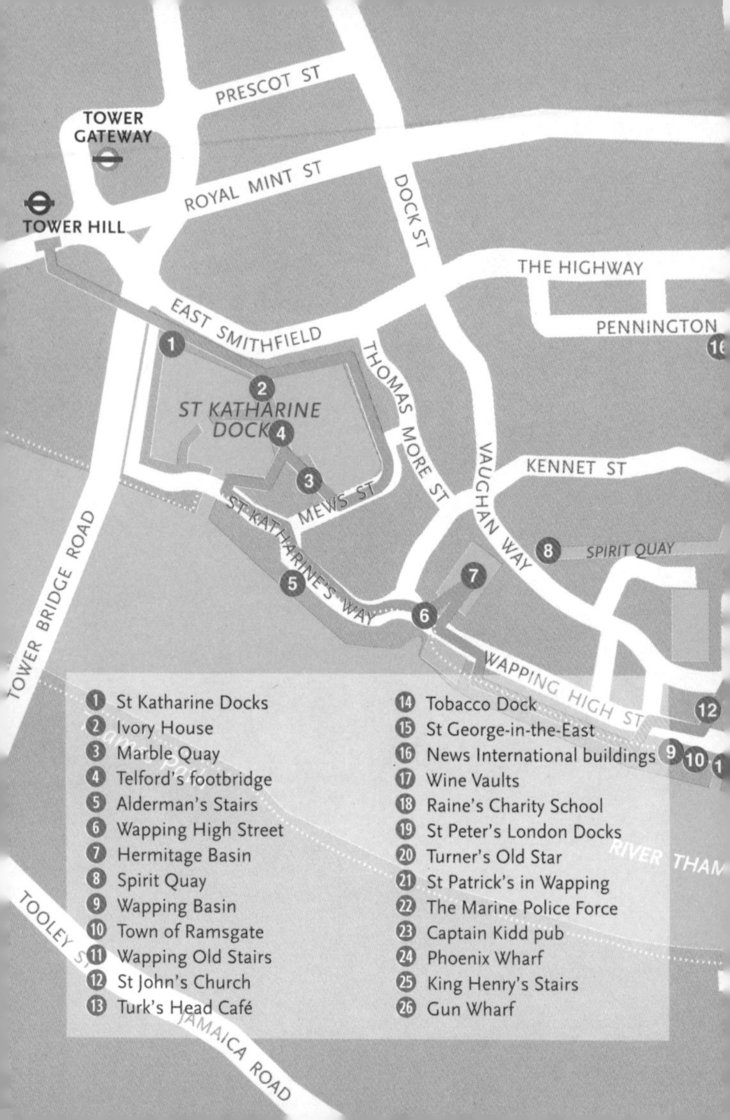

PRESCOT ST

TOWER GATEWAY

ROYAL MINT ST

TOWER HILL

THE HIGHWAY

EAST SMITHFIELD

PENNINGTON

DOCK ST

①

② ST KATHARINE DOCKS

④

THOMAS MORE ST

③

MEWS ST

VAUGHAN WAY

KENNET ST

ST KATHARINE'S WAY

⑧ SPIRIT QUAY

⑤

⑦

TOWER BRIDGE ROAD

⑥

WAPPING HIGH ST

⑯

⑫

TOOLEY ST

⑨ ⑩ ⑪

RIVER THAM

JAMAICA ROAD

①	St Katharine Docks	⑭	Tobacco Dock
②	Ivory House	⑮	St George-in-the-East
③	Marble Quay	⑯	News International buildings
④	Telford's footbridge	⑰	Wine Vaults
⑤	Alderman's Stairs	⑱	Raine's Charity School
⑥	Wapping High Street	⑲	St Peter's London Docks
⑦	Hermitage Basin	⑳	Turner's Old Star
⑧	Spirit Quay	㉑	St Patrick's in Wapping
⑨	Wapping Basin	㉒	The Marine Police Force
⑩	Town of Ramsgate	㉓	Captain Kidd pub
⑪	Wapping Old Stairs	㉔	Phoenix Wharf
⑫	St John's Church	㉕	King Henry's Stairs
⑬	Turk's Head Café	㉖	Gun Wharf

Docklands Walk Part 1

Start: Tower Hill underground station
Finish: Wapping Tube Station
Distance: 2.5 miles

The walk begins at Tower Hill underground station. From the station walk towards the Tower of London, which dominates the view to the south, and follow the signs for St Katharine Docks. You pass underneath the approach road to Tower Bridge and enter the docks on the western basin of St Katharine Docks.

This is the first of a number of docks visited on this walk that were built during the 19th century and which collectively ensured that London remained the busiest port in the world until the second half of the 20th century. In the course of the two dockland walks you will also pass through the heart of the old East End – Wapping, Shadwell, Ratcliffe, Limehouse and finally the Isle of Dogs.

❶ **St Katharine Docks** opened in 1828, one of a handful of new-style docks constructed in London after 1800. Before then the port of London (or 'Pool of London') comprised a disjointed mass of antiquated old wharves, quays and shipbuilding yards that were dotted along the banks of the Thames. As London prospered at the hub of the growing British Empire, it became clear that the old port infrastructure was unable to cope with the rapidly increasing volume of shipping.

Merchants became frustrated at seeing their ships moored idly in the Thames for days or even weeks waiting their turn to be unloaded, all the while vulnerable to river pirates and the weather. They began to push for reform, and a key turning point came in 1799 when legislation was passed permitting the construction of the West India Docks (seen later) on the Isle of Dogs. These docks set the template for what would follow, boasting acres of water that could accommodate the biggest ships and high perimeter walls behind which goods could be safely stored in warehouses.

Situated in Wapping, the site of St Katharine Docks had previously been dominated by the hospital of St Katharine's by the Tower,

View of Tower Bridge from Alderman's Stairs

founded in 1147 by Queen Matilda as a religious community and hospital for the poor and sick. In 1273 Queen Eleanor ensured the patronage of St Katharine's was reserved to the Queens of England. This protected it – unlike many other religious foundations – from Henry VIII's Dissolution of the Monasteries, and the Puritan revolution of Oliver Cromwell.

By the early 19th century St Katharine's stood as a strange medieval relic in the heart of a vast slum. The hospital and the area's 11,000 inhabitants fought a long and bitter battle against the dock's developers, but ultimately they lost. The residents were forced to leave and – with the exception of the hospital – received no compensation.

The slums were demolished and labourers, often from Ireland, arrived to excavate the dock. It became a feature of many of the docks built in this period that the immigrant workforce settled in London, seeking employment on the docks they had helped build and forming a new breed of worker – the East End 'docker'. The hospital survived its move and, today known as The Royal Foundation of St Katharine, is based in Limehouse, where it can be visited in the second docklands walk.

The St Katharine Docks Company engaged the distinguished engineer Thomas Telford (1757-1834), to design the docks – his only major London work. It comprised an eastern and western dock connected via a basin to the south that in turn fed into the Thames through a lock. The soil excavated from the site was used for the foundations of the smart houses then being built on the marshy new suburbs of Pimlico and Belgravia to the west.

St Katharine Docks specialised in luxury goods such as ivory, spices, shells, sugar, rubber, wines, perfumes and marble. The docks were surrounded by a high security wall, now largely demolished. Henry Mayhew, in his book *London Labour and the London Poor* (1851), describes the 'lofty walls' which enclosed 'an area capable of accommodating 120 ships, besides barges and other craft. Cargoes are raised into the warehouses out of the hold of the ship without the goods being deposited on the quay... in one-fifth of the usual time'. Many of the six-storey warehouses were built close to the water so cargoes could be unloaded by cranes straight from the ships, thus reducing labour requirements and the risk of theft by London's well-organised criminal gangs.

Walk along the north side of the dock. You can see to your right
2 **Ivory House** – named after the goods once kept therein – with its impressive Victorian clock tower. On your left as you move towards the eastern basin look out for a pair of elephant figures on top of the old dock gates facing East Smithfield, another reminder of the ivory trade that came through the dock (including woolly mammoth tusks dug up in Eastern Europe during the 19th century).

Carry on along the edge of the eastern basin, passing the Georgian bollards used for berthing ships. St Katharine Docks – never large enough to attract the bigger trade ships – were never a great commercial success. Struggling financially, in 1864 they were amalgamated with London Docks, their competitor in Wapping. In 1909 St Katharine Docks, along with the other docks in London, came under the common control of the Port of London Authority (PLA). They were later devastated during the Blitz and, whilst they managed to re-open, continued to struggle financially. Like the other London docks, St Katharine Docks were unable to cope with the introduction of containerisation from the 1960s. This demanded larger and more modern ports, such as Felixstowe and Tilbury, to accommodate a new generation of ships. St Katharine Docks were the first London docks to close in 1968 – all the others would follow by 1980. Today, home to a yacht marina and flanked by expensive new flats, St Katharine Docks is an affluent place once again – a prosperity that belies the difficulties faced by the Docklands generally as the area struggles to recover from the dock closures that resulted in the loss of nearly 10,000 jobs during the 1970s.

Continue round to reach ❸ **Marble Quay**, named after the fine stone once imported here from Italy. Nearby is the **Dickens Inn**, its façade a modern reconstruction of an old galleried inn but actually built on the shell of a Georgian building. Just in front of the Dickens Inn you can cross a working replica of ❹ **Telford's footbridge** that spans the eastern dock entrance. Beside this is the original footbridge itself. Over to the west you can see a branch of Starbucks that occupies the spot where the medieval Gothic church of the old hospital once stood.

Walk towards the Thames, passing the still-functioning river lock. Beside the lock stands a superb example of a Georgian dockmaster's house which once offered its occupant a panoramic view of the shipping traffic up and down the Thames.

Leave St Katharine Docks through the small curved alleyway beside the dockmaster's house, following the map along St Katharine's Way. On the right you will see ❺ **Alderman's Stairs** – the first of many stone staircases leading down to the Thames shoreline you will pass on this walk which have been in use for hundreds of years.

Soon you reach ❻ **Wapping High Street**, a thoroughfare with its origins in the late 16th century when a link was required between the quays of the City and the storage warehouses further to the east along Wapping Wall. On your left is a round red-brick former PLA building dating from the early 20th century, and behind this is **Hermitage Basin**. Both were part of the London Docks that were opened in 1805 and which once dominated this part of Wapping.

During the late 18th century Wapping was typical of the isolated villages that could still be found dotted along the north bank of the Thames. These villages, often surrounded by marshes, were populated by shipbuilders, sailors and tradesmen connected to the ship trade. However, the huge population growth of London in the 19th century, and the creation of the new docks, changed these old communities forever. Many old buildings were demolished to make way for the docks and new immigrants arrived looking for labouring work, or to become dockers.

Living conditions deteriorated during the 19th century and the districts around the East End docks experienced great poverty. This helped fuel the often terrible labour relations between the dockers and the dock owners, reaching a nadir during the bitterly fought London Dock Strike of 1889. The brutality of life on the docks was best exemplified by the infamous 'call on' which required the massed ranks of casual dockers to stand behind a chain at the dock gates and bay for the attention of the foreman in order to be selected for a day's work.

7 **Hermitage Basin** is one of the few dock basins to survive. The basins were pools of water that acted as conduits or holding areas between the Thames and the main dockyards to ensure the efficient flow of traffic. Many of the basins have been filled in since 1980 when the last of the docks in London were shut. Hermitage Basin – now surrounded by upmarket flats – is still full of water, although its channel to the Thames

has now been blocked. At the north end of the basin is a narrow strip of water called **❽ Spirit Quay** that leads to Tobacco Dock. We will visit Tobacco Dock later on in this walk so for now continue along the Thames Path.

The London Docks stretched over 90 acres and, after opening in 1805, enjoyed a 21-year monopoly requiring all vessels (other than those from the East and West Indies) carrying tobacco, rice, wine and brandy to be unloaded there. The docks – designed by John Rennie and Daniel Asher Alexander – had room for more than 300 ships, not including 'lighters', which were smaller vessels used to transport cargoes between the big ships and the shore. The whole area was surrounded by a high wall, patrolled by a private security force, and the four storey warehouses could hold 200,000 tons of goods. These goods were unloaded from the ships by a complicated hierarchy of dockers, with a fairly small permanent workforce supplemented by up to 3,000 casual workers.

Continue east along the **Thames Path** until it leads you back inland and you reach the former entrance of **❾ Wapping Basin** – the second of the three basins that connected London Docks to the Thames. The entrance has now been filled in; however, it is flanked on either side by the magnificent Georgian houses of Wapping Pier Head, built by Daniel Asher Alexander between 1810 and 1813 for officials of the London Docks. Stop for a moment and try to imagine tall sailing ships gliding past these houses on their way inland through Wapping Basin and into the dockyards further north. Custom House at number three on the west side serves as a tangible reminder of the officials who once lived and worked here.

Just past the Pier Head houses is the **❿ Town of Ramsgate** public house, named after the sailors from Ramsgate who once moored their ships nearby and arrived at the pub via the Wapping Old Stairs that still run alongside. The pub claims to date from the early 1600s and was originally called the Red Cow. It contains extensive former wine cellars once used by the Admiralty as a holding cell for those caught by the notorious 'press gangs' and forced to join the Navy. Criminals were often kept in here as well, many beginning their perilous journeys to Australia from underneath the pub.

9

9

10

⑪ Wapping Old Stairs are worth walking down, and if the tide is out you can go onto the shoreline and see the blocked-up riverside entrance to **Wapping Basin** (watch out – the steps can be very slippery). The stairs were used for centuries by pirates, smugglers, adventurers and ordinary travellers. The notorious 'Hanging Judge' George Jeffreys (1645-89) was caught on these stairs (or, according to some versions of the story, in the pub) whilst in disguise and seeking a last drink before attempting to flee the country in 1688. He was, ironically, said to have been identified, by a former prisoner he had convicted. Jeffreys died of kidney disease in the Tower of London the following year.

The bottom of the stairs is possibly the site of Execution Dock – where the Admiralty hanged pirates and smugglers for around 400 years up until 1830. The most famous victim was William 'Captain' Kidd, who originally worked for the Admiralty before targeting French ships for his own benefit. After being caught he was hanged here in 1701, though the rope broke on the first attempt. His dead body, in accordance with tradition, was left to be washed over by three tides before being tarred and hung up as a deterrent to others.

Opposite the **Town of Ramsgate** you head through a gate into the former churchyard of ⑫ **St John's Church**. Across the churchyard you can see the church tower – the only part of the building to survive the Blitz and now incorporated into an apartment block. On the right is the former church charity school, which retains its original stone figures of a boy and girl. The church was built in 1756 and the school four years later.

Continue along Tench Street passing the ⑬ **Turk's Head Café**, once a Victorian pub popular with the Irish dockers. The façade still contains its early 20th-century brewery signage advertising long defunct brands of ale. This is a good place to stop for a break and is very friendly.

Head north with the old security wall of the London Docks on your left. As you pass the John Orwell sports centre, the football pitches you can see through the gates lie on the now filled-in site of Wapping Basin. Continue up Reardon Street looking out on the left-hand wall for a plaque commemorating former Wapping resident Vice-Admiral William Bligh (1754-1817). Bligh was a great seaman, but his achievements are overshadowed by his command of the Bounty and the mutiny led by Fletcher Christian in 1789. Christian had actually been recruited by Bligh in Wapping. They drank together in the Town of Ramsgate before setting out on the ill-fated voyage.

Continue through Discovery Way into **⑭ Tobacco Dock**, which contains a Grade I listed warehouse built in 1812. As its name suggests, it served as a storage place for imported tobacco, plus other expensive goods including spirits and wine. Tobacco Dock was also the connecting dock between the now filled-in Eastern and Western Docks, and is the only substantial part of London Docks to survive after their closure in 1971 and subsequent redevelopment. Today the former warehouse stands empty despite recent attempts to convert it into an upmarket shopping arcade.

The two ships outside are replicas of an 18th-century merchant ship and an American schooner captured during the Anglo-American War (1812-1814). Leave Tobacco Dock for now, passing by the grand entrance on Wapping Lane. On top of the gates are carved figures of boars' heads and barrels, symbolic of the wine, spirits and animal furs once imported here.

Whilst hard to imagine now in this quiet part of London, the area around the docks would have once teemed with people. In 1849 Henry Mayhew described a typical morning as 'one of the most extraordinary and least known scenes of this metropolis... congregated within the principal entrance masses of men of all grades, looks, and kinds. There are decayed and bankrupt master butchers, master bakers, publicans, grocers, old soldiers, old sailors, Polish refugees, broken-down gentlemen, discharged lawyers' clerks, suspended

Government clerks, almsmen, pensioners, servants, thieves – indeed, every one who wants a loaf and is willing to work for it. The London Dock is one of the few places in the metropolis where men can get employment without either character or recommendation'.

Continue north up Wapping Lane until you reach the Highway, formerly the Ratcliff Highway, which was notorious in the 18th and 19th centuries for its high levels of crime and vice. The **Ratcliff Highway Murders** were committed here in December 1811, and were regarded as the most gruesome in the capital's history until upstaged by the Whitechapel Murders of 1888 that were carried out by Jack the Ripper.

The first of the seven murders took place at number 29 on the Highway, just east of Artichoke Hill, where a car showroom now stands. Draper Timothy Marr, his wife Celia and their child, as well as their shop boy James Gowan, were all brutally murdered in their home. The murderer struck again twelve days later at the Kings Arms Inn which once stood at 81 New Gravel Lane, now Garnet Street, killing publican John Williamson, his wife Elizabeth, and their servant Bridget Anna Harrington. In an age before a national police force existed, panic spread throughout the area and around 40 arrests were made by the authorities. A sailor named John Williams was eventually charged with the murders but killed himself in prison before trial. As was then the custom with suicides, his body was buried with a stake through its heart at a crossroads. It was later rediscovered in 1886 at the junction of Cannon Street Road and Cable Street. A local publican kept Williams' skull on display for his customers.

Cross the Highway to visit ⓱ **St George-in-the-East**, the burial place for the murder victims. The church was built between 1714 and 1729 and is one of only six churches in London designed by (Wren's great pupil) Nicholas Hawksmoor (1661-1736). It boasts a huge 160-feet tower whose clock was designed to be seen by ships on the Thames. The interior was later gutted during the Blitz, and was rebuilt in the 1960s as a modern space within Hawksmoor's shell. The church is normally open daily.

Head back over the Highway down Chigwell Hill (opposite Cannon Street Road) and then Pennington Street. On your right

18 Raine's charity school

you can see the imposing site of Rupert Murdoch's  **16 News International buildings**, known as 'Fortress Wapping', that occupy the northern half of the former site of the Western Dock. It was outside the gates that Murdoch's vicious battle with the print unions was fought in 1986, his victory sounding the death-knell for the old traditions of Fleet Street.

Walk along Pennington Street to reach, on the right-hand side, the main entrance into Tobacco Dock. Just inside the entrance are statues of a boy and a tiger on one side and a bear on the other. Both remember **Jamrach's** animal emporium, which was located nearby in the 19th century. Sailors arriving at the docks would often visit Jamrach's to sell animals collected during their voyages, and at any one time the shop might have stocked elephants, monkeys, snakes, rare birds and bears.

The statue of the boy and tiger recalls a tragedy in 1857 when a Bengal tiger being escorted by Jamrach escaped and injured a little boy. One of Jamrach's workers beat the tiger off with an iron bar but in doing so fatally injured the child. The commonly told story that Jamrach saved the boy from the tiger's jaws is sadly wishful thinking. A few days later *The Times* reported that the tiger – sold to a travelling menagerie – broke out again and killed a lion in a terrific fight.

Walk right through Tobacco Dock, passing the former **17 wine vaults** that were once the largest in London. Exit on the south side to come out near the replica ships seen earlier and continue down Wapping Lane.

A detour down Raine Street on the left leads you to the former **18 Raine's charity school**, dating from 1719. The building still

retains the original figures of a charity girl and boy on the outside and the stone lintel over the main entrance announces: 'Come in & Learn Your Duty to God and man – 1719'.

At the back of Raine Street is Farthing Fields where the workhouse of St George-in-the-East used to stand. In *The Uncommercial Traveller* (c.1860) Charles Dickens described his visit to the workhouse, a place he found to be 'thoroughly well administered by a most intelligent master'. Many of the casual dockers who failed to secure work from the foreman would have ended up here, although even for the very poor the workhouse was seen as a last resort given the typically terrible conditions that resulted in high mortality rates.

Back on Wapping Lane you pass the Anglo-Catholic church of **⑲ St Peter's London Docks**, which dates from 1866 and has its origins in an even earlier mission. Its first vicar, Charles Lowder, was known as the 'Father of Wapping' because of his dedication to the local people, particularly during a great cholera outbreak in the 1860s when he refused to leave his post.

Further down Wapping Lane take a right down Watts Street, passing ⑳ **Turner's Old Star**. This pub is thought to have once been owned by the painter J. M. W. Turner (1775-1851). Turner was drawn to this area near the Thames because of the quality of the light. He was a secretive man who maintained a number of mistresses, including Sophia Booth, a widowed landlady from Margate. Legend has it that after Turner inherited this property he converted it into a tavern and installed Mrs Booth as the landlady.

Continue onto Tench Street and retrace your steps towards the Thames, cutting through the pleasant park on your left. Just beside the Turk's Head Café take a small detour along Green Bank Street to visit ㉑ **St Patrick's in Wapping**, a fine late 19th century Catholic church whose congregation was once largely composed of Irish dockers. It was also used for some scenes in the seminal London gangster film *The Long Good Friday* (1980).

When you are back on Wapping High Street head left (eastwards), passing a number of former warehouses that have in recent years been converted into offices or flats. Even after the Georgian docks were built many of the smaller wharves and quays along the Thames bank continued to function. In the 19th century this part of Wapping was known as 'Sailor Town'. At one time sailors could choose between 37 pubs that lined Wapping High Street.

The sailors were described by the Victorian social commentator Thomas Beames in his 1852 book on the rookeries (or slums) of London thus: 'Go there by day, and every fourth man you meet is a sailor; you will hear German, French, Spanish, and even modern Greek, spoken by those whose dress at once connects them with our mercantile marine. Some are Negroes, many foreigners – but the Jersey frock – the souwester, or tarpaulin hat – the pilot coat and pea jacket – the large trousers gathered in tight at the hips – the rolling walk as though the ship was pitching beneath them – the low quartered shoes with large bows, are characteristics of a race, which, whether at home or abroad, are distinguished in a moment from the rest of the population. Public houses abound in these localities: it is difficult to conceive how so many can thrive...'. The Museum of Docklands on the Isle of Dogs seen in the second docklands walk contains a reconstruction of Sailor Town with its maze of alleyways (www.museumindocklands.org.uk).

Unsurprisingly crime was a major problem in Wapping, and it resulted in the foundation here of Britain's first police service – **㉒ The Marine Police Force** – in 1798. The original force used rowing boats to patrol the Thames and catch members of local gangs such as the River Pirates, Night Plunderers, Light Horsemen, and Scuffle-Hungers. The force was founded nearly thirty years before the Metropolitan Police, and became the Thames Division of the Met in 1839. Today the Marine Support Unit of the Metropolitan Police Service is still based in Wapping High Street, and on your right you can see the modern white design of the force's boat yard. The division's headquarters are found just a few doors along, the building dating from 1907 but is standing on the site of the original headquarters founded in 1798.

Just past the police headquarters is the **㉓ Captain Kidd** pub, once part of the workshop of the neighbouring St John's Wharf. Dedicated to the pirate mentioned earlier, it is a good place for a stop as it offers fantastic panoramic views over the Thames. It has

also been suggested that Execution Dock – referred to above – was actually located near the shoreline by the pub.

Continuing along Wapping High Street you pass **㉔ Phoenix Wharf**, **㉕ King Henry's Stairs** and then **㉖ Gun Wharf**. The latter two names recall that Henry VIII's foundries, used in the production of cannon for his Navy ships, were based around here.

If your legs can stand it you can continue to part 2 of the Docklands walk or alternatively Wapping station is close at hand. ●

23 *Captain Kidd public house*

VISIT...

The Wapping Project (see p.320)
Wapping Hydraulic Power
Station, Wapping Wall, E1W
www.thewappingproject.com

Wilton's Music Hall
Graces Alley, Tower Hamlets, E1
www.wiltons.org.uk
The world's oldest surviving
Grand Music Hall (10 min walk
from St Katharine Docks).

EAT, DRINK...

Dickens Inn (see p.300)
Saint Katherines Row, E1W
www.dickensinn.co.uk

Town of Ramsgate (see p.302)
62 Wapping High Street, E1W

Turk's Head Café (see p.305)
1 Green Bank, E1W

Captain Kidd pub (see p.312)
108 Wapping High St, E1W

12 Docklands Walk
Part 2

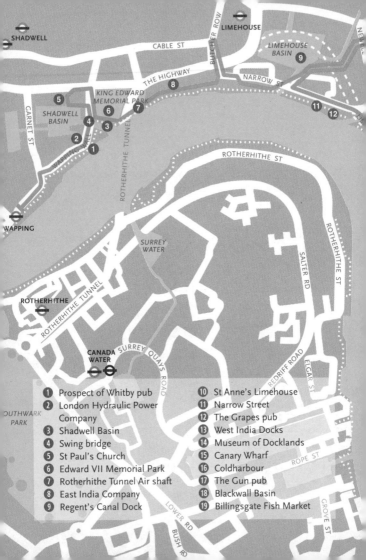

SHADWELL

CABLE ST

THE HIGHWAY

BUTCHER ROW

LIMEHOUSE

LIMEHOUSE BASIN

⑨

NARROW ST

⑪ ⑫

KING EDWARD MEMORIAL PARK

GARNET ST

⑤

SHADWELL BASIN

⑥

④ ③ ⑦

⑧

② ①

WAPPING ST

ROTHERHITHE TUNNEL

ROTHERHITHE ST

WAPPING

SURREY WATER

ROTHERHITHE TUNNEL

SALTER RD

REDRIFF ROAD

ELGAR ST

ROTHERHITHE ST

ROTHERHITHE

CANADA WATER

SURREY QUAYS ROAD

SOUTHWARK PARK

RÓPE ST

GROVE ST

LOWER RD

BUSH RD

① Prospect of Whitby pub	⑩ St Anne's Limehouse
② London Hydraulic Power Company	⑪ Narrow Street
	⑫ The Grapes pub
③ Shadwell Basin	⑬ West India Docks
④ Swing bridge	⑭ Museum of Docklands
⑤ St Paul's Church	⑮ Canary Wharf
⑥ Edward VII Memorial Park	⑯ Coldharbour
⑦ Rotherhithe Tunnel Air shaft	⑰ The Gun pub
⑧ East India Company	⑱ Blackwall Basin
⑨ Regent's Canal Dock	⑲ Billingsgate Fish Market

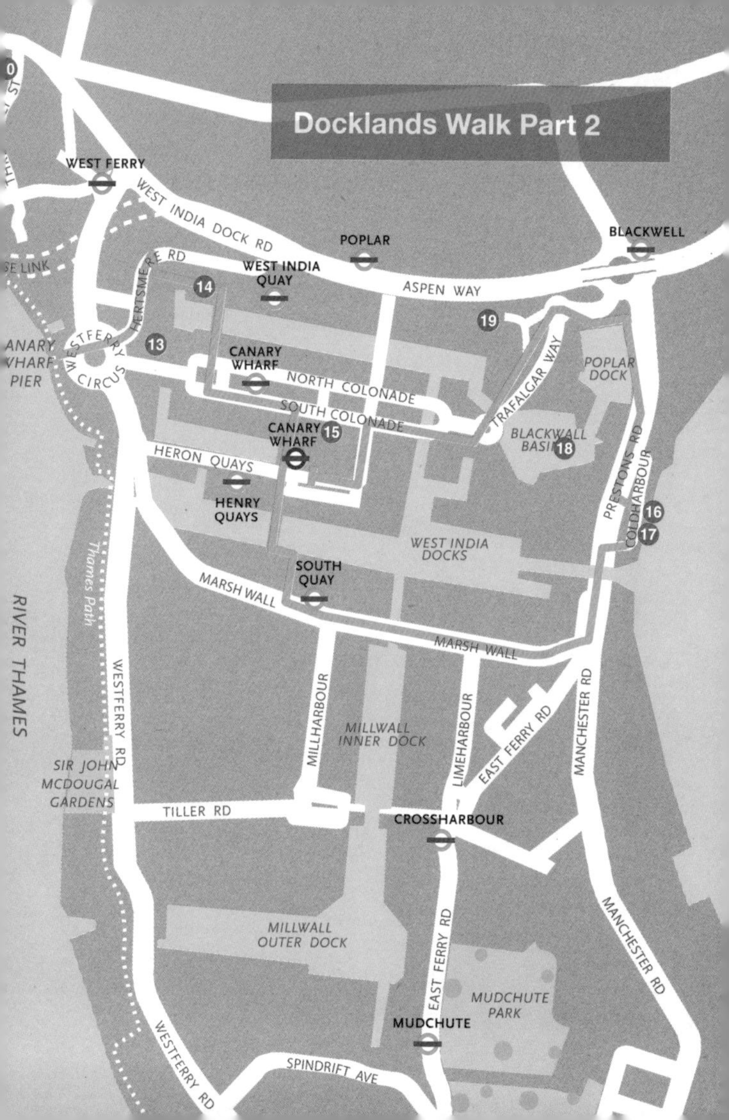

Docklands Walk Part 2

WEST FERRY

WEST INDIA DOCK RD

POPLAR

BLACKWELL

LIMEHOUSE LINK

WEST INDIA QUAY

ASPEN WAY

LIMEHARBOUR RD

WESTFERRY RD

CANARY WHARF PIER

14

13

CANARY WHARF

NORTH COLONADE

19

TRAFALGAR WAY

POPLAR DOCK

WESTFERRY CIRCUS

SOUTH COLONADE

CANARY WHARF

15

BLACKWALL BASIN

18

PRESTONS RD

COLDHARBOUR

16

17

HERON QUAYS

HENRY QUAYS

WEST INDIA DOCKS

RIVER THAMES

Thames Path

SOUTH QUAY

MARSH WALL

MARSH WALL

WESTFERRY RD

MILLHARBOUR

MILLWALL INNER DOCK

LIMEHARBOUR

EAST FERRY RD

MANCHESTER RD

SIR JOHN MCDOUGAL GARDENS

TILLER RD

CROSSHARBOUR

MILLWALL OUTER DOCK

EAST FERRY RD

MANCHESTER RD

MUDCHUTE PARK

WESTFERRY RD

MUDCHUTE

SPINDRIFT AVE

1 Hanging gibbet, Prospect of Whitby public house

Docklands Walk Part 2

Start: Wapping Tube Station
Finish: Canary Wharf underground station
Distance: 5.2 miles

Part 2 of the Docklands walk can be explored as a continuation of the previous walk for those with the stamina and time, but it can also be the first point of departure for those wanting to explore this unique area of London. The walk starts at Wapping underground station on the East London Line. Trains travelling south from here pass under the Thames to Rotherhithe through what was the **world's first river tunnel** – the Thames Tunnel – built by father and son Marc and Isambard Kingdom Brunel between 1823 and 1843. Dogged by problems and worker fatalities during construction, the tunnel was eventually opened for pedestrian traffic only and taken over by the underground in 1869.

You can rejoin the Thames Path through a red-gated entrance on the right. This takes you along the river passing some modern apartment blocks and an old anchor found during the excavation of St Hilda's Wharf in the 1980s. The path soon takes you away from the river and you come out at New Crane Stairs to see Garnet Street on the right. Writer Johnny Speight used this name for his Wapping-dwelling character Alf Garnett, star of long-running sitcom *Till Death Us Do Part*.

Bear right onto Wapping Wall road before picking up signs again for the Thames Path. Wapping Wall is built on top of the original wall constructed in late medieval times to prevent the Thames from flooding the area. On the right you will soon see the ❶ **Prospect of Whitby** public house whose origins may date as far back as the 1520s. At the rear is a hanging gibbet that recalls the justice once handed out to pirates. Now a renowned gastropub, it used to be one of many public houses in the area that swarmed with East End low-life, and was aptly nicknamed the 'Devil's Tavern'. The reputation did not deter the likes of Samuel Pepys, Charles Dickens and J. M. W. Turner from enjoying a drink here. In 1777 the name of

the pub was changed to refer to the Prospect, a collier ship from Whitby that was moored nearby for many years and which became a local landmark.

Opposite the Prospect is a stylish red-brick building formerly owned by the ❷ **London Hydraulic Power Company**. Dating from 1890, it was one of a number of local plants that provided hydraulic power to work the cranes, capstans, bridges and lock gates in the surrounding docks, and it remained in use until 1977. Today the building is home to the Wapping Project Gallery, an arts complex which is worth a visit.

Just outside the Prospect take a right and head along the Thames Path. This leads you round to the former entrance of ❸ **Shadwell Basin**, the last of the three basins on this walk that connected the Thames to the London Docks. Shadwell, like Wapping, was once a rural hamlet that supported a small-scale fishing and seafaring industry. It adjoined the Hamlet of Ratcliffe just to the east, although the latter has now disappeared as a distinct area, courtesy of extensive road building, slum clearances, and the devastation caused during the Blitz.

Walk towards the original red ❹ **swing bridge** – once powered by the London Hydraulic Power Company – and cross over to see the vast expanse of Shadwell Basin. Today this is used primarily for water sports and other leisure activities. Follow the path on the right until you reach some steps in the wall that take you to ❺ **St Paul's Church**, clearly visible above.

Shadwell was famous in the 18th century for the number of master mariners who lived there. St Paul's became known as 'the Church of the Sea Captains', 75 of whom were buried in its vaults. The explorer Captain James Cook (1728-79) was perhaps the most famous parishioner, and his son James was baptised here in 1763. Jane Randolph was also baptised here in 1720, later moving to America where she gave birth to the future US president Thomas Jefferson.

The original church fell into disrepair and was rebuilt in the 1820s as a 'Waterloo Church' – one of 600 churches built in the early 19th century following the Church Building Act of 1818. The Act's wording referred to the parish having a population of 10,000 people, 'the far greater part of them being labourers in the docks and on the River'. Inside the church look out for a list of benefactors to the charity school, which includes a number of sea captains. The former school building still stands opposite the church.

Leave the church by the main entrance and follow the map along the Highway onto Glamis Road to reach the red

swing bridge again and then head south down a narrow alleyway towards the Thames. This skirts alongside the ❻ **King Edward VII Memorial Park** on your left, built in the 1920s. Much of old Shadwell, including its slum housing, was demolished to make way for it.

As you reach the Thames Path again head eastwards and look out for a circular brick building. This is actually an ❼ **air shaft** for the **Rotherhithe Tunnel** running directly underneath. The tunnel was opened in 1908 by George Prince of Wales (later King George V).

On the rear of the air shaft you can see a ceramic tile placed here in memory of 'navigators who in the latter half of the sixteenth century set sail from this reach of the River Thames near Ratcliffe Cross'. Ratcliffe Cross was a place on Narrow Street, slightly further to the east, that marked the boundary of the Pool of London, and which also served as the starting point of many Elizabethan voyages of exploration.

Continue along the path and on your left, after the massive modern Free Trade Wharf development, you will see some fine

Georgian buildings once owned by the ⑧ **East India Company**, the great trading concern that at its peak controlled vast swathes of the British Empire including India. The Company built the warehouses in the late 18th century, although they were partly destroyed in a huge fire of 1794 that devastated much of Ratcliffe and is regarded as the most destructive fire to have taken place in London between the Great Fire of 1666 and the Blitz of 1940. Just past these warehouses on the left you can see the modern Atlantic Wharf building, which stands on the site of where – at least until the end of the 19th century – a small inlet called Ratcliffe Dock was located.

Continue on until the path heads away from the Thames and takes you to the start of Narrow Street. At this point those interested in the history of the 12th-century Foundation of St Katharine can see its current home by heading north across the busy highway and then up Butcher Row. The Foundation is on the right-hand side, but cannot be visited by the public. It is no longer serves as a hospital, and the building is mainly used as a conference centre for those involved in religious matters.

Back on Narrow Street continue east until you see a sign for the Thames Path on the right, which you follow. You soon come to the entrance of ⑨ **Regent's Canal Dock**, now known as Limehouse Basin. Walk up the stairs past Gordon Ramsay's gastropub – **the Narrow** – which occupies the old dockmaster's house. Cross the bridge to join the pathway that skirts around the dock.

Opened in 1820, Regent's Canal Dock covered ten acres and was used by seagoing vessels offloading goods distributed via England's extensive canal system. Not initially successful; it eventually carved out a niche for itself by the mid 19th century supplying coal to power stations. The dock declined because of the railways and it was later renamed Limehouse Basin. The dock continued to be used for commercial trade as late as the 1960s and today is now mainly used as a berthing place for leisure boats.

The dock is connected both to the Regent's Canal and the River Lee Navigation (via the Limehouse Cut). Follow the sign for Limehouse Cut and pass under two overhead bridges until you see an opening on the right-hand side. This leads into a little park which you walk through. At the entrance cross over Newell Street with its Georgian houses to reach ❿ **St Anne's Limehouse**.

St Anne's is another of Hawksmoor's rare group of London churches and was consecrated in 1730. Hawksmoor's Baroque building was badly damaged by fire in 1850 and later restored by Philip Hardwick. The churchyard contains an intriguing pyramid, thought to have been designed by Hawksmoor for the church tower. The architectural historian **Sir Nikolaus Pevsner** described it as a 'remarkable pyramid, of unknown date and unknown purpose'. It stands about three metres high and has the *'The Wisdom of Solomon'* inscribed upon it in both Hebrew and English. In recent years some writers have suggested Hawksmoor was more interested in Pagan or Freemasonry symbolism and see this as yet another example of his attempts to infiltrate his designs into a Christian context.

Retrace your steps from the church back to Narrow Street and continue eastwards through Limehouse, an area named after the lime oast houses that existed here from the 14th century. By 1610 half of Limehouse's population of 2,000 people were seafarers. Later it became a popular location for Chinese sailors who had been left stranded in London. Many had joined the Blue Funnel Line, a shipping company that refused its deckhands a return passage.

As a result many Chinese sailors ended up settling in Limehouse, often marrying local women and generally keeping a low profile. At the most around 2,000 such sailors lived in the area, but their use of opium created a reputation – largely exaggerated – of vice-ridden Limehouse dens where honest citizens were corrupted by drugs and young women sold into the mythical white slave trade.

Many writers and social commentators felt compelled to investigate the illicit pleasures on offer, and as a result Limehouse's opium dens feature in many books of the era including Charles Dickens's *The Mystery of Edwin Drood*, Oscar Wilde's *A Picture of Dorian Grey*, and several Sherlock Holmes novels by Arthur Conan Doyle. In the popular books of Sax Rohmer, the villain Dr Fu Manchu and his evil gang were often to be found in dens of Limehouse. The Fu Manchu stories were later made into a series of popular films in the mid 20th century, thus ensuring Limehouse became known internationally for its legendary vices.

During the first half of the 20th century, and largely goaded on by the popular press, the local authorities planned London's original 'Chinatown' out of existence. Laws were introduced to clamp down on drugs and prevent the hiring of Chinese sailors. Streets popular with the Chinese were demolished to make way for new roads. From the time of the anti-Chinese riots that took place in 1919 in East London until the 1950s, the Chinese community in Limehouse gradually disappeared. A new, more socially acceptable version of Chinatown grew up around Gerrard Street in Soho where it continues to thrive to this day. However, a rare remnant of the old Limehouse Chinese community can be seen at 50 East India Dock Road where the Chun Yee Society School is situated, hosting both a Chinese school and old people's club.

⑪ Narrow Street contains a cluster of late 17th and early 18th-century houses (see numbers 78-94) and is one of the East End's most historic streets. It has attracted a number of well-known residents over the years including David Lean (1908-91). The director of *Brief Encounter*, *Lawrence of Arabia* and *Dr Zhivago*, bought four derelict houses in Sun Wharf on Narrow Street in the 1980s. He then spent £6 million creating a fantastic river-facing house that is regarded as one of the best in London and which is still owned by his family.

Make sure you visit number 76 – **⑫ the Grapes public house**. The original inn was rebuilt in 1720 and was well known to Charles Dickens. As a boy he used to come to Limehouse to visit his godfather, who was a sail-maker living in Newell Street. His godfather often brought Dickens to the pub where he was made to stand on a table and sing to the customers.

The writer used the Grapes as the inspiration for the Six Jolly Fellowship Porters public house depicted in *Our Mutual Friend* (1865). In the book he describes 'a narrow lopsided wooden jumble of corpulent windows heaped one upon another as you might heap as many toppling oranges, with a crazy wooden verandah impending over the water... The available space in it was not much larger than a hackney-coach; but no one could have wished the bar bigger'. The description still runs true today.

Shortly after the Grapes, pick up another sign for the Thames Path and head back out alongside the river to get fantastic views of One Canada Square (better known as the Canary Wharf Tower) – the tallest building in Britain – situated on the Isle of Dogs. There is a short walk now that leads you around the beginning of the 'U' shaped peninsula that is home to the Isle of Dogs. Cross a narrow modern bridge over Limekiln Dock. If you have time, walk along the path on the right-hand side of the dock to see a building at the far end that retains its original signage for **J&R Wilson 'Ship Stores'**.

Continue past the new and distinctive Dundee Wharf on the left and soon you arrive at Westferry Circus in Canary Wharf, situated on the Isle of Dogs. For many centuries Limehouse was seen as the eastern limit of central London, with the Isle of Dogs

12 *The Grapes Public House, Narrow Street*

regarded as a marshland, largely uninhabited and rarely visited. Although it is not actually an island, the interlocking docks and canals constructed across the peninsula in the 19th century have almost made it one.

In medieval times it was known as Stepney Marsh, and the current name was first mentioned in 1588 – perhaps in reference to Henry VIII's hunting dogs (which may have been kennelled here), or the 'dykes' constructed by the Dutch engineers who drained the marshes. Until the late 18th century there were less than a handful of buildings in the whole area, but that changed when the huge West India Docks were opened on the northern side.

An Act of Parliament in 1799 paved the way for the construction of ⑬ **West India Docks**. Its owners were merchants with commercial interests in the West Indies. The momentum to build the docks was largely driven by the energies of merchant Robert Milligan (1746-1809). He had been shocked upon his return to London by the theft and delays suffered by his ships whilst they tried to offload their cargoes in the Pool of London.

By 1802 the Import Dock was completed, with the parallel Export Dock to the south finished three years later. To the south of the West India Docks ran the City Canal, a channel cut right across the Isle of Dogs to allow ships to avoid the long journey around the peninsula. However, the City Canal was never very successful and was later taken over by the West India Dock Company. The company then turned the canal into a third parallel dock and re-named it the South West India Dock.

Initially the West India Docks only dealt with goods from the West Indies such as rum, molasses and sugar. The original Import Dock covered 30 acres and was the first commercial wet dock in London. Eventually the West India Docks would cover a huge 295 acres, most of which is now covered by the Canary Wharf estate.

Ships would enter the West India Docks from the Blackwall Basin on the eastern side of the peninsula, with the smaller 'lighters' entering from Limehouse Basin on the west side (now filled in). The docks could berth up to 600 vessels at any one time, and they were surrounded by a moat and six-metre high security wall patrolled by armed guards – the first London docks to be completely enclosed. Within the walls were five storey warehouses, and the Import Dock alone contained an unbroken line of warehouses that stretched for three-quarters of a mile.

Follow the map across Westferry Circus and cross over to Hertsmere Road. Taking this road you will see an entrance on your right that will take you to the former Import Dock.

Walk slightly further along Hertsmere Road, looking out on the left for the Georgian dockmaster's house, and just past this the remnants of the dock gates where the infamous 'call on' for casual dockers took place behind a chain. Walk back to the entrance to the Import Dock. The small circular building opposite dates from 1803 and was once the guardhouse. By the entrance there is commemorative tablet that neatly describes the purpose of the docks, to offer 'complete security and ample accommodation (hitherto not afforded) to the shipping and produce of the West Indies at this wealthy port. The first stone was laid on Saturday the Twelfth Day of July, A.D. 1800, by [prime minister] William Pitt... and Robert Milligan'.

14

15

Enter the former Import Dock, flanked by some surviving Georgian warehouse buildings and modern office blocks. Immediately on the left, behind a bronze statue of Milligan, is an old sugar warehouse which today is home to the excellent ⑭ **Museum of Docklands** (open daily 10am-6pm), which explores many aspects of the fascinating history of London's docks. If you need a break, the museum has a café, and there are also plenty of other restaurants lining the Import Dock.

When finished at the museum, continue along the north quay of Import Dock and cross over the bridge into the heart of the modern ⑮ **Canary Wharf** development. This has been the most successful regeneration project in the Docklands, and in barely 20 years has begun to challenge the Square Mile as the preferred London location of many global financial institutions. You may wish to finish the walk here and leave Canary Wharf via one of the DLR stations, or the Canary Wharf underground station, all of which are clearly signposted.

Alternatively, if you have the energy to see a little more of the remnants of the old docks, carry on through Cabot Square and then head left down South Colonnade, bearing right to follow the signs for the Jubilee Line. This takes you out into an open area situated on the site of the filled-in sections of the former Export Dock. Head south and walk through Jubilee Place. As you exit Jubilee Place cross the footbridge on the other side, which takes you out over the former South West India dock. On the other side, walk down Admiral's Way to join Marsh Wall and then head east.

On your right you will see the top of the reverse 'L' of the former Millwall Dock that was opened in 1868 and specialised in timber and grain from the Baltic. Millwall Dock covered a 200-acre site right in the heart of the Isle of Dogs, and was eventually connected to the West India Docks complex in 1927 before being closed in 1980. Today the old dock is mainly used for watersports.

At this point head north off Marsh Wall and join a footpath that skirts the southern edge of South Quay. After a few minutes you will reach the eastern side of the Isle of Dogs and head north up Preston's Road, crossing a bridge that spans the eastern entrance to the docks. Shortly on your right walk up **16** **Coldharbour**, whose Georgian houses are the oldest buildings on the Isle of Dogs. The historic **17** **Gun** public house is located here, with its origins in the early 18th century. It is named after the cannon fired to celebrate the opening of the West India Docks in 1802 and legend has it that Lord Nelson, who stayed at number three (now called Nelson's House), used to come here for illicit liaisons with his mistress Lady Hamilton in an upstairs room. The Gun was also a haunt for smugglers and still has a spy-hole used to watch out for the 'Revenue Men'.

Continue north up Preston's Road looking out for ⑱ **Blackwall Basin** on your left, once the main entrance for ships entering West India Docks. Near the entrance you can see a fine Grade II listed Georgian house built for the dock supervisor by John Rennie in 1819.

Just to the north of Blackwall Basin, and reached through a small entrance in the wall, is **Poplar Dock**. Originally a reservoir and timber pond, from 1852 it became a railway dock for coal and other goods and now serves as a marina. Follow the path around Poplar Dock and on the north-west side come out onto Trafalgar Way (opposite the McDonalds).

From here bear left at the roundabout and walk towards the vast tower of One Canada Square, with the modern ⑲ **Billingsgate Fish Market** on your right. The road takes you back into the heart of the Canary Wharf complex and you soon will see signposts for the DLR or Jubilee line stations that signal the end of the walk. ●

VISIT...

Billingsgate Fish Market
Trafalgar Way, E14
www.billingsgate-market.org.uk

Museum of Docklands
(see p.330)
No1 Warehouse,
West India Quay, E14 4AL
www.museumindocklands.org.uk

GREENWICH:
National Maritime Museum
Royal Observatory
(www.rmg.co.uk)
Greenwich Market

EAT, DRINK...

Prospect of Whitby (see p.319)
57 Wapping Wall, E1W

The Narrow (see p.323)
44 Narrow Street, E14
www.gordonramsay.com

The Grapes (see p.326)
76 Narrow Street, E14
www.thegrapes.co.uk

The Gun (see p.331)
27 Coldharbour, E14
www.thegundocklands.com

18 *Blackwall Basin*

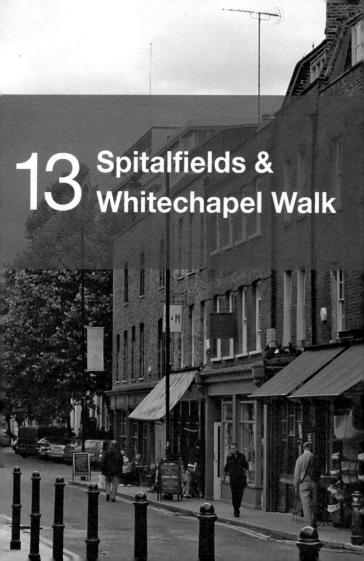

13 Spitalfields & Whitechapel Walk

Spitalfields & Whitechapel Walk

THREE

BETHNAL GREEN

COLLINGWOOD ST

HEADLAM

1. Bishopsgate Institute
2. Dennis Severs's House
3. Elder Street
4. Weaver's attic windows
5. Spitalfields Market
6. St Mary Spital Charnel House
7. Christ Church Spitalfields
8. A. Gold
9. Sandy's Row
10. Sandy's Row Synagogue
11. Artillery Passage
12. Gun Street
13. No. 56 & 58 Artillery Lane
14. Night Refuge & Convent
15. Miller's Court
16. Jews Free School
17. Jewish Soup Kitchen
18. Moorish Market
19. Christ Church School
20. Jamme Masjid Mosque

29. CH. N. Katz
30. Old Truman Brewery
31. Hanbury Street
32. Sunday market
33. Beigel Shop
34. Spitalfields City Farm
35. Eastside Books
36. Sheraz Bangla Lounge
37. E. Elfes Ltd
38. Blooms
39. Royal London Hospital
40. No. 259 Whitechapel Road
41. Edward VII monument
42. Blind Beggar pub
43. Whitechapel Idea Store
44. The Grave Maurice pub

DURWARD ST

WHITECHAPEL

RAVEN RD

OLD MONTAGUE ST

WHITECHAPEL RD

VALLANCE RD

FIELDGATE ST

FULBOURNE ST

NEW RD

CAVELL ST

GREATOREX ST

BRIXTON ST

CHESHIRE ST

45. Tower House
46. Fieldgate Street Synagogue
47. Whitechapel Bell Foundry
48. Altab Ali Park
49. Water fountain
50. No. 88 Whitechapel Road
51. Whitechapel Art Gallery
52. White Hart Pub
53. Red brick arch
54. Toynbee Hall
55. Wentworth Street Model Dwellings
56. Petticoat Lane
57. East India Company Warehouses

FIELDGATE ST

FORDHAM ST

21. Russian Steam Baths
22. S Schwartz
23. The Minister's House
24. Ten Bells Pub
25. Christ Church Spitalfields
26. Puma Court
27. Princelet Street
28. No. 19 Princelet Street

COMMERCIAL RD

Spitalfields & Whitechapel Walk

Start/Finish: Liverpool Street underground/rail station
Distance: 4.5 miles

The walk begins from Liverpool Street station and is best undertaken – if you are feeling energetic – on a Sunday morning when the three historic markets of Spitalfields, Petticoat Lane and Brick Lane are in full swing. From the station head north up Bishopsgate, passing the distinctive ❶ **Bishopsgate Institute** on the right hand side. The Institute – opened in 1894 – was designed by Charles Harrison Townsend (1851-1928). His distinctive style can be seen again later on in the walk as he was also responsible for the Whitechapel Art Gallery. The Institute to this day continues to offer a wide variety of courses aimed at adults, and its quiet library contains an unusual mix of local students and City workers during the week. Continue north and turn right onto **Folgate Street**. This quiet road, full of elegant Georgian townhouses, is the first evidence of Spitalfields's strong association with successive waves of immigrants who have passed through this area over the centuries.

At number 18 Folgate Street is ❷ **Dennis Severs's house** – an excellent example of an early 18th-century Spitalfields house. Severs was an eccentric American, now deceased, who bought the house for £20,000 in the 1970s and lovingly restored it. He laid out each room as it would have appeared to a family with French Calvinist (or 'Huguenot') origins who Severs imagined living here between 1719 and 1914. The naturally-lit interior in which visitors creep around under an order of silence makes for one of the most atmospheric attractions in London. The artist David Hockney described the experience as being comparable to a performance of one of the world's great operas.

② Dennis Severs's House, Folgate Street

The best time to visit is on one of the regular Monday night candlelight tours (booking is necessary). You can also visit on the first and third Sunday each month (between 12noon-4pm) and every Monday lunchtime following those Sundays. Check for visiting details on the website at www.dennissevershouse.co.uk (tel 020 7247 4013 between 9.30am-3pm).

The Huguenots were one of the most influential immigrant groups to settle in Spitalfields. They first began to arrive in London in the 1570s after persecution in Catholic France. The worst single atrocity they suffered being the St Bartholomew's Day Massacre in Paris in 1572 that saw around 2,000 Huguenots butchered in the streets. *Huguenot* was originally meant as a derogatory term, and possibly a corruption of 'Eidgenosse', the German word for confederate.

Many of the arriving Huguenots were skilled silk weavers, but as foreigners they were not allowed to join the established City guilds. Instead the immigrants settled outside the City walls in places such as Soho, Clerkenwell and Spitalfields and began their own businesses. The influx from France eased after the Edict of Nantes (1598), but turned into a flood after the Edict was revoked in 1685. Up to 80,000 Huguenots came to England in the following years, with half settling in London. Spitalfields proved a popular location as it had a reputation for tolerating religious non-conformists. By 1700 20,000 people living in this area were involved in the silk trade. The Huguenots lived in London as they had done in France, the first generation continuing to use French and founding nine French churches in the East End.

The Huguenot weavers originally settled in this immediate vicinity, including ❸ **Elder Street** just off Folgate Street, and the neighbouring Fleur de Lys Street. Over the years their cottages spread eastwards to Brick Lane and beyond. Some of the Georgian houses built at this time still survive, typically with large attics where the silk looms were located. The ❹ **attic windows** allowed the weavers the maximum possible light to labour under and the spaces between the floorboards were stuffed with discarded pieces of silk to stifle the noise of the looms.

Follow the map up Elder Street and Fleur de Lys Street to see some other well-preserved streets, and then head south into **Spital Square**. 'Spital' is derived from St Mary Spital, an Augustinian hospital that was founded on this site in 1197 by Walter Brune and his wife Rosia. Until it was dissolved by Henry VIII in 1538, the hospital dominated the area and its land to the east became known as 'Spital fields'. The term 'Spital' is a contraction of 'hospital'.

St Mary Spital had an outside pulpit named the Spital Cross, and by tradition sermons were preached there every Easter. This tradition was continued even after the hospital closed, and today the Spital sermons take place at the church of St Lawrence Jewry in the City.

Developed in the 1720s, Spital Square was once the finest area of housing in Spitalfields. The better-off silk merchants and master weavers lived here, although their houses were later demolished (number 37, dating from 1740, is a rare survivor). Today it is hard to imagine the extent of the French influence in places like Spitalfields during the 18th century. The Huguenots were assimilated within two or three generations into London,

5 *Spitalfields Market*

often anglicising their surnames. However, it is worth remembering that one in four Londoners is thought to be able to trace their ancestors back to these French immigrants.

Continue south to reach **5** **Spitalfields Market**, established in 1682 under a licence granted by Charles II, and originally specialising in fruit and vegetables. The current building dates largely from 1885 to 1893 and was funded by the then-owner, and former market porter, Robert Horner. The fruit and vegetable market moved to Leyton

in 1991. In recent years, despite a hard fought campaign by locals, property developers have knocked down substantial sections of the Victorian building.

A market still operates – every Thursday (antiques and vintage), Friday (fashion, art) and Sunday (general, and the busiest day). However it seems today overshadowed by the up-market shops and cafés that have sprung up in the area.

On the north side of the market look out for a staircase leading down below ground level. This lets you view the foundations of the old **6** **St Mary Spital charnel house** where the bones of the deceased were stored. A Roman burial ground was uncovered near here in 1999, the most spectacular find being a stone sarcophagus with a sealed lead coffin inside. Inside were discovered the remains of a wealthy Roman woman of the 3rd century AD. For more information about the excavations in Spitalfields visit the Museum of London (www.museumoflondon.org.uk) where many of the objects are kept on display.

Walk over to Brushfield Street to the south of the market. Ahead is one of the finest – and most imposing – church façades in London. Nicholas Hawksmoor's **7** **Christ Church Spitalfields** was built between

1714 and 1729, and is one of only six London churches he designed. Even to this day the church dwarfs the buildings around it – this was intentional as the Church of England wanted to remind the non-conformists of Spitalfields where the religious power in England really lay.

Christ Church – which can be visited later on in the walk – was frequented by descendants of the original Huguenot settlers and gravestones with French names can still be seen in the churchyard. Christ Church was shut down in the 1950s and almost demolished. However, it has recently been reopened and is now open Monday to Friday 11am-4pm if it is not in use for an event.

❽ 'A Gold' – a deli at number 42 Brushfield Street – is named after Amelie Gold, a French milliner who lived and worked here in the 1880s. The original shop sign with her name and occupation still hangs outside, a rare reminder of the textile and fashion trade that was once so important to the economy of Spitalfields.

Head down Fort Street and cross into ❾ **Sandy's Row**. On the left is the discreet entrance to the ❿ **Sandy's Row Synagogue**. Dating from 1854, it was originally a Huguenot chapel and later converted into a Synagogue by a society of Dutch immigrants known as '*Chevras Chesed v'Emes v'Menachem Avelim*' (Society of Loving Kindness, Truth & Comforters of Mourners). It is one of only four surviving synagogues in the East End when once there were over 100, and today is fighting closure due to its dwindling congregation.

Spitalfields has always been a place of great social upheaval and transformation. The silk industry went into terminal economic decline from the late 18th century as it was increasingly undercut by cheaper fabrics produced on the power-looms of the industrialised northern towns and also imports from India and China. Poverty became widespread in Spitalfields, not helped by a huge increase in the population of the East End that far outstripped the social infrastructure then available. The elegant Georgian houses once inhabited by single families were split up and turned into sweatshops and slum dwellings.

Poor immigrants have always settled where things are cheap, and during the 19th century the Jewish population of the area

grew steadily. However, after the 1880s this growth exploded as many fled the anti-Semitic pogroms then taking place in Russia and Poland. Over the next 25 years around 100,000 Jews are thought to have settled in the East End, many living in houses once occupied by earlier Huguenot immigrants.

Continue down Sandy's Row and then left along **⑪ Artillery Passage**, a narrow thoroughfare that gives a good impression of how much of London looked 200 years ago (some of the buildings date from the early 1700s). The passage, like neighbouring **⑫ Gun Street**, is named after the 'Fraternity or Guild of Artillery of Longbows, Crossbows and Handguns' who were given rights by Henry VIII to practice their archery on St Mary Spital's fields. The archers developed into the Honourable Artillery Company – the oldest regiment in the British Army – who moved their headquarters in 1658 to their current location just north of Chiswell Street in the City.

At the end of Artillery Passage look out for two Georgian houses at **⑬ numbers 56 and 58 Artillery Lane**. Both were built in 1705, with the Grade I listed number 56 the better of the pair. It has a shop front that dates from 1756 and is one of the best surviving examples of that era left in London. The houses were originally built for the Jourdains, a family of successful Huguenot silk merchants who had fled France.

At the junction with Crispin Street on the left stands the former **⑭ Providence Row Night Refuge and Convent**. Built in 1868, it provided a temporary shelter for the poor of Spitalfields and remained in use until the 1970s. It was run by the Sisters of Mercy, and was able to help 300 women and children and 50 men. The 'Men' and 'Women' signs are still visible on the brickwork outside.

Between August and November 1888 this part of the East End was terrorised by the Whitechapel Murders carried out by an unknown serial killer who became known as 'Jack the Ripper'. All of the five official victims (some claim up to 11 were murdered) were near-destitute prostitutes who lived and died in this area. Mary Jane Kelly – the fifth official victim – is believed to have lived at the Refuge when she first arrived in London in 1884. A number of the other Ripper victims also probably stayed here when they could not afford to pay for a night at one of the cheap lodging houses that were once commonplace throughout Spitalfields and Whitechapel.

Opposite the Refuge is a car park that stands on the site of **⑮ Miller's Court** in Dorset Street. This was once one of the worst slums in 19th century Spitalfields, used by the *'lowest of all prostitutes'* according to the Victorian social reformer Charles Booth. On 9 November 1888 Mary Jane Kelly was brutally murdered in a rented room in Miller's Court. It was the only time Jack the Ripper was able to carry out one of his murders without any immediate fear of being disturbed and he spent the whole night dismembering his victim, keeping the fire burning as he hung up Kelly's intestines around the room. For some unknown reason – at least officially – the murderer ended his attacks after Kelly's death. The nearest modern location to the original crime site is the unnamed service road along the north side of the car park. If you stand with the Providence Row Refuge behind you and look towards

Commercial Street, the site of Kelly's room is approximately two-thirds of the way down the service road on the left hand side – ridges marking the entrance of Miller's Court can clearly be seen on ground.

To the right of the Refuge is Bell Lane. Immediately on the right at the beginning of the lane is where the **16** **Jews Free School** once stood. It was founded in 1732 by Jewish immigrants and moved here in 1822. By the early 20th century it had become the largest school in the world with over 4,250 pupils. Former pupils include comedian Bud Flanagan, bandleader Joe Loss, diamond company owner Barney Barnato, and Morris ('Two Gun') Cohen who became a general in the Chinese army under Chiang Kai-shek. The school was bombed during WWII and later relocated to Camden.

Head down Brune Street, named after the founders of St Mary Spital. On the left you pass **Tenter Ground**, the street name recalling a time when medieval textile workers would stretch out woven cloth on frames – or 'tenters' – in this area so it could dry evenly. The phrase to 'hang on tenterhooks' is derived from this practice. The early 18th-century building on the left, originally occupied by Huguenot silk weavers, was bought for £4 million in 2008 by the artist and local resident Tracy Emin.

Continue along Brune Street to see the former **17** **Soup Kitchen for the Jewish Poor** on the left. This opened in 1902 and was one of several charity kitchens dotted throughout the East End. The original soup kitchen in

Spitalfields was opened in Brick Lane in the 18th century to help impoverished Huguenot weavers. At its peak the Brune Street Kitchen provided meals for more than 5,000 people each week. By the 1950s it was still supporting 1,200 families and only closed in 1992. Today the building has been converted into flats but retains its distinctive brick signage, including the figure of 5662 – the year 1902 in the Jewish calendar.

Follow the map to cross Commercial Street and enter Fashion Street opposite. On the right you pass an ornate building built by Abraham Davis in 1905 and known originally as the ⑱ **Moorish Market**. With around 250 small shops inside, it was designed to compete with Petticoat Lane market nearby but was never successful. The building is now home to a fashion college.

This street was once the heart of a slum full of cheap lodging houses. The Jewish writer and poet Israel Zangwill (1864-1926) lived here as a child. At the start of his influential book *Children of the Ghetto* (1892) he recalls Fashion Street as a 'dull, squalid, narrow thoroughfare in the East End... branching off in blind alleys'. The title of his hit play *The Melting Pot* passed into the English language as meaning a mix of different cultures – appropriate given the history of Spitalfields. Jack London lived in this street for about six weeks in 1902 whilst writing his devastating account of life in the East End *The People of the Abyss* (1903), and the Jewish playwright Sir Arnold Wesker grew up here in the 1930s.

Turn left onto **Brick Lane**, named after the medieval brick kilns once based here that made use of the excellent local clay. This road has in recent years become one of London's most famous streets, immortalised by books such as Monica Ali's award-winning *Brick Lane* (2003) which was also made into a film. The south side is dominated by Asian restaurants and is the centre of 'Banglatown' – a recent creation by the local Bangladeshi community modelled on the better-known Chinatowns found in many major cities.

Over one-third of the inhabitants of the London Borough of Tower Hamlets – of which Spitalfields is a part – are Bangladeshi. Of these 90% can trace their origins back to the Sylhet region of north-east Bangladesh. The Bangladeshi community now dominates

Fournier Street

much of Spitalfields in the same way as the Jewish and Huguenot communities did in earlier centuries. Many settled in this area in the second half of the 20th century, often fleeing the civil unrest that plagued what was then East Pakistan in the 1960s.

On this walk we will go up and down Brick Lane, so to begin with head northwards. On the left you pass **⑲ Christ Church School**, which dates from 1874. The original church school was founded in 1782 and the composition of its classrooms has always closely reflected the successive waves of immigrants that have settled in Spitalfields.

Continue on to reach the junction with **Fournier Street**. The corner building is the **⑳ Jamme Masjid Mosque**, the only place in the country to have been used as a place of worship by Christians (French and English), Jews and Muslims. The building – then named the *L'Eglise Neuve* – was founded in 1743 by the Huguenots and served as both a school and a chapel. As the Huguenots faded from Spitalfields the building was taken over in 1809 by the London Society. This institution was dedicated to converting members of the growing Jewish community to Christianity and offered £50 to any Jew who re-settled in a Christian district.

Despite spending many thousands of pounds the society could only claim 16 absolute converts. The society was replaced by the Methodists who occupied the building until 1897. It was then leased to the Machzike Hadath community who converted it into the Spitalfields Great Synagogue. The synagogue quickly became a focal point for Jewish life in the area and in 1912 30,000 people crowded the streets here to witness the funeral of Rabbi A. Werner.

After WWII the Jewish population in Spitalfields declined rapidly, many settling outside London after their homes had been destroyed during the Blitz. The synagogue struggled to survive against a dwindling congregation and in 1975 the building was converted for use as a mosque. The

Huguenots understood how temporary their imprint – and that of every subsequent immigrant group – would be on Spitalfields: the sundial they built on the Fournier Street side of the mosque still survives and contains the poignant inscription *'umbra sumus' ('we are shadows')*.

Opposite the mosque (at number 86 Brick Lane) is the former site of the ㉑ **Russian Steam Baths**. From the late 19th century this was where generations of local Jews would come for their weekly ritual cleansing before the start of the Sabbath. The baths closed in the early 1940s following a fire.

Continue down Fournier Street (originally Church Street), containing some of the finest Georgian houses in London. Dating from around 1720, many were originally occupied by Huguenot weavers.

In later centuries the street became run down; however, in recent years the houses have been lovingly restored and sell for millions. This has led some to suggest that the streets around Brick Lane are in danger of becoming 'embourgeoised', with the poorer residents of the area being forced to live further and further away.

One noted development in recent years has been the number of artists who have moved to the vicinity, many originally attracted by the cheap rents. Gilbert and George and Tracey Emin all have houses in Fournier Street, whilst Rachel Whiteread lives nearby. When Gilbert and George first moved here in the 1960s (their studio is at number 12) the street was mainly Jewish, and George later recalled 'The front doors were open all day. All the windows were open, so people would speak to each other from one side of the street to the other. Extraordinary antique behaviour'.

As you walk down Fournier Street look out for the old Jewish shop sign – **㉒ 'S Schwartz'** – that can be seen at number 33A. Above number 37 is an original fire protection badge, a common sight in the 18th century when there was no national fire service. Residents would pay a premium to an insurance company that operated a private fire fighting service, and erect the badge as proof of their policy. There were a number of cases recorded of crews turning up to a house fire and refusing to help the residents because they were insured by a rival company.

㉓ The Minister's House at number two is a rare example of a residential house designed by Nicholas Hawksmoor. Hawksmoor created it for the use of the minister of Christ Church Spitalfields, a function it serves to this day.

At the end of Fournier Street is the atmospheric **㉔ Ten Bells Pub**, established in 1755. Many of the prostitutes who walked the streets of Spitalfields and Whitechapel in the 1880s socialised and conducted their business here. Annie Chapman – the second victim of Jack the Ripper – was seen drinking here the night before her death. Mary Jane Kelly (mentioned above) was also a regular here and had her 'pitch' directly outside where she would wait for customers.

Hawksmoor's imposing church of **㉕ Christ Church Spitalfields** stands opposite and you may wish to visit it now. Its former church graveyard has long been known as **'Itchy Park'**, the name reflecting

its reputation as a haunt for Spitalfields' homeless since the 19th century. The author Jack London experienced a night here in 1902 whilst researching *The People of the Abyss*. He described how 'on the benches on either side arrayed a mass of miserable and distorted humanity... a welter of rags and filth, of all manner of loathsome diseases... leering monstrosities, and bestial faces'. During this era 55% of East End children died before the age of five. Sadly poverty remains a problem in Spitalfields and the homeless still congregate in Itchy Park.

Follow the map to Wilkes Street, stopping to look at **㉖ Puma Court** on the left. The almshouses halfway down Puma Court date from 1886 and contain an inscription referring to Norton Folgate. The latter was a strange district of nine acres that existed in this vicinity from medieval times until 1900. It was known as a 'liberty', meaning it was an area that was outside the normal jurisdiction of the City authorities.

Most liberties in London obtained their original privileges because they were connected to one of the great religious institutions

that dominated large parts of the capital until Henry VIII's Dissolution of the Monasteries. After this many such districts continued to benefit from these antiquated privileges, attracting criminals and debtors who were often safe from their pursuers whilst they stayed within the jurisdiction of the liberty. The great Elizabethan playwright Christopher Marlowe (1564-93) lived in Norton Folgate during the late 16th century.

Continue right up **㉗ Princelet Street. Numbers 6-10** were once home to a Yiddish theatre known as the Hebrew

26 Puma Court

Dramatic Club, founded by Jacob and Sarah Adler in 1886. A year later 17 people were crushed to death during a performance after a false fire alarm was given. The Adlers later moved to New York where they became a major influence on the American theatre and the fledgling Hollywood film industry.

28 Number 19 dates from 1719 and was originally the home of the Huguenot Ogier family who fled France to become prosperous silk weavers in Spitalfields. The building was later taken over by a group of Polish Jews in 1869 who built a synagogue at the rear. This synagogue still survives in a very fragile state and is oldest Ashkenazi synagogue in London.

During the 20th century the attic where the Ogier family had once carried on their textile business became the home to the reclusive Rodinsky family from Poland. David Rodinsky, a shy Jewish scholar, outlived his mother and sister and then one day in 1969 simply disappeared. His attic room lay unopened for several years, his fate unknown. Rodinsky has since become symbolic of how it is possible for individuals to slip unnoticed through the social safety net. His sad story has been brilliantly told in Rachel Lichtenstein's and Iain Sinclair's book *Rodinsky's Room*. Number

19 is now looked after by the Spitalfields Centre Charity. Visit the website for more information at www.19princeletstreet.org.uk.

Walk back to Brick Lane and look out on the other side for the sign **29 'CH. N. Katz'** outside Number 92. The only reminder of a shop that until just a few years ago sold string and paper bags – one of the last Jewish owned businesses on Brick Lane.

Continue north where ahead you can see the chimney and bridge of the **30 Old Truman Brewery** complex. The brewery

– originally named the Black Eagle Brewery – dominated around 11 acres of Brick Lane and had its origins in the 1660s when it came under the ownership of Joseph Truman. It was managed in the 18th century by Sir Benjamin Truman, who lived at number 91.

The Truman family connection ended in 1789, and the business was later known as the Truman, Hanbury, Buxton & Co. Brewery. It remained one of the largest and most profitable producers of beer in London. Charles Dickens refers to this prosperity in *David Copperfield* (1850) when Mrs Micawber declares: 'I have long felt the brewing business to be particularly adapted to Mr Micawber. Look at Barclay and Perkins! Look at Truman, Hanbury, and Buxton! It is on that extensive footing that Mr Micawber, I know from my own knowledge of him, is calculated to shine; and the profits, I am told, are e-NOR-mous!'.

In the 1970s the brewery employed around 2,000 people but a decline in the popularity of its beer saw production finally cease in 1988 after more than three hundred years. In recent years the old brewery buildings have been converted into over 200 units. These are typically rented by web designers, architects and artists, many of whom socialise in the bars and clubs that have sprung up all along the north side of Brick Lane.

Just before you reach the old brewery complex head left down **31 Hanbury Street**. On the left at number 22 is Christ Church Hall. This was originally built as a Huguenot chapel in around 1719,

and was later taken over by Christ Church Spitalfields. Charles Dickens once performed a book reading here, and in July 1888 it hosted a meeting in support of the 'London matchgirls' who had gone on strike at the Bryant and May match factory in Bow. The women strikers were fed up with the terrible working conditions at the factory, particularly the way in which the phosphorous used in the production process caused widespread jaw injuries. The meeting was addressed by the radical activist Annie Besant and Eleanor

Marx, daughter of Karl Marx. Against all the odds the factory owners caved in to the strikers and the victory is commemorated by a roundel on the street.

A plaque outside number 12 recalls that this was the birthplace of Jewish comedian Bud Flanagan (1896-1968), the leader of 'The Crazy Gang'. Annie Chapman – the second victim of Jack the Ripper – was found dead outside the yard of number 29 Hanbury Street on 8th September, 1888. The building has long since been demolished although Chapman's ghost is said to haunt the site of her death.

Continue up Brick Lane, which is at its vibrant best during the ㉜ **Sunday morning street market**. This has taken place since the 18th century when farmers from Essex would travel to London to sell their produce. At the north end of Brick Lane are two all-night bagel shops, another reminder of the area's traditional Jewish connections. The ㉝ **Beigel Shop** at number 155 is the oldest (and reputedly the best) in London having been founded in 1855.

Walk back down Brick Lane. This may be a good time to stop at one of the many restaurants that line the street. Just after the railway bridge over Brick Lane is Buxton Street on the left. If you have children you might want to head up here to visit the ㉞ **Spitalfields City Farm**. This covers 1.3 acres of land that was once part of a railway goods depot, and contains a variety of animals and other attractions that are popular with children. The farm is open Tuesday to Sunday 10am-4.30pm (visit www.spitalfieldscityfarm.org to see what events are on).

Continuing south down Brick Lane you might want to stop at ㉟ **Eastside Books** at number 166. This small but well-stocked shop contains a great selection of books relating to the East End and its history.

Nothing so far on the walk has presumably suggested to you that a new Messiah might live around Brick Lane, however that is what was claimed in the early 1980s by the Scottish mystic Benjamin Crème (b. 1922). He spent hundreds of thousands of pounds around the world publicising his belief that the 'Maitreya' (or 'master') had descended in 1977 from his ancient retreat in the Himalayas to live amongst the Asian community around Brick Lane. Crème even met a gathering of journalists in a Brick Lane tea shop on one occasion in the hope the Maitreya would turn up, but the local man who appeared was declared by Crème to be an imposter. For all we know the Maitreya may still be living locally.

Continuing south look out for Chicksand Street (nearly opposite where you entered Brick Lane from Fashion Street). In

Bram Stoker's novel *Dracula* (1897) boxes of the Count's Transylvanian earth were stored at number 197. This was just one of six deposits of Dracula's '*ghastly refuges*' that were made at various locations in London.

Opposite Chicksand Street look for the ㊱ **Sheraz Bangla Lounge** at number 13 Brick Lane. This is one of Brick Lane's most famous restaurants and you will see at the top of the building a deep-red brick signage displaying a frying pan motif and lettering. This is the only remaining evidence that number 13 was once a Victorian pub named *Ye Old Frying Pan*. Mary Ann Nichols – Jack the Ripper's first official victim – was seen drinking in the pub shortly before she was murdered on 31 August 1888.

Number 17 Brick Lane – slightly further on – was until mid-2008 a salesroom for the masons **37 E. Elfes Ltd**. Jewish headstones were sold here, and it was the last enterprise on Brick Lane that targeted the Jewish market. The business has now moved out to Essex. Nearby you will see the arch over the road that marks the entrance to 'Banglatown'.

Follow the map into Old Montague Street. **38 Blooms**, once the most famous Jewish restaurant in the East End, used to be based at the corner of this street and Brick Lane. The original restaurant was founded elsewhere on Brick Lane in 1912 and moved here in the 1930s. It eventually moved in 1952 to Whitechapel High Street where it remained until finally closing in 1996. For many this closure marked the real end of the old Jewish East End.

Continue along Old Montague Street. In the late 19th century the Whitechapel Workhouse Infirmary Mortuary was based here, and was

where the bodies of some of Jack the Ripper's victims were stored in 1888. At the time many hundreds of people used to crowd the mortuary entrance as a strange excitement gripped the local population and tourists alike fascinated by the Whitechapel Murders.

Head right along Greatorex Street to reach **Whitechapel Road**. Like Spitalfields, Whitechapel has long been a magnet for immigrants arriving in London and social conditions were often harsh. The Russian-born Yiddish theatre actor Jacob Adler (1855-1926), who worked at the Princelet Street theatre mentioned above, described his first impressions of the area in his memoir: 'The further we penetrated into this Whitechapel, the more our hearts sank. Was this London? Never in Russia, never later in the worst slums of New York, were we to see such poverty as in the London of the 1880s'.

Continue east along Whitechapel Road passing Vallance Road on the left. The infamous East End gangsters **Ronnie and Reggie Kray** lived as children at number 178 (now demolished). Fulbourne Street is the next road on the left. This once contained a social club (now demolished) that in May 1907 hosted a preliminary meeting of the 5th Congress of the Russian Social Democratic Labour Party. The meeting was attended by the future Soviet leaders Joseph Stalin (then called Djugashvili), Vladimir Lenin and Leon Trotsky. Stalin stayed for a fortnight at a doss house seen later on in the walk.

Walk down Fulbourne Street and then right into Durward Street. This was formerly known as Buck's Row and on the east side – just to left of the old school (now converted into flats) – is the site where Mary Ann Nichols was murdered by Jack the Ripper on 31 August 1888. Hours before her murder she had been turned away from her lodging house in Thrawl Street (seen later) because she could not afford a few pence to pay for a bed. Nichols was reported as saying 'I'll soon get my doss money, see what a jolly bonnet I'm wearing'.

Return to Whitechapel Road. Opposite is 🟢 **The Old Royal London Hospital**, which was opened in 1757. The hospital contains a little-known museum in the crypt of its former church (the entrance is on Newark Street). It contains exhibits on dentistry, nursing, and the lives of the nurse Edith Cavell and Joseph Merrick. The museum is open Monday to Friday 10am-4.30pm. On the Fulbourne Street side of Whitechapel Road at ⑩ **number 259** you will find an Indian sari shop. In the 1880s this same building housed a gruesome waxworks and 'freak show' featuring Joseph Merrick (1862-1890) – better known as the Elephant Man. Merrick suffered from a rare medical condition that gave rise to a grotesque appearance, and he was

sometimes paraded in the shop window under a placard announcing him as the 'Deadly Fruit of Original Sin'. In 1888 the same shop cashed in on the Whitechapel Murders by charging people to view figurines depicting each of the Ripper's victims.

Sir Frederick Treves, a surgeon at the hospital, came across Merrick here and his intervention ensured that Merrick lived out the remainder of his short life under Treves's care. Merrick's skeleton is now preserved in the hospital's museum, although it is not on display.

Cross over to the hospital side, passing on the north side of Whitechapel Road a ⑪ **monument to Edward VII** (1841-1910). This was erected in 1911 by the local community in memory of Edward's support for the country's Jewish population. Despite criticism from some anti-Semitic quarters, Edward accepted a number of wealthy Jews into his entourage, particularly members of the Rothschild and Sassoon families and Sir Ernest Cassel.

Continue up Whitechapel Road (on the side of the hospital). On the right is the entrance to **Sidney Street**. The East End has always been a hotbed of radicalism and this reputation was cemented by the **Sidney Street Siege** of January 1911. The incident

began when a gang of Latvian revolutionaries bungled the robbery of a jewellers in nearby Houndsditch, killing three policemen in the process. The gang managed to escape and led by Peter Piaktow – nicknamed 'Peter the Painter' – they hid at 100 Sidney Street. However, they were soon discovered and the resulting siege was a disaster. Under the command of Winston Churchill, then Home Secretary, the house ended up on fire and two of the gang died inside. However the mysterious Peter the Painter disappeared and to this day the fate of this East End legend is unknown. The original building was later demolished but the site stands about halfway down on the east side near Sidney Square.

Cross over to the other side of Whitechapel Road (opposite the Sidney Street entrance) where you will find the ㊷ **Blind Beggar** public house. It was here on 9th March, 1966 that gangland boss Ronnie Kray shot and killed George Cornell – a former friend of the Krays who had left them to work as an 'enforcer' for their great rivals the Richardsons. Kray was convicted of the murder in 1969 and imprisoned; in the same year his brother Reggie was jailed for murdering Jack 'The Hat' McVitie. In June 1865 the Methodist minister William Booth preached his first open-air sermon outside the pub, the first act of the East London Christian Association, which later developed into The Salvation Army.

Returning west along Whitechapel Road (on the same side as the Blind Beggar), look out for the multi-coloured glass fronted **43** **Whitechapel Idea Store** at number 321. This is Tower Hamlets' innovative take on the library, and the striking building – opened in 2005 – received a nomination for the prestigious Stirling Prize for architectural design.

Heading westwards, at number 269 is **44** the **Grave Maurice**. This was also a popular haunt of the Krays in the 60s, and where they once held a 'parley' with their rivals the Richardsons. The singer Morrissey – formerly of The Smiths – used a photograph of himself standing outside the pub on his compilation album *Under the Influence* (2003). The pub regularly attracts fans following the 'Morrissey trail'.

Cross over Whitechapel Road (on the same side as the hospital), following the map along New Road. Turn into Fieldgate Street and look out on the right for the gothic red brick **45** **Tower House**. Now converted into expensive flats, this was once a cheap hostel for men that was described by Jack London in *The People of the Abyss* as 'the Monster Doss House'. Joseph Stalin stayed here in 1907.

Ahead on the right is the former **46 Fieldgate Street Great Synagogue**, founded in 1899 and recently closed because of the decline in the local Jewish population. In marked contrast the vast East London Mosque that literally overshadows the former synagogue appears to be thriving with the surrounding streets often crowded with people on their way to attend prayers.

Just past the mosque is one of the most extraordinary commercial enterprises in Britain – the **47 Whitechapel Bell Foundry** at number 32/34 Whitechapel Road. Originally established in Whitechapel in 1570, but with its origins dating as far back as 1420, the foundry has occupied its current building since 1738. The foundry is the oldest manufacturing company in the country and its most famous products include the original Liberty Bell (made in 1752) and Big Ben at the Palace of Westminster (made in 1858). Whilst the Liberty Bell is not that well known in Britain, in America it is a great symbol of the American Revolution. According to tradition it was rung on 8th July, 1776 to summon the citizens of Philadelphia for the reading of the Declaration of Independence.

During the week (9am-4.30pm) you can visit the foundry to view a small display on its history kept in the foyer. Tours are also

possible on certain Saturdays. It is best to visit the foundry's website for details as tours may need to be booked due to popularity (see www.whitechapelbellfoundry.co.uk).

Although probably not worth a detour on this walk unless you are particularly interested in Jack the Ripper, Henriques Street (formerly Berners Street) lies a couple of roads down to the south of the foundry (just on the other side of Commercial Road). This was where on 30th September 1888 Elizabeth Stride became

Whitechapel Market, Whitechapel High Street

the third official murder victim of Jack the Ripper. During the Whitechapel Murders the police believed the Ripper might be a local character known to prostitutes as 'Leather Apron'. Leather Apron had a history of assaulting prostitutes as they plied their trade, and he was eventually identified as John Pizer. Pizer lived at 22 Mulberry Street – just off Plumber's Row beside the foundry. However, despite being arrested he was able to provide cast-iron alibis that ensured he was never charged.

Return to Whitechapel Road and walk westwards. Shortly on the left-hand side you will see the **48** **Altab Ali Park**, which you walk through. This is dedicated to a local Bangladeshi man who was murdered in a racist attack in 1978. At this time the local Bangladeshi community had been subjected to a long-running campaign of intimidation from right-wing extremist groups. One effect of the murder was to galvanise the community into standing up to such tactics, and as a result the impact of the racist groups (many based on the north side of Brick Lane) was drastically curtailed.

The park covers the site of the parish church of **St Mary Matfelon**, which was destroyed during the Blitz and not rebuilt. Old tombs from the church can still be seen in the park, as can the outline of St Mary's foundations. It was St Mary's lime-washed exterior – known as the White Chapel – that gave this area its name in medieval times. The south exit of the park has a **49** **water fountain** that was part of the old church and was moved here in 1879. It is a reminder of

49

the days when the East End was often afflicted by cholera epidemics due to the poor quality of the water supply. Public fountains like this were important as they provided a rare hygienic alternative for the local population.

On the right-hand side of the road at **50** **number 88** look out for a small Jewish coat of arms above the current shop, once occupied by the **Jewish Post & Express** newspaper in the 1930s. **Number 90**, now occupied by a Burger King restaurant, was the site of the Jewish **Blooms** restaurant mentioned earlier.

The **50** **Whitechapel Art Gallery** is nearby at number 82. Its origins lie in the 1880s when a local vicar named Samuel Barnett (see Toynbee Hall below) organised a number of free art exhibitions for the working classes of Whitechapel, and the building was completed in 1899 to a design by Charles Harrison Townsend. From the start it focused on contemporary art, and one of its most famous exhibitions was held in 1938 when Picasso's anti-war painting *Guernica* was put on display. The gallery has recently been extended to incorporate the neighbouring building that housed the Whitechapel Library between 1892 and 2005. For many generations of immigrants the library was the only place they could access books easily and it became known as the 'university of the ghetto'.

Head up Gunthorpe Street, with the **52** **White Hart Pub** on the corner. Severin Kosowski, a Polish immigrant who changed his name to George Chapman, worked as a barber in the basement of the pub and because of his surgery skills became a major suspect during police investigations into the Whitechapel Murders. He was not charged, but was later convicted of poisoning three of his common-law wives and hanged in 1903. This street, then known as George Yard, has another Ripper connection as it was here that a local prostitute named Martha Tabram was found murdered on 6 August 1888. Although not one of the five 'official' victims, her horrendous injuries have led many to suggest she was murdered by Jack the Ripper.

In 2006 Scotland Yard's Violent Crime Command unit, using experts who deal with modern day serial killers, sifted through the evidence collected by the police back in 1888. Using modern techniques they came up with a photo-fit of the Ripper suggesting he was between 25 and 35 years old, stood between 5ft 5ins and 5ft 7ins tall, and lived locally. Unfortunately this description matches a number of the dozen or so people often cited as likely suspects.

Ahead is Wentworth Street and opposite you can see a **53** **red brick arch** dating from 1886. The arch was originally part of the entrance to the Charlotte de Rothschild Model Dwellings. These were built by the **Four Per Cent Industrial Dwellings Company**, which had been founded the year before by a group of wealthy Jewish philanthropists led by Sir Nathaniel Rothschild. The company's object was to provide decent, low cost accommodation as an alternative to the terrible slum properties that prevailed in the vicinity. 'Four per cent' refers to the expected rate of return for shareholders – much less than would be expected for a normal commercial property company. By offering a lower return, rents charged to tenants could also be lower. Within 11 years the company had built accommodation for 4,000 people.

Opposite the arch is **54** **Toynbee Hall**. It was opened in 1884 by Samuel Barnett and named after a young academic named Arnold Toynbee who worked alongside Barnett in trying to help the area's poor. The hall became a hot-house for social reform and attracted a large number of volunteers from Oxford and Cambridge. The politicians Clement Attlee and William Beveridge were among those who spent time working here during their early careers. Marconi's first demonstration of the wireless in the UK took place here, and Toynbee Hall was also the location of the meeting that brokered the end of the 1926 General Strike. The institution continues to provide help to the less well-off inhabitants of the area. It also contains a small arts centre with a pleasant café.

Follow the map along **Thrawl Street** and then into **Flower and Dean Walk**. In the 1880s these streets were part of a slum, or 'rookery', with Flower and Dean Walk described by a contemporary as 'perhaps the foulest and most dangerous street in the whole metropolis'. Three victims of Jack the Ripper lived in the common lodging houses that once dominated the area – Mary Ann Nichols (mentioned above – the first official victim) lived in Thrawl Street whilst both Elizabeth Stride and Catherine Eddowes (his third and fourth official victims) lived on Flower and Dean Walk (then Street). Today the walk contains modern flats and houses that were part of the first purpose-built development for Bangladeshi families.

Whilst some locals find the frequent Jack the Ripper tours in bad taste, there is no doubt the murders were significant in focusing world attention on the poverty of the East End. The London historian Jerry White has written of how Jack the Ripper did 'more to destroy the Flower and Dean Street rookery than fifty years of road building, slum clearance and unabated pressure from police, Poor Law Guardians, vestries and sanitary officers'.

Follow the map across Commercial Street and continue down Wentworth Street on the other side. On the left look out for **Goulston Street**. Just along this street on the left-hand side stand the ⑤⑤ **Wentworth Street Model Dwellings**, built in 1886. On 30th September, 1888 Catherine Eddowes was murdered by Jack the Ripper in nearby Mitre Square. Shortly after, by the doorway between number 46 and 44 Goulston Street, a section of Eddowes's blood-stained apron was found. Nearby was a chalked message: 'The Juwes are the men that Will not be Blamed for nothing'. Before a photograph could be taken, the police had wiped the message clean as they were concerned an anti-Semitic riot might break out. At the time tensions in the East End were running high because of the murders, with many speculating the killer was an immigrant who was being protected by his own community. The significance of the message has never been understood. It has since given rise to many conspiracy theories, including one that suggested the word 'Juwes' was not a misspelling but a term used in Masonic rituals thus indicating the Masons were in some way linked to the murders.

Soon you reach Middlesex Street, more famously known as  **Petticoat Lane**. A market has been held here – and in the surrounding streets – every Sunday morning for centuries. In medieval times it was known as Hog Lane and was fairly prosperous. However after the Dissolution of the Monasteries in the 1530s many of the sick who had previously been looked after at St Mary Spital were left to fend for themselves and they congregated here. Around the same time clothes dealers were moved on from their traditional site on London Bridge and set up their pitches here instead – the silk petticoats sold by members of the rag trade giving rise to the street's famous name.

In the 19th century Petticoat Lane became dominated by poorer Jewish tradesmen. Soup kitchens were opened nearby to help them, and the Salvation Army and the Jewish Board of Guardians were both based on the north side of the Lane.

The Victorian authorities changed the name to Middlesex Street in the mid 19th century in an attempt to dissociate the area from the rag trade, however to this day Petticoat Lane is the name by which it is most commonly known. It is thought Charles Dickens's inspiration for Fagin in *Oliver Twist* (1838) was a real-life local Jewish 'Prince of Fences' named Isaac 'Ikey' Solomon (1785-

56

1850). His frequent encounters with the police were often reported in the papers, and he lived in Gravel Lane off Middlesex Street.

Follow the map up Middlesex Street then Harrow Place before reaching Cutler Street. On the right you can see the huge former warehouses of the **57** **East India Company**, the vast international trading company that was founded in 1600 and later effectively ran India until the Indian Mutiny of 1857. The warehouses once received imports from China, India and the Far East that had first been unloaded at the Company's East India Docks at Blackwall and were transported here along Commercial Street (whose construction the company helped finance). The warehouses originally covered five acres, employing 400 clerks and ten times that many warehousemen. It was the import of these cheap fabrics that helped bring about the economic decline of the silk weavers of Spitalfields.

Follow the map through Devonshire Square to reach Liverpool Street station and the end of the walk. ●

VISIT...

Dennis Severs's House
(see p.338)
18 Folgate St, E1
www.dennissevershouse.co.uk

Museum of Immigration & Diversity
19 Princelet St, E1
www.19princeletstreet.org.uk

Whitechapel Gallery (see p.369)
77-82 Whitechapel High St, E1
www.whitechapelgallery.org

EAT, DRINK

Beigel Shop (see p.359)
155 Brick Lane, Spitalfields, E1

SHOP...

Brick Lane Market (see p.359)
Brick Lane, E1
Sun 6am-1pm (streetmarket)
Sun 10am-5pm (Upmarket & Backyard Market)

Spitalfields Market (see p.343)
Commercial St, E1
Tue-Fri 10am-4pm,
Sun 9am-5pm
www.visitspitalfields.com

Petticoat Lane Market
(see p.372)
Middlesex St &
Wentworth St, E1
Sun 9am-2pm

INDEX

Index

About us:

Metro is a small independent publishing company with a reputation for producing well-researched and beautifully-designed guides on many aspects of London life. In fields of interest as diverse as shopping, bargain hunting, architecture, the arts, and food, our guide books contain special tips you won't find anywhere else.

How to order:

The following titles are available to buy from our website (P&P free). Alternatively, you can call our customer order line on 020 8533 7777 (Visa/Mastercard/Switch)

www.metropublications.com

LONDON'S PARKS AND GARDENS
COVER MORE THAN TWENTY-FIVE PERCENT OF THE CAPITAL – THAT'S A LOT MORE GRASS BETWEEN TOES THAN ANY OTHER CITY IN EUROPE

LONDON'S CEMETERIES
SPEND THE DAY WITH KARL MARX, ENID BLYTON, KEITH MOON AND MANY MORE

LONDON'S CITY CHURCHES
SEE THE SCORCH MARKS OF THE GREAT FIRE, OR VISIT AN ALTAR BY HENRY MOORE

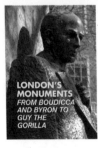

LONDON'S MONUMENTS
FROM BOUDICCA AND BYRON TO GUY THE GORILLA

LONDON'S HOUSES
FROM WORKHOUSE TO ROYAL PALACE, COME IN, CLOSE THE DOOR AND STEP BACK IN TIME

LONDON'S HIDDEN WALKS
EXPLORE LONDON AND DISCOVER HOW 2000 YEARS OF HISTORY HAVE SHAPED THIS CITY
Volume 2